MW01004108

# BEYOND IDENTITY

## Finding Your Self in the Image and Character of God

### Dick Keyes

*Wipf and Stock Publishers*
EUGENE, OREGON

Wipf and Stock Publishers
199 West 8th Avenue, Suite 3
Eugene, Oregon 97401

Beyond Identity
Finding Your Self in the Image and Character of God
By Keyes, Dick
Copyright© January, 1998  Keyes, Dick
ISBN: 1-59244-150-5
Publication date: February, 2003
Previously published by Paternoster Press,  January, 1998 .

Unless otherwise stated, Scripture quotations are taken from the
HOLY BIBLE, NEW INTERNATIONAL VERSION
Copyright © 1973, 1978, 1984 by the International Bible Society.
Used by permission of Hodder and Stoughton Limited. All rights reserved.
'NIV' is a registered trademark of the International Bible Society
UK trademark number 1448790

# Contents

*Acknowledgments*                                          v
*Foreword*                                                 vii
*Introduction*                                             ix

1 Identity under Attack                                    1
2 Identity Lost                                            32
3 Identity Found: A Healed Relationship                    73
4 Identity Found: A Restored Reflection                    102
5 Reconciliation: Toward a Higher Honesty                  138
6 Anger                                                    171
7 Servants and Martyrs: Identity and the Family            218
8 The Problem of Living with Myself                        250

*Notes*                                                    260
*Index*                                                    270

To my wife and children
Mardi, Christopher, Timothy, and Benjamin

'You come of the Lord Adam and the Lady Eve,
and that's both honor enough to lift up the head
of the poorest beggar, and shame enough to bow
the shoulders of the greatest emperor on earth.'
– C.S. Lewis
*Prince Caspian*

# Acknowledgments

*Certain authors, speaking of their works, say, 'my book,' 'my commentary,' 'my history,' etc. They resemble middle class people who have a house of their own, and always have 'my house' on their tongue. They would do better to say, 'our book,' 'our commentary,' our history,' etc., because there is in them usually more of other people's than their own.*

(Pascal, Pensées, #43)

Those 'other people' who have had a real part in this book are too numerous to mention here or even in the notes at the end. However, I would be remiss not to give credit for that handful of people who have in one way or another had special contributions to make. Francis Schaeffer has had a profound influence on me spiritually, intellectually, and personally. Jay Adams rekindled from disillusionment my hopes of seeing a fruitful interaction between theology and psychology. Os Guinness has been a constant source of stimulation with his ideas and of encouragement to publish these thoughts. Also, countless people to whom I have spoken individually and in groups will never know their contribution to the shaping and sharpening of these thoughts into something coherent.

David and Susie Ursell welcomed me into their home in Gloucestershire where I did the bulk of the writing away from the busy life of L'Abri, and my parents then offered me a similar refuge in this country to complete the work. Jim Manney and the staff at Servant Publications have made many useful suggestions and done a great deal of hard work.

My wife and family have been a source of strength and encouragement throughout the many years that the book has been forming.

Dick Keyes
Southborough, Massachusetts

# Foreword

Perhaps you have seen those television commercials in which some limber young thing declares her belief in a low calorie concoction because, as she puts it, 'I believe in me.' These ads always make me chuckle. Although I admire the sound self in the body beautiful as much as the next person, I'm old enough to realize there has to be something more to existence than me and my identity. 'A man by himself is in bad company' someone once wrote. We could just as well add, 'a man in search of his identity is traveling the wrong road.' You don't have to go very far along that road to notice how quickly the landscape becomes flat, parched, and unpromising. The more you find out about your self the more you realize how very insufficient it is.

The point, as Dick Keyes shows with wonderful good sense in this book, is that 'any worthwhile discussion of identity must reach beyond identity.' That is, it must reach beyond the narrow and confining categories of psychological and media models of selfhood because all these models 'are smaller than the one you were made for.'

Oh yes, there is to be sure such a thing as identity, but it's a good deal richer and more mysterious, and, at the same time, more solid than our personality theories allow for; and to achieve it requires a much more brutal honesty than any therapist, let alone any ad man, would dare encourage us

in. But I'll leave the description of that remarkable trans-
formation of the self to Mr. Keyes, and simply observe that
one reads his account with a real sense of recognition ('Yes,
that's what life is like') as one does not when reading the
psychological theories.

In addition to recognition, one finds refreshment here.
The refreshing fact is we are not left with the sad fate of
having only ourselves to believe in, or, for that matter, with
the ridiculous fate of being overly concerned with questions
of personal identity. The question, 'Who am I?' which seems
so pressing when we are young is not really the crucial
question to ask. After all, as Mr. Keyes makes clear, our
true identity is hidden in God and won't be revealed until
we are with God. We are not, right now, in a position to
appreciate or even guess at our real potential. In the mean-
time a better question to ask is, 'What must I do to do God's
will?' That is the part we should play. The cultivation of
ourselves is a business better left to God. He will do an
enormously better job at it than we will. But let me step
aside and let Dick Keyes make his very convincing case.

– William Kirk Kilpatrick

# Introduction

It is fair to ask why we have yet another book on the subject of personal identity. Is not the proliferation of such books itself a symptom of one of the difficulties that confronts our culture? In a self-obsessed society, just talking about the self runs the high risk of contributing more to the problem than the solution.

W.H. Auden wrote to an earlier generation, 'miserable, wicked me, how interesting I am.'[1] Many of our generation might adapt this to say, 'confused, wonderful me, how exciting I am.' Despite a psychological triumphalism, a self-defeating preoccupation with the self has obstructed true growth and ruined many lives.

Some have denounced our generation as too introspective and self-indulgent, but this denunciation, though probably true, has not shed much light on our problems nor made them go away. To offer help one must enter the self-knowledge discussion at least enough to make contact with its vocabulary and then move out of it to more promising ground. The psychological issues become a springboard to consider life from a better vantage point with a wider horizon.

What do we see beyond the strictly psychological questions? Humankind stands alone, a fragile, vulnerable creature, in this tiny corner of what seems to be an infinite space.

Politically, as some gain more power, others have less freedom and more fear. On an individual level, hopes and expectations are boundless and self-contradictory. Members of the most materially privileged society in history, we are plagued by anxiety and frustration. Accident, disease, and death will claim us, and we know it – or do we? We are indeed the 'glory, jest, and riddle of the world.'[2]

How can we best understand this riddle? There are many current models for describing people, some of which I will touch on in these pages. I have not approached the questions of identity from the statistics of experimental psychology, but simply as a Christian observer of the modern individual and society. I will use the categories of Christian theology to both understand and challenge those in that society. You will find a view of history that spans Creation, Fall, and Redemption and will confront terms such as God, the image of God, sin, and salvation.

It is legitimate to request that this theological base be defended and justified, since for many today it has lost plausibility or no longer even commands interest. This justification is a worthy task, but it has been done by others better than I could do it here.[3] I should add, however, that I am unembarrassed about working from a theological foundation, since this foundation has a solid intellectual base. Those who boast of a scientific neutrality in these wide psychological issues are not to be respected so much for their objectivity as suspected for their naivete. They might claim freedom from philosophical bias in their study of human life and nature, but they in fact work from an impoverished philosophy, adopted unconsciously or uncritically. This philosophy then inevitably affects the shape of their thought whether they are aware of it or not.

I will make no attempt to establish the truth of the Christian faith here. It is my hope that for those who do not share this faith, these chapters will carry a compelling logic of their own in the light of history and personal experience, and that they will make the time and find the energy for further investigation into that faith's claims.

I have tried in this book to build a bridge from the theological and philosophical wealth of the Christian view of humanity to the very practical experience that each one of us has living with ourselves. The Christian view is grand and extravagant, with its emphasis on our likeness to God himself and the drama of his care for us. Our experience of ourselves is too apt to be shabby, fraught with confusion, doubt, and self-hatred. The Dutch philosopher Herman Dooyeweerd wrote, 'An image cannot be anything in itself. Man ex-sists; that is to say, he cannot find himself except from a standpoint outside of himself, in his relationship to his Origin.'[4] Our struggle for identity in all its breadth can thus be best understood in terms of the character of God and of our interaction with him. Our identity comes from a source beyond itself. It is an identity derived. This book is about how a complex of dynamics is at work moving us from believing these magnificent ideas toward the ability to live them out in flesh and blood.

The first four chapters deal with the question of identity directly – from defining the terms and a discussion of the preoccupation with identity today, to a biblical understanding of the loss and regaining of identity. The next two chapters on honesty and anger focus on two pressure points at which different strategies of life show dramatically different psychological results. Then a chapter on identity and the family points to the danger of substituting family members for God himself as the source of identity. The final chapter deals with facing recurrent failure.

There are many things this book does *not* do. This is not a book on how to give or receive counseling. It will not give you a quick fix for all the difficulties that you might have. Knowledge alone, even if it is true, does not itself transform us. It must be taken in with thoughtfulness and lived out with integrity. This book does not endorse any one of the models of counseling or schools of psychology that are current, even though I make use of certain models in these pages. Neither do I attempt to describe the formation of identity through childhood and adolescence. Instead I focus on the dynamics of choices, feelings, and courses of action that can affect us at almost any age. Finally, it is most certainly not the last word on the subject. For me it has been an exciting exploration in which I have been the one to gain the most. But it is an attempt to put a good hard scratch on the surface of a vast subject. There is much room for future fruitful digging.

# ONE

# Identity Under Attack

*. . . intellectual doctrines about the self don't just sit around in unreadable scholarly journals. They wind up in people's heads.*[1] (M. Brewster Smith)

*The age-old function of religion – to provide ultimate certainty amid the exigencies of the human condition – has been severely shaken. Because of the religious crisis in modern society, social 'homelessness' has become metaphysical – that is, it has become 'homelessness' in the cosmos.*[2] (Peter Berger)

*A man's spirit will endure sickness; but a broken spirit who can bear?* (Prov. 18:14)

The word 'identity' literally means absolute sameness. It comes from the same root as 'identical.' When it is used psychologically, 'identity' refers more to a self-sameness, internal cohesion, and self-respect. Finding your identity is therefore not like finding a lost shoe or glove, nor is it coming up with a perfect character description or definition of yourself. It is found rather in living in the midst of a constantly changing inner and outer world and growing in a sense of peace with oneself, with God, and with other people. As such, it is a continual process of housecleaning, consolidation, and reorganization.

The term 'identity crisis' is widely used today not just of individuals, but of nations and institutions as well. We hear that Africa is experiencing a crisis of identity, as is the church, the family, and even the profession of psychiatry. This is not just the overworking of a popular phrase. Institutions as well as individuals need a sense of integration, a measure of self-understanding, a shared idea of what they are and what they are trying to do. At a time when social change is proceeding faster than ever before, it is not surprising that identity crises are found almost everywhere. Individuals and institutions are seeking a knowledge of their boundaries, purpose, and value.

## A Map of the Territory

Let us first map out some of the boundaries of our discussion. I will point to four kinds of awareness. These are not given as a survey of levels of consciousness. They are simply four of the ways that we experience ourselves. By contrasting them we can get an understanding of the specific question of identity.

### Simple Experience

Much of the time we are not particularly aware of ourselves doing things. We work, eat, drive the car, go shopping without thinking about the fact that we are doing them. We can go through the whole range of human activity – whether it be with intensity or relaxation – without observing ourselves. But this simple or non-reflective experience is not the only way we relate to ourselves. Simple experience inevitably produces thoughts and situations that force us to reflect on ourselves. A human being is both the observer and the observed; our minds can and will bend back on themselves. People can think about themselves.

## Images of Self

Because I can think about me, I can experience myself and be aware of it. I might ask myself 'What am I sitting here at a desk for?' 'What direction is my life taking?' 'Am I a success or a failure?' I am also aware of all kinds of feelings about myself. They might range from despair, guilt, and shame to joy, elation, and satisfaction. As I reflect on myself I cannot help forming images of myself, little mental self-portraits in different situations, attitudes, and emotional states.

Think of some of the images you have of yourself. You will find that they are very diverse. Compare your image of yourself when you are in a rage with yourself when you are sad; when you are accelerating behind the wheel of a fast car with yourself in a dentist's chair;[3] when you are laughing at some one with when you are laughed at; when you see someone stopped by a police officer with when you yourself are stopped; when you have great joy of success with when you are caught stealing money from a friend; when all your plans are being carried out flawlessly with when a subordinate defies you. These self-images are not easy to integrate with each other. If this is so, in relatively trivial situations, imagine how much more the problem arises in the midst of life-jarring events. Compare your image of yourself when you are being thanked for saving a person's life, with when you have permanently injured someone through negligence; when you discover that your love for a member of the opposite sex is returned, with when your spouse informs you that your marriage is finished; when you have inherited a fortune, with when you have lost your job; when you get a clean bill of health from the doctor, with when you are told that you are terminally ill.

The images you have of yourself are self-contradictory and disorganized, an ever-shifting collage. But the very diversity of these images creates a need to find some kind of coherence among them. The coherence or integration of these many images, such as it is, is your sense of identity.

## Identity

We quite often hear some one say, 'I wasn't myself yesterday.' Who is that self that didn't seem to be around yesterday? Our daily experience demands that we establish a certain self-sameness amid the many diffusing forces acting on us. Having a role to identify with is not enough. You have different roles with different people. You cannot relate in the same way to your best friend as to your grandmother, or to your parents as to your children. You have as many roles as images of yourself. And yet there is one self that was once three years old and might live to be eighty or more. With all the radical changes of mind, body, and environment over a lifetime, it is somehow the same you.

A true and positive sense of identity has two sides. I will be coming back to these often in the course of this book. The first side is the one that I have already mentioned – a sense of internal coherence or integration of the self. The second is an acceptance of that self as having value.

A person with a strong and true sense of identity will experience peace with self, others, and God. This person will have a certain self-forgetfulness, a lack of self-absorption and self-consciousness. By contrast, the person with a weak sense of identity is painfully concerned with him or herself. This person is keenly conscious of being one who is fragile, unreal, and unsubstantial and feels like a loosely held together

collection of roles played to the audience of others' expectations and determined by forces outside of their control. They
might describe themselves as masses of contradictory selves
or as several actors on a stage without a script or director.
This lack of cohesion usually goes together with feelings
of self-hate. Complaints of 'I don't know who I am' often
go along with 'I can't stand myself.' The person with a
negative and disintegrated attitude toward self is apt to see
others as threatening competitors. Their successes only
point to personal inadequacy, their failures comfort with
the thought that maybe this person is not so bad after all or
at least that there is partnership in misery.

People with a weak identity are apt to be what Erik
Erikson calls 'identity-hungry,'[4] that is, in relationships with
others they try to find or fortify themselves, whether by
bragging, self-assertion, manipulation, or self-pitying with-
drawal. Other people exist as means to buttress their weak
and dependent sense of self, not as persons in their own
right. Motivated by fear and anxiety they are like a baby
bird in a nest with a huge open mouth pointed to the sky
shouting 'feed me!' 'make me feel like a person!' They may
even get a perverse satisfaction out of being hated – at least
they have been noticed. We cannot exaggerate the psychological pain in a disintegrated sense of identity. The questions and doubts are not remote, but are urgent.

The areas that work for or against our sense of identity
can be formulated in many ways. I have found four factors
emphasized in the Bible that are useful tools to understand
our own experience. These factors are morals, models,
dominion, and love. We will discuss these factors in depth
in this part of the book. Look at them briefly.

One of the main shaping forces on our identity is our
moral values. From these come our sense of meaning and
purpose in life. Some things are more valuable than others.
Something is worth living for; perhaps something is even

worth dying for. Aleksandr Solzhenitsyn made this comment about Bertrand Russell's famous statement, 'Better red than dead':

> All my life and the life of my generation, the life of those who share my views, we all have one standpoint: better to be dead than a scoundrel. In this horrible expression of Bertrand Russell there is an absence of all moral criteria.[5]

If, as Solzhenitsyn asserts, there is something so valuable that it is worth more than life itself, then this value will have a profound effect on how we live our lives and on the formation of our identity. Our moral values are not just principles 'out there' somewhere, but, if we take them seriously at all, they become part of us. A good example of this is given in the words of Thomas More in Robert Bolt's play *A Man For All Seasons*. Thomas More was being pressured even by his own family to approve of Henry VIII's marriage to Anne Boleyn. To do this would have been a denial of his understanding of the word of God, of his own faith. To his own daughter's pleadings, More replies:

> When a man takes an oath, Meg, he's holding his own self in his own hands. Like water. (He cups his hands) And if he opens his fingers *then* – he needn't hope to find himself again.[6]

Thomas More stood firm and was executed on false charges. His observation is profound. If he had violated his moral values, he would have lost something of himself as well. Had he changed his moral values to suit the occasion, he would have emerged as a far less substantial human being. Someone who will betray their own values is somehow not solid. This theme is powerful in the wisdom literature of the Bible: 'Like a muddied spring or a polluted fountain is a righteous man who gives way before the wicked' (Prov. 25:26). Of critical importance is not only what the values are, but also how do we relate to them. Do we actually live by our values? When we fall short of them, how do we handle that failure?

*2* The second shaping factor to our sense of identity is models. We all have models, heroes and heroines. These people may be real or imaginary. We do not think just in terms of propositions and commands, but also in pictures, stories, images, things to aspire to. Here is where your imagination thrives. Your models are those people or images of people that you would like to be like, it would be heroic to be like them. As we shall see, our sense of identity is shaped by who these models are, how our models relate to our morals, how we handle it when we fall short of them.

*who is your model*

*3* A third factor is dominion. According to Genesis 1:26, dominion over the earth is very closely tied to being made in the image of God. Dominion simply means mastery over some bit of the world to some degree. I understand this in the widest possible sense, to include any kind of mastery. For example it would include a child learning mastery over his or her own body in learning to crawl, walk, talk, or ride a bicycle. It would include designing an airplane, writing a poem, or making a relationship grow. In the modern world especially, our use of language is one of the main areas of dominion. As images of God we are created to have dominion; this is who we are. If this dominion is entirely thwarted by others or aborted by us, it has a negative effect on our sense of identity. We are apt to feel helpless, useless, and to hate ourselves and others.

*ex*

*4* Lastly there is the factor of love. This is closely related to dominion, but needs to be treated separately. Love given and received is vital to our sense of self. Modern psychology has told us of our need to be loved. The biblical writers say this as well, but put the emphasis also on our need to love. If we do not love we are very much less than we were made to be. If we do love, our sense of identity grows.

Morals, models, dominion, and love are critical areas
bearing on our identity on both fronts, the sense of self-
acceptance and of internal coherence. But morals, models,
and the ability to have dominion and love do not come out
of thin air. Where do morals come from? How do we know
what is heroic? In what way do I express dominion and love,
and to what end? 'Identity' is a psychological concept, but
it quickly raises these other questions which lie outside the
scope of psychology. Just as our simple experience led to
self-reflection and images of the self, and the many diverse
images of self led to the need for identity, so also any
worthwhile discussion of identity must reach beyond
identity. Allen Wheelis put this bluntly, 'Values determine
goals, and goals define identity. The problem of identity,
therefore, is secondary to some basic trouble about value.'[7]

### Beyond Identity

A table or a chair just 'is,' but a human being needs to feel
that he or she exists in terms of something, some standard or
point of integration. You see, a woman could be single, often
be depressed, could earn an average income, be resentful of
her father, and have an optimistic view of her country's
future. However, these are temporary features of her life. Any
one of them can change and none of them is large enough or
solid enough to be the core of her identity. But the question
remains, what *does* she relate to? How does she come to grips
with the reality which is her? To adequately deal with these
questions she needs to know what kind of world she is living
in, and what her place in it is, she needs to know what she
values, whether she has any conscious control over her life,
and if there is any self worth searching for. These questions
push us beyond the normal categories of psychology; we are
talking of world views, of philosophy and theology. One
writer speaks of each of us having a 'master story' – some

kind of picture of what the world is like and how it works. In the light of this story we interpret the meaning of our lives. [8] Ernest Becker suggested that this higher level of meaning demanded contact with something transcendent:

> There is no 'harmonious development,' no child-rearing program, no self-reliance that would take away from men their need for a 'beyond' on which to base the meaning of their lives. [9]

Humans will always compute their values in terms of something, whether that something is worthy or able to bestow value on them or not. It is only when people reach beyond humankind that they can get any conclusive affirmation of themselves.

Jesus pointed out this very thing in the Sermon on the Mount. He knew that everyone has treasure, something that is the most important thing in his life. The main issue, he said, is where that treasure is.

> Do not lay up for yourselves treasures on earth, where moth and rust consume and where thieves break in and steal, but lay up for yourselves treasures in heaven, where neither moth nor rust consumes and where thieves do not break in and steal. For where your treasure is, there will your heart be also. (Mt. 6:19–21)

What is of interest to a discussion of identity is the very last sentence: 'For where your treasure is, there will your heart be also.' Everyone has some kind of treasure. Everyone also has a heart – the inmost core of the self, your psychological and spiritual center of gravity. Jesus says that your heart will move to reside wherever your treasure is. In other words, you make a symbolic extension of yourself outside yourself. If your treasure is a new suit, or car, that is where your heart is. If the boundaries of your self encompass that suit or car, your sense of identity is at stake when they are damaged. Hence your disproportionate rage if soup gets spilled on your suit or your car is scratched. Ernest Becker gives the analogy of an amoeba which can extend its cell wall to surround and enclose a foreign body. A material object can become an invisible symbolic extension of my self and my identity is therefore as vulnerable as the fate of the object. Think of the men who threw themselves off the top of buildings when the stock market crash came in 1929.[10] When money was their treasure, life was taken away, their heart was gone and their life became unbearable.

We can find our treasure in either of two places – in God or in something that God has made on earth. We are living in a society that for the most part puts its treasure on earth, in possessions, job, status, public admiration, money, power, self-knowledge, or self-growth. We can make any-thing sacred. We sacralize it by giving it such importance in our priorities. Think of how sacred money is in our society. Can you imagine asking all your friends how much money they make in a year and what their net assets are? Many people today would feel that the question was impertinent or indecent, even though it is a perfectly straightforward factual question asked by a friend. Why is this? It is because today money is something sacred, its power is great and mysterious. Talking about how much of it you have is a private matter like one's religion, too personal to be discussed with good taste in public.

Chesterton said, 'when a man ceases to worship God he does not worship nothing, he worships anything.' The only thing that is beyond identity for many people today is the material, created world in all its impermanence and unpre-dictability. If your treasure is there, your heart is there too, and your psychological safety hangs on the contingencies of this world – weather, opinion, or stock market.

Jesus contrasts treasure in this world to treasure in heaven. Here our treasure is safe; no one can steal it. His claim was, first, that the God in heaven is really there. He exists; he is not just the object of some psychological technique of self-integration. Jesus claims also that God alone can bear the weight of your identity. Only he can give an adequate basis for the morals, models, dominion, and love which are the foundation of self-coherence and self-acceptance. Only he is great enough to do justice to your uniqueness and the vast diversity of your experience in his created world. If your identity is rooted in God himself then he can give you a sense of both coherence and self-acceptance amid the rapid change of this world and in the face of death – the ultimate threat to identity.

Erik Erikson, although not taking a specifically Christian viewpoint in his work, wrote:

> How did man's need for identity evolve? Before Darwin the answer was clear; because God created Adam in His image, as a counterplayer of His identity . . . I admit to not having come up with any better explanation.[11]

Erikson is saying that the need for identity makes sense within a Christian world view – with God as creator and human beings as his image. That is not to say that finding a sense of identity is easy for those who are Christians, but that the questions are those that you would expect to find if we were made for a relationship to some one greater than ourselves.

Although the problem of identity is as old as humankind itself, there are many reasons why it is especially urgent in the last half of the twentieth century in the West. These relate both to the world of ideas and also to changes in social structures.

## The Loss of a High View of Humankind

Gradually and for many reasons, Western culture has cut itself off from the Christian faith in its radical, vital, and biblical form. Many welcome this as the cutting of an umbilical cord enabling human beings to come of age as independent and autonomous beings directing their own destinies. Nevertheless the abandonment of Christian faith has left us with many intractable problems. Matthew Arnold still speaks for many in his famous lines, 'Wandering between two worlds, one dead / The other powerless to be born.'[12] No longer do we have a foundation on a philosophical level for our feelings about ourselves – namely, that we have dignity above that of a stick, stone, or an animal. No longer do we have an overall purpose for our lives, or a standard for our moral choices. The high view of humanity as the image of God has not survived the subtraction of God from the equation. In Erikson's terms, human experience demands nothing less than Deity who has lent a halo to mortals. Without this God to whom we correspond, we are alone, cut loose and corresponding only to the chemicals of which we are made.[13] The closely interrelated disciplines of philosophy and the sciences have spearheaded these changes. Scientific theories were interpreted in an increasingly secular climate of thought. None of the discoveries themselves needed to threaten Christian belief. But within the framework of Enlightenment and Post-Enlightenment thinking, they were thought to cast serious doubt on the truth of the Bible and the existence of God, thereby undermining the plausibility of belief in humanity as the image of One greater than ourselves. Three snapshots from the history of science show the high view of humankind to be hanging by an increasingly slender thread, snipped at by the scissors of both disciplines.

First is the discovery of the vastness of space, that the earth is not the center of the universe or even of the solar system, and that humankind therefore is but a speck of dust in the midst of an infinite emptiness. The work of Galileo and Kepler was a greater threat to Aristotle and church authority than to the Bible, but it nevertheless undermined people's attempt to derive human significance from the geometry or size of the universe. The consequence, as R.C. Zaehner pointed out, is that man's 'quantitative nothingness must be compensated for by his qualitative uniqueness which set him apart from every other form of creation.'[14]

This very qualitative uniqueness was the next to go, at least cut away, in the minds of many of those who accepted the arguments in the writings of Charles Darwin. Suddenly the distinction between human beings and animals became doubtful. Our questions of identity once made sense; now they seem out of character with our origin and nature. Existentialist literature sees our need for identity as something that alienates us from the rest of the world. We have evolved into misfits. Animals, who never raise such questions, are far better adapted to a godless environment. Gone is the qualitative uniqueness. We are one with the animal – but we cannot feel or act that way.

The third step is in the same direction. Human beings are seen to be a mechanism – a cog, albeit a complex and disruptive cog in the machine of the universe. Jacob Bronowski wrote:

> We sense that there is no break in the continuity of nature. At one end of her range the star has been linked with the stone; at the other end man has been put among the animals. What now remains is between these ends to make a single chain of Animal, Vegetable or Mineral along which nature becomes one with her creatures. An unbroken line runs from the stone to

the cactus, and on to the camel, and there is no supernatural leap in it. No special act of creation, no spark of life was needed to turn dead matter into living things. The same atoms compose them both, arranged only in a different architecture.[15]

Christians can and should challenge some of these views as poor science and philosophy. But apart from the truth or untruth of these ideas, they have a profound and often disruptive effect on the view of self and others for the one who takes them seriously. The fact that some of the major schools of psychology today hold to a mechanistic view of humanity explains why those schools are of little help to the person grappling with problems of identity.

Ernest Becker describes the same shift in different terms, and laments its impact on humanity. For the last half million years, he says, human beings have believed in two worlds, one that you could see and one that you could not. The material world that you could see was where you lived your daily life. The invisible world was a greater and more powerful world upon which this material world depended for its origin, coherence, and power. The meaning of our lives, and our source of coherence and value, was in terms of the invisible world. With the Enlightenment and the science and philosophy of the last century, we are suddenly told that the invisible world does not exist. It never did. Yet our need for coherence, value, and heroism still remain, so we then must derive these from the visible, material world.[16]

Much of the agony of our modern world results from this effort to find ultimate meaning in the material world whose own meaning is neither apparent nor ultimate.

Life seems an accident, its span useless, death unfair. But this is largely because we live only on the visible dimension; our lives are an intensified self-seeking for fulfillment and posses- sions, largely because we believe there is nothing else, and life is so precarious.[17]

The irony of this is often missed. The promises of the Enlightenment were prodigious. Under the banner of reason humankind was to come of age and discover our true nature and fulfillment, free from the shackles of religious superstition. The Enlightenment would liberate us to be ourselves for the first time in history, to find our true identity, standing on our own two feet without the help of God. Yet the result was to turn human beings to material gadgetry for meaning and heroism. We had previously been a counterplayer to God, our identity a reflection of God's image. Now modern people must try to remake themselves 'in the blueprint of a manufactured identity.'[18] We must try to conjure up some basis for our identity from within ourselves and from the world around us. The sociologist Hans Mol, reflecting on the work of Simmel, underscores the bitter irony:

> To him the bequest of modern rationalist individualism was man's inability 'to preserve a sense of the wholeness and identity of self against the very currents which were supposed to both liberate and emphasize this wholeness and identity of self.'[19]

The Enlightenment view of humankind and the world, promising a new and greater sense of identity, has instead proven to be one of the main enemies of what sense of identity is left. The savior turned out to be the destroyer from which many who see the issues most clearly flee in disarray.

The Enlightenment idea which destroyed much of the basis for human identity was the notion that everything outside human beings, whether it be the values of specific societies or contact with something transcendent, is only relative and time-bound. Religion is seen as the groping of a culture toward resolving the perplexities of the human condition. Thus all religions are true, but only in that they truly reflect this search. But all religions are also false because there is no God who is able to make himself known. The truth of religion

is therefore only a psychological or sociological truth, justified by the beneficial results to the individual or society,
rather than by an authentic relationship with a real God.
Some feel that this is a valid re-interpretation of religion for
the twentieth century. Yet the vast majority have choked at
this miniaturized faith and concluded that the emperor has
no clothes. They have given up hope of finding a foundation
for their lives in anything transcendent.

Without a transcendent point of reference, something
truly beyond our identity, we ourselves shrink. Every discipline for the study of humanity built on that premise
contributes to the shrinkage. Rollo May protests against the
reductionism of academic psychology in a fanciful account
of a psychologist appearing before St. Peter at the gate of
heaven. Peter condemns the psychologist, not for distorting
data on his PhD thesis, but for a deeper reason:

> You have spent your life making molehills out of mountains –
> that's what you're guilty of. When man was tragic, you made
> him trivial. When he was picaresque, you called him picayune.
> When he suffered passively, you described him as simpering;
> and when he drummed up enough courage to act, you called
> it stimulus and response. Man had passion; and when you were
> pompous and lecturing to your class you called it 'the satisfac-
> tion of basic needs,' and when you were relaxed and looking
> at your secretary you called it 'release of tension.' You made
> man over into the image of your childhood Erector Set or
> Sunday School maxims – both equally horrendous.[20]

Psychologists are not alone in making molehills out of
mountains. Our whole modern view of reality tends to see
knowledge as real and reliable only when it is quantifiable
and put on a table or a graph. However, those aspects of
our lives that are most distinctively human are least suited
for reduction to numbers.[21]

We cannot minimize the psychological impact of these ideas. Modern people may avoid the despair of some of the existentialists simply because our emotions revolt against what our minds seem to tell us. Our emotions react against seeing ourselves as machines. We may therefore avoid despair, but not confusion. When God is eliminated, we are miniaturized. Our stature cannot survive the loss of God from our world view.

## The Loss of Heroes

The destruction of a system of moral absolutes has been compounded by profound confusion about models. Today there is little shared sense of what it is to be heroic. Ernest Becker, who has examined the fate of heroism in modern society as much as anyone, sees all humans as trying to be heroes, that is, to be significant in some final sense. This was a fulfillable dream when people could believe that a personal relationship with God was possible. Now that this possibility seems no longer open, heroism has become a profound problem. The job of any society is to create some kind of an agreed hero-system by which people can feel heroic in their contribution to that society. Our society has now lost this and we face a crisis in heroism. In Becker's view:

> The crisis of middle- and upper-class youth in the social and economic structure of the Western world is precisely a crisis of belief in the vitality of the hero-systems that are offered by contemporary materialist society. *The young no longer feel heroic in doing as their elders did, and that's that.* [italics mine][22]

A crisis of heroism is no small problem. When there seems to be nothing to aspire to, there is great potential for destruction, both for individuals and for society.

To make matters worse, heroism has become separated from moral values; often morals and models work against each other in the same person and in the same society. The heroes and heroines of music, film, and literature are only rarely heroic for their moral qualities. Rather they are heroic for their rebellion against the values of society, for their freedom from restraint and limitation. The worst in them is often pictured as being desirable. This is a drastic change from the mainstream of Western cultural history. How rare are writers like C.S. Lewis whose genius as a writer of fiction lay in his ability to make moral goodness attractive and heroic.

The other side to the separation of heroism from morality is illustrated by a story about two women talking over their back fence. One asked the other, 'What do you think of Mrs. So-and-so?' After a long pause the second woman responded cautiously, 'I think she's a good person.' With a look of satisfaction the first woman replied, 'That's what I thought you would say. I don't like her either.' Moral goodness today is often portrayed as something unheroic – unattractive, deadly dull, excruciating.

The heroism of the materialist consumer society is tarnished for many people today. William Kilpatrick writes:

> It is a pity that when the young are looking for dragons to slay we hand them computer cards to fill out. They would like to feel that they are useful to society and that their existence does make an immediate difference. They would be involved in a great enterprise, but we tell them that their importance lies in getting good grades and otherwise keeping out of the way. [23]

Modern heroism is superficial. 'In the future,' said artist Andy Warhol, 'everybody will be famous for at least fifteen minutes.' [24] Many people see this superficiality and they are cynical about it. I have often heard young people reflect on their inability to identify with anyone. They say, 'Well, I don't want to be like my parents, I don't want to be like any of my teachers or my doctor either. I certainly don't want to be like any of the politicians that I know of. Actually, I can't think of anybody that I would like to be like.' They seek their identity negatively, as an effort to *not* be like any of the potential models that surround them.

It would be wrong, however, to say that heroism was dead. There are enough posters of the stars of film and music on bedroom walls to show that it is alive though not well. To be famous is to be heroic. Susan Margolis wrote that 'today the gifted as well as the deranged among us are struggling to be famous the way earlier Americans struggled to be saved.'[25] The problem is that the various forms of today's heroism are inaccessible to the vast majority of people. Despite Andy Warhol's assurances, not everyone can be famous. Those that are heroic for their resistance to society are few and they do not always live very long. Those who exemplify freedom from restraint – like the James Bonds and Clint Eastwoods – are difficult to imitate without going to jail or to the emergency room. Only a few can make enough money to get a sense of heroism from their balance sheet and even then it is easily lost. The heroism of physical beauty is possessed by few and even those who have it soon lose it. Talented heroes in entertainment and sports possess skills out of the reach of the average man or woman. How many people will ever have the 'right stuff' when all is said and done? The vast majority of people will never actually be heroic *on their own terms*, and they know it.

How then does heroism function? Very often it is expressed in daydreaming rooted in frustration. Heroism has been a source of aspiration, a powerful dynamic to motivate people to excellence, and yet watching a football star make a ninety-yard run rarely inspires more than a journey to the refrigerator for another can of beer. This kind of heroism spawns fantasies of self-glory that ultimately turn against you. Real life seems so very drab and dull by comparison. It is too easy to reject yourself and your life as falling hopelessly short, 'I just don't have what it takes.' Because of its very triviality, modern heroism more often than not consigns people to frustration with themselves and their lot in life. Sam Keen points this out:

> It may be harder for modern man to be a hero. In tribal cultures, heroism had to do with repeating archetypal patterns, following in the footsteps of the original heroes. The hero was not supposed to do anything new. We have thrown away the past and disowned traditional models. So the terror of the modern hero is that he has to do something new, something that has never been done before. We are justified only by novelty. I think this is why modern man (and with women's liberation, modern woman) is anxious and continually dissatisfied. We are always trying to establish our uniqueness.[26]

This split between heroism and morality is a new development in the wider cultural understanding. Think of Bunyan's *Pilgrim's Progress*, a book illustrating Christian heroism in the particular model of the Puritans. It has provided generations of men and women with a sense of the heroic that was accessible to them. You could be heroic not only in the dramatic moments of the crises of life, but in the day-to-day details. You could be a cosmic hero by living the life of faith because you would be doing the will of the God who made the cosmos.

## Changes in Social Structures

Changes of social and economic structures in Western society over the last hundred years have been enormous.

They have not been independent of the changes in the history of ideas, but are inextricably intertwined. I will touch on a few of the most obvious factors.

Technological society in the West, with its modern industrial system, urbanization, communications, and travel, has had a profound impact on the average citizen's sense of identity. Much of this impact is negative. Technological society has a morality which values efficiency and profitability more highly than human needs. The harshness of modern civilization is somewhat relieved by the awareness that in the long run it is uneconomic to treat people too badly. It would be wrong to say that the world of business is given over to exploitation. It is to say, however, that the internal logic of short-term technical efficiency must be consciously leaned against if people are to be valued.[27] The world of technology is one in which people are often compared unfavorably with the machine. Machines can work faster, they don't go on strike, nor do you have to pay them pensions. Instead you can repair them and depreciate them against taxes as they get older.

Many complain of a sense of powerlessness in their jobs. Significant decisions are usually made at levels so remote from the average worker that they feel helpless to effect change. Their areas of dominion or mastery are so small by comparison to their dependence on the technological system (for food, heat, water, electricity, entertainment) that they are apt to feel helpless victims of a huge system to which they personally contribute little.

Another important factor is the range of choice for the young person today. Young people in earlier generations found considerable security in carrying on in the steps of their parents. Boys who entered the job market at the time of either of the world wars had almost no choice but to join the military, and those who entered it during the depression were happy to get any work at all. Now there is a far greater range of choice for the young man or woman with a certain level of education, not only in a job, but in what kind of person he or she chooses to be. But this is a mixed blessing. Some have termed it 'overchoice.' There is such freedom that it can provoke anxiety. They do not feel that they can make serious decisions with that many possibilities, and long for some one to tell them what to do. A real problem of identity is brought on with the person who has no basis for identity other than a future job and yet the job could be in a number of different areas.

Finally, modern social change has broken down the institutions that previously provided social continuity and support for the individual's sense of identity. I am thinking here particularly of the changes in the role of the family, the church, and the local community which stood as mediators between the individual and the mass collective of society. The isolated individual now faces the mass alone.

The sources of the breakdown are both in the world of ideas (e.g. the loss of divine authority for the family and the church) and in the everyday structures of society (e.g. the impact of urbanization and industrialization). Think of the number of families that move their home every three to five years. Imagine the effect of this on a community which is urban and therefore already more anonymous than its rural counterpart of a hundred years ago. Think of the change from the time when the home was the basic economic unit in which each member of the family played a part, to modern society where the public and private worlds are sharply divided. The family is in the private world, and might have nothing to do with what any members of it do in their workplace. Think also of its effect on the church, which becomes a place which people pass through, as they pursue the call of upward mobility.

I do not want to suggest that the result of modernization has been entirely or even overwhelmingly negative. Yet we need to see its negative side so that we can better understand the struggle for identity today.

## Attempts to Manufacture Identity

These social and ideological changes tend to either directly attack the possibility of rooting identity in God, or at least detract from the plausibility of doing so. People, cut off from God, must manufacture their own identity. In Jesus' words, we lay up treasures for ourselves on earth. It should not surprise the Christian that the effect of our feverish attempts to do this would be destructive.

A vast economic and media machine semi-consciously enforces the ultimate importance of superficial and degrad-ing morals and models. How is a person to resist this? We are prey to a network of influences that insist that one's personal worth depends on physical appearance, youthful-ness, money, gadgets, and ability to impress people. Even if we are successful in meeting these demands, they will destroy us. The person who possesses some of these qualities is condemned to be valued only in terms of beauty, money, and success. The person who has the courage to rebel against them is judged worthless by society. This judgement is a powerful deterrent to rebellion.

An integral part of these degrading standards is the intolerance of deviation. Conformity rules many people's search for identity. Even non-conformity must adhere to rigid standards. Some would not be caught dead without a dinner jacket; others will never appear in public without tattered blue jeans. Conformity, a familiar feature of most discussions of identity since David Reisman's *The Lonely Crowd*, involves an enslavement to the whims of the group, a commitment to which many mass movements owe their strength. Only in acceptance by the group does one find the self-confidence needed to face life. Allen Wheelis wrote:

> Without meaningful goals modern man has, understandably, no sense of direction; for he does not look where he is going. Like an anxious soldier on a drill field he covertly watches those around him to make sure he stays in step. He sticks to the group, and where the group will go next nobody knows.[28]

Of course the person who sells his soul to a group has not solved the problem. There still remains nagging anxiety and inauthenticity.

Modern people have not manufactured a viable identity. This is true not only for those who find their way to psychiatrists and psychotherapists but for the mass of men and women in society. They see themselves in Willy Loman of Arthur Miller's *The Death of a Salesman*, the man who 'never knew who he was,' and his many varied successors in films, drama, music, and fiction. They send books of popular psychology – making extravagant promises – rocketing onto the best-seller lists. But the promises go unfulfilled. The human attempt to manufacture an identity apart from God has failed. To say that modern people have not manufactured a viable identity does not mean that they have not tried. They have tried and tried hard. Let us consider the two main directions that people have moved to try to find some sense of self.

### New Victorianism

The New Victorianism differs from the old in being less overtly and self-consciously moral, more sexually liberated, and basing its values more on prevailing practices than on principles. It resembles the old Victorianism in its deeply rooted materialism. Personal security is to be found in one's possessions, a house at least half paid for, life insurance, investments, and prospect of job advancement. These ma-terial goods promise to provide the adequacy and sense of self that is lacking.

The New Victorian tries to achieve these ends by clear goals, careful planning, and determined hard work. The only way to get ahead in a highly competitive society is by having more dedication, discipline, and will power than the next person. The New Victorian's identity is found in a job or means of economic security. The question asked of the child, 'What are you going to be when you grow up?' means, 'What job will you have?' or 'How will you earn your living?' The job, house, achievements, or other measures of status define you. Many people experience great anxiety in writing their resumes for just this reason. They know that they are judged as whole people by what is recorded on the piece of paper. Failure is not part of the program. The only comprehensible reason for it is a lack of determination.

In this way work takes on a religious character. It is the means by which you can establish yourself in this world and know where you stand. Henry Ford, one of the heroes of modern technology, wrote:

> I do not think that a man can ever leave his business. He ought to think of it by day and dream of it by night. . . . Thinking men know that work is the salvation of the race, morally, physically, socially. Work does more than get us a living; it gets us a life.[29]

Calvin Coolidge wrote in the same vein: 'The man who builds a factory builds a temple. The man who works there worships there.' Although these words have the quaint ring of the older Victorianism, much of the same attitude lingers on, masked by modern cynicism, unabashed greed, and a more sophisticated use of leisure time.

To the New Victorian, the larger questions, such as the existence of God, the purpose of life, the nature of humankind, or the reality of death, are seen as irrelevant – the province of dreamers, idle diversions from the task of getting ahead in the real world. This is true of the New Victorians whether they are inward and defensive, fighting to keep what they have, or daring and used to taking risks. Neither has time in their busy schedules to look beyond the ever pressing needs of the world that they have created for themselves. Middle-aged New Victorians show little sympathy for anyone experiencing problems of identity, particularly for the identity crises of adolescence. They see these questionings as the fruit of idleness and affluence at just the time when young people have the whole world before them, 'opportunities that I never had when I was your age.' The New Victorian's attitude closely resembles that of a Pharaoh of ancient Egypt when he was asked if his Jewish slaves could go for a three days journey into the wilderness for religious reasons. He replied:

> Moses and Aaron, why do you take the people away from their work? Get to your burdens! And Pharaoh said, 'Behold the people of the land are now many and you make them rest from their burdens!' The same day Pharaoh commanded the taskmasters of the people and their fore-men, 'You shall no longer give the people straw to make bricks, as heretofore; let them go and gather straw for themselves. But the number of bricks which they made heretofore you shall lay on them you shall by no means lessen it; for they are idle; therefore they cry, 'Let us go and offer sacrifice to our God.' Let heavier work be laid upon the men that they may labor at it and pay no regard to lying words. . . .' (Ex. 5:4–9)

Struggles of self, purpose, and religion squander what would otherwise be economically productive time and energy.

Although in discussing the questions of identity New Victorians might insist that they never had the problem, experience shows that it occurs for them at a later time. For a man, it sometimes arises in the self-doubts of mid-life or at retirement when in the words of his wife he 'doesn't know what to do with himself.' He finds it difficult to derive a sense of identity from a pension check. The feminist movement, to its credit, has highlighted the issue of identity throughout a woman's life. But it has also shown the way for women to fall into the worst of the identity-through-competitive-success syndrome typically associated with the man's world.

There has been much bitter and incisive criticism of New Victorians. They are said to be 'bourgeois fossils,' beset by 'work addiction,' have a 'foreclosed identity' and be guilty of 'copping out of the human race.' They treat life's largest issues of meaning, love, and truth as luxuries to be indulged in only after economic security is established, a time which never seems to arrive. Their lives are over before they ever asked what they were about. In the words of W.I. Thompson: 'if a man could not survive the subtraction of his job from his identity, then there wasn't really much to him in the first place.'[30]

A person is obviously more than a job. One can quit or be fired and does not thereby cease to exist. Yet the New Victorian values have spread beyond those who seem obviously to be success-oriented to affect almost everyone. People move from job to job driven by the inward conviction that financial success and possessions will bring a sense of identity, but never seem to find a job that provides them with an adequate self-definition. For the same reason, those who are ashamed of the low status of their jobs or who are frustrated and inhibited in them will take a more distant and cynical attitude toward their work. For them, their identity is rooted more in their private lives – the use of their leisure time to accumulate possessions and have experiences that validate the self and supply a sense of freedom and self-determination.[31] Still others reject the New Victorianism completely and seek identity in a reaction to it. These are the New Romantics.

## The New Romanticism

The New Romanticism is the polar opposite of the New Victorianism. The older Romantic Movement rebelled against the anti-human tendencies in Rationalism, certain strands of Christian theology and the impact of the Industrial Revolution. Similarly, its newer form lashes out against the technological demands and obligations of the New Victorianism. While the New Victorian says that your identity is to be found in what you do the New Romantic says that your identity is in what you feel yourself to be. Feelings rule. The Romantic's personal emotions are the highest authority. Spontaneity is the Holy Grail. They are convinced that the inner goodness of human beings can emerge if they are freed from prescribed moral systems, organized religion, and the octopus of technology. One of their first principles is that whatever is worth doing can be achieved without much effort. Planning as a means of getting what you want is compromise. Real virtue is found by simply letting go and following wherever emotions lead. To exert oneself to accomplish something is to be inauthentic, the hypocritical pawn of others' expectations and demands. Their goal is complete spontaneity and freedom, a perfect integration of feelings and action. This is where the New Romantics hope to find an identity that is really their own.

Unlike the New Victorians, the New Romantics place a high priority on finding their identity. Work is a luxury to be indulged in only after they have got their heads together. They may work, but only when the work does not involve obligation, responsibility, or commitment lasting more than a few weeks. They stay at it as long as it stimulates or excites them . . . in short until it requires an effort to continue. As with many romantics before them, obligation is the ultimate enemy.

The New Romantic, like the New Victorian, has many critics. To these critics they are drop-outs, parasites living off others' hard work. They are held up as examples of grotesque and dangerous self-indulgence. Peter Berger despaired at the prospect of American universities becoming 'vast identity workshops,' places where 'for four years or less students sit under the trees with their shoes off and engage in the not so arduous task of finding out who they really are.'[32] Among the critics are burned out New Romantics. After living that way for three years, one woman concluded, 'I find that I'm exactly the person I used to be. There was no other poetic inner *me* waiting for me.'[33] Erik Erikson wisely questions the whole psychological basis of New Romanticism:

> If to those who seek identity, Norman Brown advocates 'Get lost' and Timothy Leary 'drop out,' I would suggest that to get lost, one must have found oneself, and to drop out one must have been in.[34]

The New Victorianism and the New Romanticism represent a deep rift in modern world views and lifestyles. Each side rejects the other, but neither has found a true sense of identity. I have deliberately cast them as caricatures, overemphasizing their differences that we might better understand their force. More realistically, most of us have elements of both within us, setting up a tug of war. They are powerful cultural forces drawing people in opposite directions, one to domination by achievements and possessions, the other to domination by emotions. It is not simply a clash between generations, but between mentalities and lifestyles of people of many ages. The conflict runs through twentieth-century literature, film, and drama. Herman Hesse, who said of himself, 'I have become a writer but I have not become a human being,' built many of his novels around this tension. *Narziss and Goldmund* is a contrast of two characters. There is Goldmund who responded to the vital forces within him, defied all obligation and moral principle and dedicated his life to sensual and artistic self-fulfillment. Although Hesse's sympathies were clearly with him, Goldmund died intensely aware of how transient and empty it had all been. The other character, Narziss, a paragon of ecclesiastical and academic responsibility and achievement, was left wondering if he had ever known what it was to live. Hesse seems to suggest that the choice we have is between being psychologically stark naked and being in a strait-jacket.

Some have seriously suggested that the only valid way to escape the deadening effects of the machine world is insanity. A more popular source of relief is sex. The New Victorian sees sex as the chief humanizer of technology, which otherwise seems to leave so little room for the human. The New Romantic also glorifies sex. *Playboy Magazine* and its counterparts unite the poles in their combination of sex and technology into one gospel. Yet the absence of a true sense of identity has put great weight on human sexuality to support the unsteady human ego. In the words of Rollo May, sex has become 'something to do when we can think of nothing to say to each other,' the body is asked to 'compensate for the abdication of the person.'[35]

Neither New Victorianism or New Romanticism is Christian, nor is one more Christian than the other. At the time of my writing, the balance in Western culture is certainly shifting toward the New Victorian. We need to be especially alert to its seductions while not rebounding to the other side. Each has some positive elements and many negative ones. Both are part of the problem which stems from the severing of the sense of identity from the Creator. A true solution must start from a different basis and build in a different direction.

The questions of identity which we have discussed in this chapter are not new. However, they arise with a special urgency in the last half of the twentieth century. Finding your true identity is not as simple as finding a lost object. It means finding an internal coherence and self-acceptance rooted in the God who made us all. In the following chapters we will look in greater detail at both the destructive and constructive factors at work in this search.

# TWO

# Identity Lost

*Most of our life is in large part a rationalization of our failure to find out who we really are, what our basic strength is, what thing it is that we were meant to work upon the world.*[1] (Ernest Becker)

*Our God in the heavens; he does whatever he pleases. Their idols are silver and gold, the work of men's hands. They have mouths, but do not speak; eyes but do not see. They have ears, but do not hear; noses, but do not smell. They have hands but do not feel; feet, but do not walk; and they do not make a sound in their throat. Those who make them are like them; so are all who trust in them.*
(David, Ps. 115:3–8)

The Bible makes an extraordinary affirmation that human beings are not only a creation of God, but that they were created in the image or likeness of the Creator himself. This correspondence between God and humankind did not origi-nate in the wishful imagination of early people, but in the imprint left by the creative act of God. The Christian claim is that human beings are in fact the counter-player of His identity and that the meaning of their lives is found in terms of interaction with their Creator. We have seen how the broken relationship between humanity and God is a critical factor in our problems of identity. Now let us consider the loss of identity in the light of biblical knowledge about both creation and fall.

## Identity Before the Fall of Humankind

Humankind bears the image of God in two ways. Adam was like God in the way he was and also in what he did, in his being and also in his doing. Theologians have called these two aspects the natural or ontological likeness, and the moral likeness of God respectively.

### Humankind, the Image of God by Nature

The Christian faith holds that every person, no matter how good or bad he or she might be, is the image of God. They bear the stamp of God's nature however they might choose to live. This is the ontological likeness of God. The biblical writers do not spell out exactly what aspects of human nature correspond with those of God. In fact the issue is not raised in this technical way at all. We are the image of God as whole persons in our whole being (Gn. 1:26–7).

It is not that certain parts of our nature reflect God and others do not, nor is it the case that the divine image is something that is located within us somewhere. We are told, however, that while we were made in God's likeness the animals were not. This may mean that we can point to a certain focus of God's image in those qualities of human nature that separate us from animals. These qualities are notoriously difficult to define with precision, yet all of us instinctively know that the differences between us and animals are impossible to avoid. It seems that only human beings are aware of themselves as selves. Only they are able to reflect on themselves and their own experiences. From this self-awareness comes all the creative, moral, rational, and religious capacities that are part of what we call human personality.

People are aware of themselves in a way that they cannot be aware of others. There is a central 'I am' in each of us that seems the core of our consciousness. This 'I am' corresponds to the nature of God who described himself as 'I am that I am' (Ex. 3:14). Our 'I amness' can be a source of glory and joy, or of pain and confusion in the despair of those who actually envy the animals.

A human being is the image of God in his or her being, however we may choose to use our abilities. A cruel and heartless person is as much the image of God in this sense as the person who is kind and loving, not because these qualities have nothing to do with the divine image, but because we are ontologically the image of God irrespective of how we use or misuse our gifts and abilities. Indeed, the Bible shows us that God puts great value on human beings even after they have rebelled against him. It is wrong to murder anyone, good or bad, because all humankind are made in God's image (Gn. 9:6). Sinful humankind is in the image of God despite our sin (Gn. 5:1–3; Jas. 3:9). When we insult a poor person we insult our Maker (Prov. 17:5). The value of any human being does not come from goodness or creativity, a contribution to the state, the economy, the size of a bank account or even the number of one's press clippings. Our value is because we carry in our whole beings the image of God.

### Humankind, the Image of God by Our Lives

In the original creation, humankind was also the moral likeness of God. When they were created, Adam and Eve perfectly reflected God's nature not only in their being but in their life and behavior. They were perfectly righteous in the way they used the gifts and abilities that God had given them. Since they were in God's likeness, God gave them a task to do analogous with his own.

They were to have dominion over the earth, to subdue it (Gn. 1:26–7), by being creative in it as God was Creator of it. Human activity then was to be a mirror reflection of God's, both in what we did and in how we did it. Dominion involved action, not just reaction. Human beings shared in a limited way God's transcendence over the natural world. The whole scope of human creativity is rooted in this dominion or mastery over the world. Adam and Eve had work to do in the garden, a God-given lordship over the place where God had put them. It came naturally to them to carry out this dominion in obedience to God. They were able to be holy as God was holy.

We might say that Adam and Eve enjoyed perfect integration, integration between themselves and God, between man and woman, and between themselves and the rest of God's world. Humankind enjoyed fulfillment internally also because our being, feelings, abilities, and actions were integrated with one another. 'And God saw everything that He had made, and behold, it was very good' (Gn. 1:31). A fundamental foundation stone of the Christian faith is that as humankind reflects God's character we thereby realize our own true character, identity, and individual selfhood. Ours is not a manufactured identity but an identity derived from our Maker.

## Identity and the Fall

The third chapter of the book of Genesis tells the story of how humankind sinned. By rebellion against God they chose not to reflect the nature of their Creator in obedience, but rather to usurp his throne, authority, and the moral direction of creation. It was a fundamental change in the orientation of Adam's life. He had been created to live for God; now he attempted to establish his existence and life as independent from God.

Several non-Christian thinkers have remarked on the irrepressible human desire to be God. Bertrand Russell wrote, 'Everyman would like to be God if it were possible; some find it difficult to admit the impossibility.'[2] Jean-Paul Sartre made a similar observation: 'man is the being whose project is to become God . . . To be man means to reach toward being God.' This is not some innocent illusion, like a child pretending to be the fire chief. This drive to be God is the ultimate source of human evil, the root of our misery, apalling self-centeredness and cruelty.[3] Of course this drive is exactly what the Bible points to as the essence of original sin. This sin is pride, the desire to displace God and occupy his throne. This was precisely the nature of the temptation, 'when you eat of it your eyes will be opened, and you will be like God, knowing good and evil' (Gn. 3:5). The original sin is refusal to be and live as a creature and instead to pretend at knowing better than God himself, to set oneself up as the ultimate judge. H.R. Niebuhr puts it well:

> All human action, all culture, is infected with Godlessness, which is the essence of sin. Godlessness appears as the will to live without God, to ignore Him, to be one's own source and beginning, to live without being indebted and forgiven, to be independent and secure in one's self, to be Godlike in oneself.[4]

The original sin is not always expressed in conscious animosity toward God. More often it is a polite relegation of God to irrelevance. Nevertheless, it is still an expression of humankind's cosmic rebellion against our Maker – human beings taking our stance in independence from anything greater than ourselves. Shirley MacLaine illustrates this attitude well in a 1977 *Washington Post* interview,

'. . . the most pleasurable journey you take is through yourself . . . the only sustaining love involvement is with yourself. When you look back on your life and try to figure out where you've been and where you are going, when you look at your work, your love affairs, your marriages, your children, your pain, your happiness – when you examine all that closely, what you really find out is that the only person you really go to bed with is yourself. The only person you really dress is yourself. The only thing you do have is working to the consummation of your own identity.'[5]

The first sin fractured the harmony of Adam's life and destroyed the integration he enjoyed before the Fall. In its place came alienation in his relationship with God, with his wife, with nature, and within himself. Adam and Eve felt threatened by the presence of God and hid from him. Their environment no longer suited them perfectly but frustrated them in every area. The whole of creation was abnormal, and their moral reflection of God was twisted and bent. Physical and psychological suffering now became part of life, true guilt and shame an everyday experience.

The most inescapable and painful result of sin in the world is death. We cannot overemphasize or forget the abnormality of the intrusion of death. Humankind was made to have dominion over the earth, but our rebellion gave the earth dominion over us – 'you are dust and to dust you shall return' (Gn. 3:19). Death threatens to negate our identity itself; it is the final enemy to human ambition and psychological safety. It is the end of our dominion on this planet. In the words of William James, death is 'the worm at the core' of human happiness.[6] Since the Fall, much human thought and behavior has been an effort to either forget or deny the reality of death. We see it in the form of 'death-defying' feats of daring as well as in forced light-heartedness. Even the Christian, who has an answer to death, seldom takes his own death seriously today. Zilboorg writes:

> In normal times we move about actually without ever believing in our own death, as if we fully believed in our own corporeal immortality. We are intent on mastering death . . . A man will say, of course, that he knows he will die some day, but he does not really care. He is having a good time with living, and he does not think about death and does not care to bother about it – but this is purely intellectual verbal admission. The affect of fear is repressed.[7]

Death is God's indelible and inescapable stamp of 'Failure' on our attempt at Godhood. As such it is a source of embarrassment, confusion, and agony to those whose hope is in their own self-sufficiency. It remains as God's silent, tangible and ever-present witness that we cannot be independent and secure in ourselves. Yet we as a race have not given up the attempt at Godhood. The same sin of pride which was at the heart of the Fall fuels a continuing rebellion. Humanity still tries to make good on Satan's promise that 'you shall be like God.' A great tension is created between our expectations and ambitions for ourselves and the reality of death in a fallen world. The writer of Ecclesiastes concluded,

> For of the wise man as of the fool there is no enduring remembrance, seeing that in the days to come all will have been long forgotten. How the wise man dies just like the fool! (Eccl. 2:16)

But death is a problem only because 'he has put eternity into man's mind' (Eccl. 3:11). Death would not be so outrageous were it not for all the human expectations that it negates. We have illusions of being God, our minds can span millions of years, and yet w e will become dust. From the perspective of modern existentialism, Ernest Becker writes:

> Man is literally split in two; he has an awareness of his own splendid uniqueness in that he sticks out of nature with a towering majesty, and yet he goes back into the ground a few feet in order to blindly and dumbly rot and disappear forever. It is a terrifying dilemma to be in and to have to live with.[8]

This tension between the desire to be God and the realities of human life in the world is not a far-away philosophical problem. It is a tension between our desire to be the center of the world, and a world order that was not even in its original perfection designed with human beings at the center. It reaches into the most practical areas of our lives. Daniel Boorstin touched on this when he wrote about the extraordinary level of expectations in American society:

> When we pick up our newspaper at breakfast, we expect – we even demand – that it bring us momentous events since the night before. We turn on the car radio as we drive to work and expect 'news' to have occurred since the morning newspaper went to press. Returning in the evening, we expect our house not only to shelter us, to keep us warm in winter and cool in summer, but to relax us, to dignify us, to encompass us with soft music and interesting hobbies, to be a playground, a theatre, and a bar. We expect our two-week vacation to be romantic, exotic, cheap and effortless. We expect a far-away atmosphere if we go to a near-by place; and we expect everything to be relaxing, sanitary, and Americanized if we go to a far-away place. We expect new heroes every season, a literary masterpiece every month, a dramatic spectacular every week, a rare sensation every night. We expect everybody to feel free to disagree, yet we expect everybody to be loyal, not to rock the boat or take the Fifth Amendment. We expect everybody

to believe deeply in his religion, yet not to think less of others for not believing. We expect our nation to be strong and great and vast and varied and prepared for every challenge; yet we expect our 'national purpose' to be clear and simple, something that gives direction to the lives of nearly two hundred million people and yet can be bought in a paperback at the corner drugstore for a dollar.

We expect anything and everything. We expect the contra- dictory and the impossible. We expect compact cars which are spacious; luxurious cars which are economical. We expect to be rich and charitable, powerful and merciful, active and reflective, kind and competitive. We expect to be inspired by mediocre appeals for 'excellence,' to be made literate by illit- erate appeals for literacy. We expect to eat and stay thin, to be constantly on the move and ever more neighbourly, to go to the 'church of our choice' and yet feel its guiding power over us, to revere God and to be God.

Never have people been more the masters of their environ- ment. Yet never has a people felt more deceived and disap- pointed. For never has a people expected so much more than the world could offer.[9]

The terrible irony of the Fall is that we expect more than Eden and yet can only realize far less. Even when our power over nature and other people has reached undreamed of heights through technology and the modern state, our basic problem remains, 'we are like the beasts that perish' (Ps. 49:13). Not only will we perish, but 'when his breath departs he returns to his earth; on that very day his *plans* perish' (Ps. 146:4).

The Fall's blow to human identity is clear. Instead of naturally reflecting our Creator in a perfect world, we are bearing a twisted image of God and live in a fallen world which yields to our dominion only in a limited and double edged way for the short time until we die. The Fall affects our identity in three ways. First, it breaks the relationship between us and God. God becomes a threat and human beings dislike him. Second, it distorts the image of God that we bear. We become unlike God. The moral likeness between God and ourselves is now distorted, for which we are guilty. Thirdly, the whole creation including humankind groans under the abnormality of a world infected by sin and death.

But an important distinction must be made between our worth and our worthiness. Sinful people, unworthy as we are, are not worthless. Because of sin, humankind is unworthy of the blessing of God in any form. We deserve only judicial punishment for our rebellion against God. But this is not to say that we have lost all worth or value. We are still God's image although we have marred that image morally. God still loves us and wants us to be saved and come to a knowledge of the truth (1 Tim. 2:4). We still have dignity as human beings, image-bearers of God, even though we might not know who we are or the reason for our dignity. Worth and worthiness are often confused in Christian teachings. But merit – what a person deserves – is very different from value, what a person is worth. Some Christians, rightly trying not to minimize the sinfulness of human beings, have wrongly called people worthless. We do not honor the Creator by belittling the highest part of his creation on earth – humankind. Although our moral imageness is perverted and spoiled by sin, we are still God's image by nature, and therefore of value in the sight of God.

How does the Fall affect the four factors which shape our sense of identity – morals, models, dominion, and love? It is clear that the Fall has left its legacy in each of these areas.

## A Problem with Morals: Guilt and the Fear of Honesty

There are two aspects to the human moral problem. First is the experience of guilt; second is what we do about that experience of guilt.

*Guilt*

Modern thought relentlessly undercuts the reality of guilt.
Moral philosophers might say guilt is impossible because
there are no longer moral absolutes and standards. Some
psychologists deny guilt because, they say, all human acts are
determined, not freely chosen. Other psychologists claim that
people do wrong because their inner anxieties obstruct their
basically good intentions and so should not be treated as
guilty. A politician might refuse to call political outrages
dishonest, but rather see them as irregularities, indiscretions,
or miscalculations. These claims and rationalizations dilute
an awareness of guilt. But by dispensing with inconvenient
rules, modern people have lost a moral basis for all decisions.

   By contrast, the Bible is quite clear that moral guilt is real.
Sin means objective moral guilt before a holy God. Sin is
rebellion. The apostle John wrote, 'Everyone who commits
sin is guilty of lawlessness; sin is lawlessness' (1 Jn. 3:4). Sin
is also falling short of a standard. Paul wrote, 'All have
sinned and fall short of the glory of God' (Rom. 3:22–3).
Falling short of God's standards is something of an under-
statement because it assumes that people are actually aiming
at those standards. If the truth be known, we seldom aim
seriously at God's perfect standards. But even when we do
aim at God's moral law, we fall short. Jesus himself had
some of the most unsettling things of all to say about sin
and guilt. He denied any suggestion that sin is a superficial
or external problem. He said, 'For out of the heart come
evil thoughts, murder, adultery, fornication, theft, false
witness, slander' (Mt. 15:19). True moral guilt is real, and
it comes from problems within us.

   Moral guilt needs to be taken seriously in contrast to the
many modern forms of our self-congratulation. But that is
not to say that all feelings of guilt correspond to real guilt
before God. There is a complex relationship between guilt

feelings and true moral guilt. I will mention a few of the forms of this relationship. We can have feelings of guilt when we are in fact guilty of breaking the commandments of God. Our feelings then accurately reflect a true state of affairs. We can also feel no guilt when in fact we are guilty. In this case our emotions do not reflect the true state of affairs. Thus we can peacefully sleep as Jonah did in the ship while sailing as fast and as far as he could from carrying out God's task for him. Then we might have strong feelings of guilt about things that are not wrong at all in the sight of God. These can come from impressions left on us at an early age that certain things are 'not done,' such as playing cards, going to the theater, relaxing and enjoying oneself, or experiencing our own sexuality. These guilt feelings are false guilt, and the pseudo-moral standards that cause them must be exposed for what they are – otherwise we leave ourselves in confusion, unnec- essary suffering and also divert our attention from what might be real moral issues that we should deal with. False guilt can also be more diffuse and unspecifiable, pervading one's whole existence. This could be the result of having played or been forced into the role of the one who always took the blame for any failure or conflict.

Even after separating out as best we can the false guilt that we feel, we will be left with true guilt, and most of us will feel it in some ways. Since the feeling of guilt itself is a feeling of unacceptability, it is very uncomfortable and attacks the side of identity which is self-acceptance. It undermines our confidence in ourselves as solid people, able to live out what we know to be true and valuable.

### The Fear of Honesty

The same pride that moves humankind to sin makes it hard for us to face our sin openly. Our failure to face our moral failure magnifies the effect of that failure on our lives. Just as the cover-up in the Watergate scandal caused more trouble than the original crime, so our cover-up of our sin can be worse than the sin itself.

The cover-up began in the garden. As soon as they sinned, Adam and Eve were unable to face God, each other, or themselves. They felt confused, guilty, and naked. Their dishonesty before God in the garden was not premeditated or malicious deception. In response to the Lord's terrifying interrogation, they seemed to lie quite spontaneously as a natural way of coping with the threat of personal exposure. This response sets the pattern for much of human history. More often than we care to admit, deception is the way we cope with threatening situations and personal guilt. Dishon-esty can come as naturally as the reflex action of blinking the eye or raising the hand to protect the face. As we look through the pages of the Bible we will see the legacy of this first deception in others' lives and in our own. Although it is morally wrong and inexcusable, deception of the self and others is very easy to do, and comes quite naturally to Adam and Eve's descendents.

One of the commonest ways to deny one's sin is to shift the blame onto others. Adam started it when he said to God, 'The woman whom thou gavest to be with me, she gave me the fruit of the tree and I ate' (Gn. 3:12). The woman, in turn, blamed the serpent. We all continue their tradition. To avoid the pain of facing ourselves and having others see us as we are, we shift the blame to some one else.

Criticizing others solves two problems at once. It takes our minds off uncomfortable thoughts about ourselves, and, further, focuses the blame for all woes safely in the inade-quacy of someone else. Criticism easily serves as a cover-up for guilt, anxiety, and self-hatred. A classic illustration is found in the Old Testament account of Israel's King David, Bathsheba, and Nathan the prophet (2 Sam. 11:12). David, leader of the army, as well as king, was at home while his

army was fighting a battle against a foreign city. One afternoon he made love to Bathsheba, the wife of one of David's
soldiers who was away in battle. Bathsheba became pregnant. After unsuccessful efforts to have her husband get credit
for the pregnancy, David arranged to get rid of him by having
him killed in battle, then married Bathsheba and they settled
down as if nothing had ever happened. After a time God sent
Nathan to David, ostensibly to ask his verdict in a legal
matter. The problem that Nathan presented was this: there
were two men, one rich with many sheep and cattle, the other
poor with only one ewe lamb who lived as one of his family.
A traveller came to visit the rich man. Rather than taking one
of his own many sheep to provide a meal, the rich man took
away the poor man's lamb, killed it, and prepared it for his
visitor. Nathan asked the king's opinion on what legal steps
ought to be taken in this matter:

> Then David's anger was greatly kindled against the man; and
> he said to Nathan, 'As the Lord lives, the man who has done
> this deserves to die; and he shall restore the lamb fourfold,
> because he did this thing, and because he had no pity.'
> Nathan said to David, 'You are the man.' (2 Sam. 12:5-7)

Several things about David's reaction to the story are
significant. First, his moral outrage at what the man had
done was overzealous. The death penalty was beyond the
prescribed punishment for sheep stealing in the law of the
land (Ex. 22:1). David's covered-up guilt had made him
cruel and high-handed. Even more significant is the type of
crime that David wanted to over-punish. It was precisely
when showed a carefully scripted picture of himself that he
flew into such a rage and said, 'The man deserves to die.'
Self-hatred smoldered inside David. He lashed out at another man who had violated common decency, but his
self-hatred was at the root of his anger.

Are we not often bothered most by those who have our own faults? We feel a certain perverse relief from our own sense of guilt and inadequacy if we can criticize someone with the same inadequacies. The anger we are afraid to direct at ourselves can be projected and transferred else-where, thereby temporarily freeing us from its weight. Or as Elizabeth O'Connor wrote, 'What we repress in our-selves we will project onto the neighbor and try to destroy there.'[10]

On the surface, it might seem that David had gotten away with adultery and murder until Nathan came to him. However, many biblical scholars maintain that in Psalms 32 and 38 David looks back to this particular period during which his sin was undeclared even to himself. Although this cannot be proven conclusively, the account of intense psychological suffering in these psalms suggests that his self-hatred was being worked out in the form of internal self-punishment.

> When I declared not my sin, my body wasted away through my groaning all day long.
> For day and night thy hand was heavy upon me; my strength was dried up as by the heat of summer. (Ps. 32:3–4)

Ultimately, shifting the blame does not work. It may seem to spare us the pain of self-knowledge and public humili-ation, but the price is internal disintegration, subconscious or semi-conscious guilt, and anger and depression. Listen to David's own words:

> My wounds grow foul and fester because of my foolishness, I am utterly bowed down and prostrate; all the day I go about mourning.
> For my loins are filled with burning, and there is no soundness in my flesh.

I am utterly spent and crushed; I groan because of the tumult of my heart. (Ps. 38:5–8)

A close cousin to blameshifting is hypocrisy, another expression of the fear of honesty. Hypocrisy is simply the application of high moral standards to others while applying low standards to ourselves. James wrote in his letter:

> But be doers of the word, and not hearers only, deceiving yourselves. For if any one is a hearer of the word and not a doer, he is like a man who observes his natural face in a mirror; for he observes himself and goes away and at once forgets what he was like . . . If any one thinks he is religious and does not bridle his tongue but deceives his heart, this man's religion is in vain. (Jas. 1:22–4,26)

James describes someone who hears God's word, agrees with it, but does not do it. Here I would draw attention to its profound consequences to our sense of identity. Notice how James's terminology is built around the disintegration of the hearer's personality. First of all, hearers deceive themselves (v. 22). Consequently, they do not know them-selves because if they ever do get a glimpse of themselves as they really are they at once forget what they were like (vv. 23–4). Finally hearers deceive their hearts (v. 26), a particularly grave deception because the heart is the very center of the person's being. James says that hearers allow deception to penetrate the core of their personalities. They see reality through a double-standard and becomes like the 'double-minded man, unstable in all his ways' (Jas. 1:7–8). David Belgum points out that hypocrisy is more serious than other sins because it is 'a method of dealing with sin which prevents a solution . . . It prevents one from facing reality objectively.'[11] If the hypocrites are aware of the hypocrisy, they may think that they are getting away with something.

Nothing could be farther from the truth. They squander one of the most valuable assets they have – their own integrity.

The self-deceiver is vulnerable. As people follow the path of blameshifting and hypocrisy, they become accus-tomed to deception. They deceive themselves more than others. The more dishonest they are with themselvs the more threatening honesty becomes. They must not only conceal acts and feelings that they are ashamed of, but also the deceptions and denials of those acts and feelings. Again this is deeply destructive to one's sense of identity. Karl Menninger wrote:

> The human conscience is like the police; it may be eluded, stifled, drugged, or bribed, but not without cost. We know some of these costs. [12]

One of these costs is vulnerability of the sort that we saw in David. O.H. Mowrer asks:

> What could more naturally produce a feeling of unreality about oneself, and life in general than the practice of deceit and misrepresentation? [13]

You cannot indulge in such deception without undermin-ing yourself and also your relationships with others. By fearing to face yourself or have others see you as you really are, you develop a huge stake in self-protection and are therefore threatened by relationships in which you are not in complete control. Could it be that all of us have at least an intuitive suspicion of the truth of Jesus' words, 'Nothing is covered up that will not be revealed, or hidden that will not be known' (Lk. 12:2)?

Take for example the incident of Joseph and his brothers in the book of Genesis (Gn. 37:39–43). In an act of exas-peration and jealousy, the brothers had sold their little brother, Joseph, into slavery. Years later when the brothers came to Egypt looking for food they were imprisoned and accused of being spies, not recognizing that it was in fact Joseph (his appearance changed) who was accusing them. Their first response was to assume that God was punishing them for their guilt against Joseph:

> Then they said to one another, 'In truth we are guilty concerning our brother, in that we saw the distress of his soul, when he besought us and we would not listen; therefore is this distress come upon us.' (Gn. 42:21)

They had all been feeling guilt for years over their sin: when disaster struck them, they instantly concluded that it was the result of the 'long forgotten' sin. Reuben chimed in, 'Did I not tell you not to sin against the lad?' (v. 22), as if their sin had just happened the previous day. All this time they had been carrying about the sense of guilt causing them anxiety, self-doubt and dread of God's judgment. Their imprisonment simply pried it into the open.

Paul in his last letter warns that treacherous and godless people will come and make easy prey of 'weak women, burdened with sins and swayed by various impulses, who will listen to anybody and can never arrive at a knowledge of the truth' (2 Tim. 3:6–7). Paul's warning could almost be a check-list of crumbling identity. I suggest that the crucial problem is that the weak women are burdened with sins. Sin that burdens is sin that is not faced directly and dealt with by taking it to God and (if necessary) other people. It is sin that is run away from, and hidden, but at the same time carried around one's neck in the form of insecurity, fear, dread of discovery, and lack of confidence in oneself. Everything else follows: weakness, lack of discernment, and being a hapless victim of other people's strong opinions and false teaching.

The Samaritan woman whom Jesus met at the well (Jn. 4) is another good example. After her conversation with Jesus she rushed away and said to the people in the city, 'Come, see a man who told me all that I ever did' (v. 29). Jesus had actually done no such thing. He had simply told her about the one thing that she had been trying to conceal. Perhaps it seemed to her like 'all that I ever did' because she had let her whole identity be defined by sins that she would not honestly face.

Finally, we can see the more positive side of the honesty question in Proverbs 10:9: 'He who walks in integrity walks securely, but he who perverts his ways will be found out.' Deception brings vulnerability, but integrity brings security. Integrity does not mean sinlessness, but among other things, honesty about our sin. It therefore belongs not just to the angels, but to any of us who is willing to face our sin and weakness before the living God.

## Shame: A Problem with Models

We feel shame but seldom talk about it.[14] Perhaps we are ashamed to; shame is too close, too personal. Another reason is our assumption that shame is the same thing as guilt, so that we have understood shame when we have dealt with guilt. This is not so. We will begin by comparing shame with guilt, then look at its particular relationship to models and finally get to the root of the experience itself as it bears on our quest for identity.

### Shame and Guilt

You may remember that we mentioned the importance of models or heroes and heroines to our sense of identity. They are the targets of our aspirations and represent for us honor and glory. Just as guilt is a falling short of moral norms or commandments, shame is a falling short of our models, our sense of what it is to be heroic. Both guilt and shame have in common that they are feelings of unacceptability, so they are easily confused. But they point to two distinguishable standards of self-evaluation – one based on morals (guilt) and the other on models (shame): The difference between shame and guilt becomes clearer when we look at the opposite of these words in biblical thought. The opposite of guilt is innocence, a state of being blameless or guiltless. The opposite of shame, however, is not innocence, but rather glory and honor. This is clear in many places in the Bible. Look at two examples from the Old Testament:

> I will turn their glory into shame. (Hos. 4:6–7)

> Let us lie down in our shame and let our dishonor cover us; for we have sinned against the Lord our God. (Jer. 3:25)

An experience of shame is therefore an experience of being dishonorable or inglorious.

There are three ways that guilt and shame can relate to each other: First, they can overlap; we can feel both shame and guilt at the same time for the same reason. For example, if you have lied you can feel guilty because the lie was morally wrong and you can also feel ashamed of the lie. You thought you were strong enough to admit a mistake but you found yourself lying to protect yourself. You felt both guilt at having done wrong and shame at being so weak.

Second, shame and guilt can be independent of each other. You may be ashamed of something that is not wrong or that is morally neutral. For example, many people are ashamed of being poor. They will not take you (if they think you are richer) to their home – 'I'd rather die than let you see where I live' – and they will not let you know about their financial need. Others are ashamed of not being a success, and they will exaggerate the importance of their jobs. But a different person in a different social setting might feel ashamed of being rich. Most of us at some time are ashamed of our bodies or part of our bodies. We have the wrong color skin, the wrong shape to our nose, we sink in or hang out in the wrong places, we are too fat or too thin, too tall or too short, our clothes don't fit, or we are physically uncoordinated. We feel shame for what we say and how we say it. We are ashamed of our accent, bad pronunciation, the joke that no one laughs at, and the serious remark that everyone does laugh at. We can be ashamed of love that is unreturned. We can be ashamed of being dependent on others' care because we are sick. All of these things are in themselves morally neutral; we cannot apply moral categories to them. Nevertheless, the moral neutrality does not reduce the pain of shame. In fact our feelings of shame at tripping and falling in front of other people can be more painful than feelings of guilt after outright dishonesty.

Thirdly, shame and guilt can work against each other. We can be ashamed of doing something that is morally right or ashamed for not doing something that is morally wrong. An outstanding example of this is found in Raskolnikov, the chief character in Dostoyevsky's *Crime and Punishment*. Raskolnikov was dreadfully ashamed at not having the courage to kill an old lady. It was this shame as much as anything that ultimately drove him to kill her. Many Christians have had the experience at points in their lives of being ashamed of knowing Jesus Christ and being identified as Christians. Here shame and guilt are antagonists.

Shame is therefore not merely false guilt, but it is a pointer to a different standard or self-measuring system – the heroic. Thus, shame and guilt can interact in these diverse ways – working side by side, independently or in opposition to each other, depending on the way our morals and models relate.

### Models

We think in pictures, images, stories, and myths, of heroes and heroines as well as in logical sequences. All of us have models of some sort, real or imaginary people with whom we identify. Our models represent in flesh and blood what to us is heroic or glorious. Maybe very few of us are like Oliver Cromwell who, when asked whether he wanted to have his warts included in an official portrait, is said to have replied bravely that he should be painted, 'warts and all.' Your model self is an ideal self-portrait with no warts. It is the person or people that you would want to be and, maybe, that you are a little bit already.

James Thurber's 'The Secret Life of Walter Mitty' is a famous short story because it shows this inner world of imagination jarring radically against the real world in a way that is both amusing and tragic. Walter Mitty is a mousy little man always being tongue-lashed by his wife. Mitty, however, has a vivid imagination; he is an expert daydreamer. On a trip to town with his wife, Mitty imagines himself as the dashing commander of an eight-engined Navy hydroplane, taking it through the worst storm in twenty years of Navy flying. He is suddenly interrupted by the voice of his wife, 'Not so fast! You're driving too fast! What are you driving so fast for?' Driving past a hospital on his way to the parking lot, he sees himself as a world-renowned surgeon called in by other surgeons to save the life of a millionaire banker and personal friend of President Roosevelt. Just as he is about to operate, another voice breaks in:

'Back it up, Mac. Look out for that Buick!' Walter Mitty jammed on the brakes. 'Wrong lane, Mac,' said the parking lot attendant, looking at Mitty closely. 'Gee. Yeh,' muttered Mitty. He began cautiously to back out of the lane marked 'Exit Only.'[15]

Thurber pulls Mitty down from his imaginative glory and heroism to real-life shame, and each time lets him wander back to his imagined glory once again. It strikes the reader as pathetic, but also is disturbing because it is not so far from what we see in ourselves. The world of Walter Mitty's models is his secret world. So it is with most of us. Our models are more difficult to articulate than our morals and usually much more private.

Our heroes are often completely unrealistic as a guide for life. Here we can see the impact of the Fall on our imagina - tions. Too easily our imaginations serve our own vanity so that our models would lead us away from what is morally right and also worthwhile. Evil has an inherent attraction for us, and this is nowhere so true as in the formation of our models. But at the same time heroism today is typically quite inaccessible to the normal person, and these models frustrate and tyrannize us. Consumer advertising thrives on our longing to be something different than we are. It makes us frustrated with the drabness of our appearance, life-style, and possessions and urges us to identify with a model who does not have our problem. Media women are always beautiful and poised; media men never make foolish mistakes or experience drudgery. These people affect all of us.

The power of media models struck me when I watched a television show on which a well-known actor appeared. In his film roles, this man was always poised and cool. He always said exactly the right thing at the right moment. I envied this actor because one of my frustrations with myself is that although I can usually think of the right thing to say, the words come to me a day later. On the television show, this man had no script, but was just trying to be his charming self. However, as I watched I could see that he was just as nervous, inarticulate, and awkward as I would have been in a similar situation. I was delighted. A little bit too delighted. I realized that I enjoyed the actor's discomfort only because his film roles had power over me. It came as a great relief to realize that the tyranny of that model was at least temporarily broken.

A good way to discover who your own models are is to ask yourself what kind of things make you feel ashamed. Every time you experience shame, there is a hero or heroine that you have violated. It may not be a certain individual who is a hero or heroine for you, but perhaps the idea that certain kinds of things are heroic.

However unrealistic or unhelpful our heroes or heroines are for us to aspire to, they end up having a great influence on our lives, sometimes more influence than our moral standards. Sex roles are very important, and usually come from our models more than from moral principles. In our culture there are still varied and rigid stereotypes of masculinity and femininity and what kinds of occupations, feelings, and actions are appropriate to both. One of the hallmarks of our time is the polarization of sex-stereotypes. There are some men whose attachment to the macho model would not allow them to be seen hanging up laundry or changing diapers. Others have no trouble with this at all and are the ones who provide the main care of the children while their wives work outside the home. Female stereotypes today are even more polarized. Some women feel threatened by their own competence, their models being women whose husbands provide it. They would never get their hands dirty under the hood of a car or change an electrical plug. Their polar opposite, on the other hand, would never stay at home with the children when she could have a career because that would be squandering her potential. None of these restrictions necessarily come from lack of ability, but from the narrowness of stereotypes which have become internalized into models. Violating these models will produce shame.

The prophet Isaiah reserves biting scorn for a hero-system still prevalent today: 'Woe to those who are heroes at drinking wine, and valiant men at mixing strong drink . . .' (Is. 5:22). There are many for whom the model of a big time sinner is heroic and they do not have the courage to violate it. I know many who have refused to believe in Jesus Christ not because they didn't know that he is true, but because they could not bear to part with a certain macho image.

### The Experience of Shame

Shame is what you experience when you suddenly realize that you have fallen short of your models. You have behaved unheroically. You thought you knew the sort of person you were, the kind of person who would never say or do *that*. But you *have* said it or done it. 'I cannot have done that, it isn't me! But I *have* done it. It is me.'

Shame is a major theme of existentialist literature. Jean-Paul Sartre gives a classic description of it. Whether moved by jealousy, curiosity, or vice, I am eavesdropping on some one, looking intently through the key-hole of their door. Suddenly I hear footsteps in the hall behind me. Some one has been watching me.[16] Here is an experience of shame. You are not a peeping-Tom, some kind of voyeur. And yet, there you are, caught at it. Not only are you exposed in the eyes of another, but more importantly you are exposed in your own eyes. You didn't think that you were that kind of person, but as it turns out, you are.

Public humiliation or embarrassment is not intrinsic to shame. Shame is at root a loss of trust in yourself. You are not so glorious or heroic as you thought. Shame jars your sense of your own identity, your certainty about who you are at some bedrock level. You wish intensely that you were someone else, more heroic.

The biblical writers often speak of shame as confusion of face or being disoriented. Shame is like rottenness in one's bones (Prov. 12:4). The Bible often associates shame and nakedness, not because our bodies are shameful, but because nakedness represents total exposure with all self-illusions stripped away. At the beginning, Adam and Eve were naked, but were not ashamed. After their rebellion their first response was to feel shame at being naked. Their bodies were the same bodies, but their relationship to God, to themselves, and to each other had radically changed. They had suddenly lost trust in themselves and their understanding of the world.

The twenty-ninth and thirtieth chapters of the book of Job contain one of the most moving descriptions of shame. Job contrasts the man he used to be with the man he had become. First, he recalls his previous stature in society.

> Men listened to me, and waited, and kept silence for my counsel.
>
> After I spoke they did not speak again, and my word dropped upon them.
>
> They waited for me as for the rain; and they opened their mouths as for the spring rain.
>
> I smiled on them when they had no confidence; and the light of my countenance they did not cast down.
>
> I chose their way, and sat as chief, and I dwelt like a king among his troops, like one who comforts mourners (Job 29:21–5).

The contrast with his current state is painful, and Job's shame is intense:

> But now they make sport of me, men who are younger than I, whose fathers I would have disdained to set with the dogs of my flock.

What could I gain from the strength of their hands, men
whose vigor is gone? . . .
A senseless, a disreputable brood, they have been whipped
out of the land.
And now I have become their song, I am a byword to them.
They abhor me, they keep aloof from me; they do not hesitate
to spit at the sight of me. (Job 30:1–2, 8–10)

This is an honest picture of a man of faith who has let his
idea of the heroic be tied too much to his position above
others in society. When that status was taken away, he
agonized in shame. Although Job did not know it at the
time, he was participating in a far greater struggle in which
he would emerge in true heroism.

Shame strikes directly at our identity by showing us that
we are not who we thought we were. It attacks our self-acceptance because at the center of it is the feeling of self-rejection. Shame shrinks your identity. Recall a time when
you felt intense shame. Your whole being seems to be
reduced to that one shameful act. Nothing else you have
ever done matters. Only the shameful act sums you up. *That*
is who you are.

## Crossfire

Often we are bundles of contradictions at a deep level. Our
morals and models are sometimes at loggerheads. We may
get our morals from the Sermon on the Mount and the Ten
Commandments, and our models from Hollywood. This
conflict between morals and models, between values and
heroes, undermines our identity by pulling us in opposite
directions.

For example, the chance comes along to lie to get ahead
in your job. Your moral principles tell you 'no,' so you will
feel guilt if you lie anyway. But if your model for yourself

is the aggressive, clever success-oriented man or woman, you may feel shame if you don't lie to get ahead. 'You are soft,' the voice says, 'the sort of person that never does make it. You aren't tough enough. People like you never get ahead.' You are caught in a crossfire between guilt and shame. One or the other will get you – or both will if the crossfire immobilizes you in anxious indecision. However it works out, life becomes a whirlpool of confusion and self-hatred.

Perhaps we can see this very problem in King Herod's dealings with John the Baptist (Mk. 6:14–29). John had rebuked Herod for his adulterous marriage to Herodias, who had been his brother's wife. Kings were not used to being treated that way, so John was imprisoned. Herodias hated John and wanted him dead, but Herod kept him safe in prison because he respected John as a righteous and holy man who spoke with an integrity that attracted him. Then Herod had a birthday banquet; Herodias's daughter danced so beauti-fully that Herod rashly promised to grant her any wish, 'even half of my kingdom.' At her mother's prompting she asked for John the Baptist's head. This put Herod in a crossfire. What was he to do? He knew perfectly well that it would be morally wrong to kill John and that he would be guilty if he did so. On the other hand, if he backed away from his public promise to his step-daughter, he would face shame and be exposed as a fool, for all at the party to see. Herod was 'exceedingly sorry' (v. 26) but chose to act according to his models and grant her request. Of course this act assaulted Herod's identity anyway. It exposed him as such a weak and confused man that he could not risk backing down to do the right thing – even from a foolish promise. Later, when Herod heard of Jesus, he assumed that Jesus was John the Baptist come back from the dead to haunt him.

Sometimes we are also caught in a conflict between different models; we can feel ashamed of being ashamed.

For example, if you feel ashamed of knowing Jesus Christ, you might quite understandably feel ashamed of that shame. You would like to be the sort of person who is thought well of by people who disdain Christians. But you also want to be the kind of faithful Christian who would never dream of being ashamed of Jesus Christ. You are caught between two different kinds of shame, each arising from the violation of a different model. You cannot win. You are caught each way in a crossfire that guarantees self-rejection.


## The Loss of Dominion

God created Adam and Eve to have dominion over the earth and to subdue it to the glory of God. This was a command not to exploit the earth but to work creatively in the world out of gratitude to God and as an expression of their stature as creatures in his image. When they had finished trying to shift blame for the Fall onto someone else, God did not bother to argue with them; he simply pronounced judgment on the whole of creation for the disobedience of humankind (Gn. 3:14–19). From this point on, pain, toil, frustration, and finally death were in the fabric of human existence. They had forfeited their right to their God-given task to subdue the earth. Now the earth would subdue us, a truth that every graveyard echoes. No longer was the earth a place that was fit for human beings. Now it threatened them, impinged on them, refused to yield to their control. In the end, the earth would swallow up its erstwhile master.

However, humankind did not lose its dominion completely. Within the limitations of the curse that God has laid down, people still exert control on their environments. But now it is a double-edged control bringing mixed blessings with it. Dominion has in part been transformed to domination. The natural world and fellow human beings bear the scars of this domination.

Before the Fall, we saw ourselves as under God, bearing God's image and deriving a sense of identity and coherence from God. But now we identify ourselves with creation instead of our Creator. Our whole orientation is downward toward what is less than ourselves, rather than upward toward what is greater. This change of orientation has many psychological results.

## Slaves of Sin

Humankind after the Fall is no longer master of itself. The Bible says we are 'slaves of sin.' In certain very important ways, we are not active but have become passive, reactive.

> The righteousness of the upright delivers them, but the treacherous are *taken captive* by their lusts. (Prov. 11:6)

> You were led astray to dumb idols, however you may have *been moved*. (1 Cor. 12:2)

> So that we may no longer be children, *tossed to and fro and carried about* with every wind of doctrine . . . (Eph. 4:14, emphasis mine)

This passivity in itself is a denial of the human likeness to God. We were created to subdue our environment to God's glory; now we allow ourselves to be acted on by things around us. Ironically, displaying their capacity for self-deception, men and women often experience this passivity as supreme selfassertion. Jude writes:

> They boldly carouse together, looking after themselves; waterless clouds, carried along by winds; fruitless trees in late

autumn, twice dead, uprooted; wild waves of the sea, casting up the foam of their own shame; wandering stars for whom the nether gloom of darkness has been reserved. (Jude 12–13)

Notice the tragic contrast between subjective experience and objective reality. In their own minds they 'boldly carouse.' They are enlightened, brave, very pictures of the modern hero. They fear no one and answer to no one. But Jude uses striking images to describe their true passivity: light and feathery clouds driven by the wind, hopelessly uprooted trees, waves driven by the wind in every direction, stars wandering aimlessly without sense of direction or purpose. Created for dominion, people find themselvs subject to forces more powerful than they are.

### Control by the Emotional Mandate

Our emotions are among the most powerful of these forces. Our emotions change more easily and quickly than our minds do. We all have had the experience. In the morning we nurse resentment or are depressed by the weather, and life is miserable. By evening, the weather clears, we are flattered, noticed, end up being the life of the party, and we feel as if the world is a wonderful place. This change in our feelings is caused by events outside of our control. We do nothing to bring it about.

The trouble comes when we allow our emotions to rule our lives. We sometimes do this in the name of honesty. Instead of just having feelings that go up and down dramatically, we allow our whole being to change according to how we feel – by emotions that change with outside situations, inward impulses, or the rise and fall of our level of blood sugar. When we feel tired we won't work. When we feel afraid of being rejected by friends we will do what they expect us to do, right or wrong. When we feel anger at some one we lash out. When we feel depressed, we withdraw. When our emotions rule, we forfeit the control of our lives. Self-control gives way to the emotional mandate.

The classical Greeks noted the power emotions have, and shunned them. They saw emotions as bad because they were unruly, irrational, and therefore liable to mislead. By contrast, the Bible does not see strong feelings as necessarily bad or dangerous, but sees that some feelings are true and good in a certain circumstance and others are false and destructive. Strong feelings at the right time are good because they reflect God's character. Other feelings are bad, not because they are strong, but because they oppose the will of God. Thus we cannot agree with those today who would polarize the discussion between those who are for emotions and those who are against them. Emotions are part of our make-up as God's creatures and every emotion has its right and wrong expression.

We must make one qualification. The writers of the Bible often describe a destructive life pattern as one controlled by feelings, passions, and desires. Emotions are to be rejoiced in, but we should not be in the grips of the emotional mandate. Emotions become destructive not when they are strong, but when they are allowed to set the course of our lives. Look once again at some biblical examples:

> A man without self-control is like a city broken into and left without walls. (Prov. 25:28)

A city without walls is helpless, without defences against outside attack. Consider how this image applies to a father whose child knows how to get him angry. The child can make his father angry whenever he wants – at his own will, not his father's. The father, lacking self-control, is under his child's control. He is a city without walls.

For we ourselves were once foolish, disobedient, led astray, slaves to various passions and pleasures, passing our days in malice and envy, hated by men and hating one another. (Tit. 3:3)

. . . we all once lived in the passions of our flesh following the desires of the body and mind, and so were by nature children of wrath. (Eph. 2:3)

Abstain from the passions of the flesh that wage war against your soul. (1 Pet. 2:11)

The theme common to all of these passages is the disintegrating effect of letting the emotional mandate have its way.

## The By-passed Self

People, made in the image of God is made to act creatively in their environment. However, the one who is in the grip of emotional demands is primarily acted on by the environment; and life becomes a series of reactions to various stimuli which confront this person from within and without. The truth is that the inner self does not set the course of this person's life; the 'I am' which is the very focal point of being the image of God, is by-passed. Is it any wonder that he or she experiences problems of identity? Stimulus and response are for this person like two ends of a see-saw: stimulus begets response without thought or decision – unmediated by the self. This person's inner self has become a spectator to its own life. They react to pressures and become what each situation makes of them instead of acting on the basis of who they are and what they know to be true. Their way of life is in conflict with who they are, the image of God, made to have dominion over the earth. In short, they live as if they had no identity.

Let us say that you lose your temper easily. If you are under your emotional mandate, anger felt is anger expressed. Your judgment is not at its best when you are angry. When you let off steam, you may hurt others psychologically – even physically. Even though you never intended it or chose it, your anger could alter the direction of your life. Or consider people who are ruled by the fear that their circle of friends will reject them if they do not do what they want. This can lead to a life of crime, an unwanted pregnancy, a life out of control. People in these circumstances do not choose the circumstances; the circumstances just 'happen.' This is why so many who live under their emotional mandate have a sense of unreality about themselves and their lives. In a real sense, they stand aside and observe their lives going past.

### A Common Solution Makes it Worse

Many people in this dilemma choose a way out that makes the problem worse. This happens when the person decides, 'All problems have come from trying to act out what everybody else wanted me to do. Now I'm going to do exactly what I feel like doing, nothing more and nothing less.' Their plan is to purge themselves of all inhibitions and restraints that they think have stifled their growth.

As you will recall, this is the hope of the modern romantic: I am what I feel, and following my feelings will lead me to my true self. This is a prescription for disaster. Following our feelings blindly in this way subjects us even more to the pressures of our peer group, friends, the weather, and other outside influences. I have heard people in the midst of this kind of search for identity tell me, 'I can only feel "myself" when I am drunk or stoned.' They reject self-control coming from the inner choosing self, and yet feel 'real' only when they have something foreign working on their brain chemistry. This simply equates authentic selfhood with absence of internal control or intention. It reduces human life to the level of animals.

Trying to find one's identity by following feelings is like trying to drive a car with the accelerator and the brake on the floor at once. It mistakes one of the causes of the problem for the solution. James Taylor's song of several years ago illustrates this:

> Sail on home to Jesus won't you good girls and boys. I'm all in pieces, you can have your own choice, but I can see a heavenly band. Full of angels coming to set me free. I don't know nothing 'bout why or when, but I can tell you that it's bound to be, because I could feel it. I guess my feet know where they want me to go, walking on the country road. [17]

Taylor scorns those who would find a home in Jesus, confesses to be at a loss in terms of his own identity, and then puts all hope in a glorious future that he has no rational hold on at all, but which he can feel. He is not in control, yet his feet seem to know where to go next. One of the greatest dangers of this attempt to find identity is its seductive false logic. At the very moment when our emotions tyrannize us, they give us the illusion of complete freedom, just as those who 'boldly carouse together, looking after themselves' (Jude 12) are recognized by God as being helpless and impotent. It does not seem to occur to us that this freedom is only on the very lowest level of our personality, and that our inner self is not so much free as just derailed.

### Life as the Path of Least Resistance

Those whose feelings control them avoid making decisions. To them, life is not made up of decisions and actions, but instead becomes the path of least resistance. This path always tends to avoid situations that involve conflict or difficulty. We do not usually 'feel' like confronting a person who is angry at us, resolving a conflict with our boss, or taking an exam for which we are unprepared. Those ruled by their feelings will try to avoid such situations, but will lose self-respect and integrity.

Ingmar Bergman pounds this point home at the end of his film 'A Passion.' He depicts a character who has led a life of evasions and lies. Toward the end, he moves painfully back and forth, unable to make a decision, and the composition of the film begins to deteriorate. The character is partially obscured by white dots on the screen and then he is gone. Albert Camus makes the same point in his novel *The Stranger*. After going through various events in life, including the funeral of his mother and sexual experiences, the protagonist shoots and kills a man. Throughout, there is a dreadful grayness and unreality about him. His life is something that happened to him; he himself never acted deliberately or made a decision. He was a stranger first of all to himself, he did not even know whether he had shot the man out of self-defense or murderous intent. Although there was a marked absence of strong feelings, he simply did what he felt like doing at each point. The stranger was a man, the image of God, acting as less than a man.

Those who do not make decisions will not face their own futures. If emotions rule them, thoughts about the future are often taboo. They imply a decision that might bind them, and they do not know how they will feel when the time comes to act on such a decision. Instead, they do not think about the future, postpone any decisions and wait for the future to become the present. Then they will see what they feel like. No decision is necessary; it is made for them when the time comes. They are in a life-pattern that is instability personified.

Following one's feelings is one of the more common ways people today lose dominion over their lives, but it is by no means the only way. For example, many people are over-scrupulous, always concerned to do the right thing in other people's eyes. They are controlled by other people's expectations. They may assume that if they are living their lives right, others will always be happy with them. By this reasoning, if others are not happy with you, it is your fault. Final security comes from acceptance by others, and the only way to be sure of such acceptance is to comply with the loudest person's expectations even when they conflict with one's own needs and obligations to others. Such compliance to others' wishes is not love or true service to them, and it certainly is not dominion over one's own life. It is a permitted domination of one person by others. If you are in this position, the chances are that guilt and anxiety are the strongest motivations in your life. Sometimes parents can exercise extraordinary manipulative control even into the adult lives of their children, by exploiting anxiety and guilt – usually without realizing it.

If you are a scrupulous, people-pleasing person, your identity is undermined in two ways. First, because you have little expression of legitimate dominion, you may have a feeling of unreality about yourself, of being a non-person. You feel that you don't matter yourself, but only have value as you are making others happy. Second, you usually smolder with unrecognized anger against the persons you are trying to please. This anger can mature into resentment and self-hatred.

There are many such patterns among us, many ways in which we fail to act in our environment as God intended, using the gifts that he gave us. In later chapters we will try to see our way toward some solutions.

## The Disintegration of Love

The disintegration of love is both the inevitable result of the erosion of morals, models, and dominion, and also a significant aspect of the loss of identity in its own right. We grow as individuals and find our identity not by ourselves but in the context of many different relationships – with parents, brothers and sisters, older relatives, spouses, children, associates, and friends. The way we learn to interact in these different relationships does a great deal to form our identity. But the shadow of the Fall lies over all our relationships, touching every area.

First, there is the problem with morals. Our moral problem is not only that we are in sin and therefore are guilty before God, but also that we are in sin and guilty before each other. There are two sides to our moral problem – the sin itself, and the way we deal with the sin. Sin against another person brings alienation. But it damages the relationship far more when we cover it up and do not admit it. If you refuse to admit your sin as sin, you might be able to present an outward appearance of composure, but inwardly you may be running away, anxious, threatened by others' presence, manipulating them, withdrawing from them out of defense. You may even compensate by overconfidence and bragging. The consequences for the quality of your love are obvious when you do this to your spouse, your parent, your child, or your friend.

There is also a 'love problem' with our models. To love as Jesus taught, we must fly in the face of many of our modern hero-systems. Many of today's models are heroic because they live without commitment, obligation, responsibility, or even emotional involvement. They are heroic for exploiting others sexually, psychologically, and financially. They are heroic precisely because of these lapses; their appeal is in the power that is gained through exploitation.

By modern standards, biblical love seems very unheroic and dull. To love with your whole heart you must have your own hero-system that is closer to the models of the Bible. Otherwise you will be pulled in two directions at once – toward Christian love on the one hand, and to the attractiveness of power-through-exploitation on the other.

Christian love demands sustained commitment; this re-quires a certain level of dominion over ourselves. William Kilpatrick has written: 'Love is simply a decision that in some essential ways we will not change; that come what may, we will stick by certain commitments.'[18] Thus the many ways we relinquish dominion over our lives makes love impossible. When our goal is honoring and expressing our own feelings, our commitment to others is inevitably short-changed. Kilpatrick quotes from several want ads in newspapers:

> Looking for woman friend, 20's, pretty, educated, to share occasional meetings of sex and warmth.

> Male grad, 22, seeks warm, gentle, honest, funloving female to show me the city. My interests are varied, active, expanding – no limitations or expectations, closeness is all I seek.[19]

These show the current wisdom about love: it is a feeling, subject to change without notice. Closeness and warmth are in; commitment is out. But love which is warmth without commitment is love without involving anything finally solid within you. It is radically less than Christian love.

If dominion is forfeited through compliance, there is an inability to love of a different sort. If your security rests on other people being happy with you, it will be unthinkable to stand up to them. Love sometimes requires that we do stand up to those who would make demands on us, for their own good as well as for our own.

To understand the impact of the loss of love on our identity there is no better place to turn than the start of 1 Corinthians 13,

> If I speak in the tongues of men and of angels, but have not love, I am a noisy gong or a clanging cymbal. And if I have prophetic powers, and understand all mysteries and all knowledge, and if I have all faith, so as to remove mountains but have not love, I am nothing. If I give away all I have, and if I deliver my body to be burned, but have not love, I gain nothing. (1 Cor. 13:1–3)

No matter how spectacular, gifted, or dedicated a person I might be, without love it is all ashes at God's feet. The subtraction of love is the great subtraction. No matter how much else I have or do, it comes to nothing without love. It is much like multiplying by zero in mathematics. No matter how large a number we multiply by zero, the result is always the same – zero.

Paul points out three things that are true of the person who does not love: 'I am nothing,' 'I gain nothing,' 'I just make noise.' This is a vivid picture of a shattered identity. Neither nihilist literature nor the theatre of the absurd says anything more degrading about human beings than Paul has said about those who have no love. They are nothing, they achieve nothing, they are without purpose or meaning. They are just a loud nuisance.

Why should the loss of love be so disintegrating to our identity? Because humanity is made in the image and likeness of God, and God is love (1 Jn. 4:8). Those who do not love violate not only God's commandments but their own identity – their own nature and calling. Love is not a technique or a feeling to fall in and out of, but is something rooted in the highest order of reality that there is – in the character of God himself. It is more real and solid than the ground that we stand on.

In summary then, let us remember that humankind as the image of God has an identity rooted in and derived from the Creator. The Fall has affected us in three ways. It has spoiled our relationship to God, our reflection of God, and our environment. Where human beings once had a close relationship with God, now there is rebellion, distrust, and unbelief. People are personally alienated from the One who is the source of their existence. Where we once perfectly reflected the character of God in our behavior, now our lives portray a twisted and distorted likeness of him. Where once the environment perfectly matched our needs, now it is beset with disaster, sin, and death.

There is no virtue in minimizing the agony of the suffering in a twisted world. But the salvation of Jesus Christ is even greater and more wonderful than the Fall is horrible. It is to that salvation that we now turn.

# THREE

# Identity Found: A Healed Relationship

*All the intolerable sufferings of mankind result from man's attempt to make the whole world of nature reflect his reality, his heroic victory; he thus tries to achieve a perfection on earth, a visible testimonial to his cosmic importance; but this testimonial can only be given conclusively by the beyond, by the source of creation itself which alone knows man's value because it knows his task, the meaning of his life.[1]* (Ernest Becker)

*For the mountains may depart and the hills be removed, but my steadfast love shall not depart from you, and my covenant of peace shall not be removed, says the Lord, who has compassion on you.* (Is. 54:10)

*For the Son of man came to seek and to save the lost.* (Lk. 19:10)

We live at a time when many ways are proposed to find humankind's lost identity. The psychological sciences, which occupy the place of cultural influence held by philosophy and theology a hundred years ago, offer no shortage of approaches to fulfillment, wholeness, self-actualization, and peace of mind. How do we face the basic issues of human identity without falling back into the very things which caused the loss of identity? At this point we need to have a firm grasp of basic truths.

We have seen how the Fall has ruined our relationship with God, ruined the reflection of God in us, and spoiled the environment we inhabit. This chapter will deal with the healing of our relationship with God; the next will deal with the restoration of God's true reflection in human lives. The third part, a spoiled environment, is well beyond the scope of these pages and will have to wait for other authors.

## Identity and Truth

The real need is not so much for a psychotherapeutic technique, but for an approach to identity deeply rooted in the nature of humankind. This approach is found in the biblical teaching about God and human nature. To highlight the Christian view with greater clarity, we will look first at several alternate attempts to establish our essential humanness.

As we have already said, each of us senses an 'I amness' which is the center of our conscious self. We also intuitively feel that we are of more value than animals and stones, even if our level of self-acceptance is very low. The question is – what is this self? To what does it correspond? Are we really of more value than an animal or stone, or is the conviction that we are different just sentimentality? Is there some aspect of our nature that is essentially human, around which everything else turns as around a pivot, and which also establishes our value? Where is our point of final integration?

One of the most famous 'I am' statements was made by the French philosopher Descartes. He said, 'I think therefore I am.' This statement was not so much a definition of what is essentially human as it was a philosophical starting point from which Descartes hoped to build certain knowledge.

Nevertheless Descartes was part of what became a philosophical movement which tended to say that what was distinctive about humanity was our critical faculty, our power of reasoning.

As we have seen, the Victorian, new or old, says, 'I am what I will,' 'I am what I can do,' or 'I am what I own.' For them, their achievements, hard work and their possessions are the center of their lives.

The Romantic's 'I am what I feel' is also familiar. The self that is rooted in the emotions seeks to both honor emotions and to establish some unity in the midst of them.

An existentialist such as Jean-Paul Sartre repudiates the very notion that human beings have an essence which they can discover. He said that human beings exist only when they are able to say 'I am what I am not.' By this he means that humans exist authentically only as they constantly *dis*identify themselves from anything that can be said about them. To allow oneself to be identified with something – with one's profession, for example – is to become a thing or an object.

The marriage of Western psychology and Eastern religion has created another answer to identity, one that is increasingly popular today.[2] Put simply, this is the claim that 'I am the All,' or that 'I am one in being with the universe.' To lose our sense of alienation, we are told to rid ourselves of the idea and experience of being a separate individual. As we learn to identify ourselves with the rest of the universe in its unity, then everything will fit into place.

These are just a few of the many ways that people try to locate their sense of 'I amness.' None of these answers rests on scientific foundations; all rely on religious and philosophical faith-commitments about the nature of humankind and the universe. All have one thing in common: they turn inward on humanity itself to find essential human qualities and the source of identity. They would have human beings look only to themselves to account for theirs experiences of themselves. They are all more sophisticated ways of saying with the daughters of Babylon, 'I am and there is no one besides me' (Is. 47:8).

By contrast, the Christian turns to God. God identified himself to Moses as 'I am that I am' (Ex. 3:14). God is dependent on nothing and on no one for his origin, existence, and meaning. Notice that he does not say, 'I create therefore I am' or 'I am omnipotent therefore I am' or even 'I am God therefore I am.' He does not need to identify himself with any*thing* external to himself, and he need not justify himself to any one. He alone can say 'I am that I am,' a statement of completely self-sufficient, self-contained identity.

This makes every human claim to self-sufficiency vain arrogance. Every human being is at every point dependent on God who holds in his hand the breath that every person breathes (Dan. 5:23). C.S. Lewis wrote:

> A human creature revolting against its creator is like the scent of a flower trying to destroy the flower – it is revolting against the very source of its power, including the power to revolt.

Humankind makes the claim of independent identity not only in arrogance but to our own degradation.

In looking to a healed relationship with God for our identity I want to make it clear that I do not mean to use God or, worse still, the idea of God, as a technique for self-acceptance. This would be to use God as a religious means to a psychological end, as a way to boost our image of ourselves in a higher form of egotism and pretension. Christian truth leads us in the other direction. Peter told us, 'Humble yourselves therefore under the mighty hand of God . . .' (1 Pet. 5:6). God is not a theological means to a higher psychological end. God is not a means to any other end. God is the Alpha and the Omega, the beginning and the end. Our true identity is found in accepting our status as creatures of this infinite Creator God and in rooting our sense of identity in his. Our identity is an identity derived.

## God the Redeemer

It is not possible for finite and guilty humanity to heal the breach in our relationship with God. The God of the Bible shows himself to be not only the Creator, but also the Redeemer of his people. Their salvation is at his initiative.

Redemption is necessary because people have sinned and true moral guilt stands between us and God. This guilt does not mean that we are worthless, but it does mean that we are unworthy of acceptance by God or any blessing from God in any form. In short, we deserve judgment.

'The gospel' was the short-hand term that Jesus and the apostles used to describe the Christian message. It is an accurate word because it means 'good news.' The good news is that God treats the believer not as our sin deserves, but as God's love through Christ requires. The Christian is one who knows that he or she deserves God's condemnation. The Christian also knows that he or she has received and will receive blessing, not because of anything he or she has achieved, but by God's mercy alone, accepted by faith.

To illustrate, I will tell you a parable. There was once an orphan roaming the streets, hungry and penniless. He stole a car and after a brief drive lost control and crashed into a tree. The police quickly found him and brought him to court where he discovered that the car he had stolen and wrecked had been the judge's car. There was no question of covering up his guilt; so he was told that he had to pay a stiff fine along with damages or else go to jail. At this point a strange thing happened. The judge came down off the bench and said to the boy, 'Since you have no money, you will have to go to jail, but I will offer you an alternative. My son is willing to pay the fine for you out of his own pocket. He will do this for you under two conditions. First, you must simply plead guilty to what you have done and accept his payment on your behalf as a free gift; second, you must let me adopt you into my family so that I would be your father and he would be your brother. This would not require you to be a perfect son, but to accept your status in my family and to let me help you try to lead a better life.'

If you are familiar with the basic facts of the Christian gospel you will not need a great deal of imagination to interpret the parable. Jesus came into the world as the Son of God. His purpose was not to condemn us; nor did he leave us with just his teaching and example, neither of which we can live up to. His purpose was rather to pay the debt that our sin incurs, to bear it on his own back and be destroyed by it voluntarily rather than letting it destroy us. Each person faces the choice of the orphan. Will he take his own punishment on himself by denying his guilt, the reality of the jail, the existence of the judge, the love of the son, or in any other way rejecting the gift of God? Or will he accept the free gift of forgiveness and adoption? This puts in a nutshell the choice we have through the offer of good news of the gospel of Jesus Christ.

Jesus himself taught that he had come primarily to die, not needlessly or as a gesture of sympathy with our suffer-ing, but to 'give his life as a ransom for many' (Mk. 10:45). As he died he cried out, 'My God, my God, why have you forsaken me?' (Mt. 27:46). This verse used to trouble me. If Jesus crumbled at the last minute, what credence can we put in his promises to us for peace in life, death, and beyond? But I noticed that the gospel writers were not in the least embarrassed by these words. Their meaning became clearer when I began to see that Jesus meant exactly what he said. God *had* forsaken him at his time of greatest need. God

abandoned and condemned him, not for his own sin, but
for the sin of any who would ever trust in him, that they
might not be condemned. When God saw him on the cross
he treated him as the worst sinner who had ever lived,
pouring out on him the punishment due to millions of
people for their sins. Although Jesus was without sin himself, by his own choice he put himself under judgment for
the guilt of others. Thus God condemned sin in a way that
would allow sinners to go free. Not only was justice done,
but mercy was offered. God turned his back on the crucified
Jesus so that through the risen Jesus he might turn his face
toward us.

No one becomes a Christian by being born in a certain
place, into a certain family or by trying hard enough, but
by personally putting trust in the Son of God in much the
same way that the orphan had to put himself into the hands
of the judge and his son. This involves choice on the part of
the person who becomes a Christian, but the Bible makes it
clear that it is also an act of God so radical that it is like
being born again. John explains it in this way:

> But to all who received him, who believed in his name, he gave
> power to become children of God; who were born, not of blood
> nor of the will of the flesh nor of the will of man, but of God.
> (Jn. 1:12–13)

The Holy Spirit of God enters into the believer at the point
of his or her acceptance of this gift of salvation, living
within the believer and making a bond between us and
Jesus Christ. The bond or union of his Spirit with the
Christian's is never broken, either by subsequent sin or
even by the death and decomposition of the body. The
Christian's conscious sense of identity passes through
death and survives its separation with the body, living with
God until the day of the resurrection.

One of the most important things to understand is that this salvation cannot be earned, merited, deserved, or paid for. It was purchased at the high price of the death of the eternal Son of God, but it is offered to us absolutely free. If we are to accept it at all we must accept it on these terms, not with any self-righteous pretensions to have earned a part of it. Faith is the step of accepting the free gift of salvation for yourself and entrusting your life to God. The apostle Paul put it this way:

> For by grace you have been saved through faith; and this is not your own doing, it is the gift of God – not because of works, lest any man should boast. (Eph. 2:8–9)

This is borne out by the words of Jesus to the criminal who died beside him on the cross (Lk. 23:39–43). The man had a life of crime behind him and, since he only had a few minutes to live, no life of Christian service to promise. All he could do was to ask for mercy. Yet Jesus told him, 'Today you will be with me in paradise.'

Exactly because our salvation does not depend on our own achievements, the Christian can be *certain* of God's forgiveness. It rests not on the Christian's unpredictable performance, but on the reliability of the word of God. The God who knows us through and through, who sees through us as through glass, says as judge, 'Case dismissed' – not because we are innocent, but because we pleaded guilty and some one else took the punishment for us. We are thereby legally justified by faith (Rom. 5:1); the bond which stood against us with its legal demands is cancelled (Col 2:14). God intends the Christian to live in the confidence that he or she is forgiven already, not in the fear of being rejected for not doing well enough.

The free offer of forgiveness through Jesus Christ is God's solution to our moral problem. This solution is hard on our pride, but the legal problem of guilt is resolved. Either we do or do not accept God's offer of free forgiveness.

The problem of shame, a violation of our models, is not so clearly resolved. In fact many conclude that the problem is irresolvable. Some existentialists have said that shame is just there and nothing can be done about it. It is part of the sickness of being a human being. Or, as Helen Lynd wrote, 'an experience of shame . . . cannot be modified by addition, wiped out by subtraction, or exorcised by expiation.'[3]

The Bible teaches that although there is false shame, not all shame is false. We experience objective, true shame for doing something shameful – that is, dishonorable in the sight of God. Perhaps this was something of what Isaiah experienced in the temple when he saw the Lord sitting on a throne, high and lifted up. He said 'Woe is me! For I am undone' (Is 6:1-5). He felt unhinged, exposed, transparent before the gaze of the God who made him. If any of us were to meet God as Isaiah did, the encounter would make any previous experience of shame seem like child's play. God sees through all our sham, deceit, pretense, and respectability. Our whole sense of self would be threatened. Any sense of being heroic would be exposed as pretension.

What then does God do about our shame? He does not forgive it because so many of the things for which we feel shame are not moral problems which would need to be forgiven. God's answer is acceptance. God accepts us personally in our shame. If you think for a minute you will see that acceptance is something beyond forgiveness. You can forgive some one and still not enjoy spending time with them or having them on your vacation with you. God's forgiveness is a legal act: We have broken the law and we plead guilty. The penalty for the crime is taken by another, and we are acquitted. But the gospel goes beyond this. God not only forgives, but he *accepts* us *personally*, wanting to be with us because he loves us. In all our confusion, sin, and shame God welcomes us, not out of duty, but because he loves us.

A passage out of Laura Ingalls Wilder's children's story *Farmer Boy* gives a suggestion on a human level of God's acceptance of his children in their shame. The story is about a boy called Almanzo who was later to become the author's husband. While at a village fair with his father, he saw a crowd around a stall containing some animals that Almanzo had never seen before. Almanzo, who later discovered that the animals were mules, went to investigate:

> Almanzo left Father, and wriggled and squeezed between the legs until he came to the bars of the stall.
> Inside it were two black creatures. He had never seen anything like them. They looked something like horses, but they were not horses. Their tails were bare, with only a bunch of hair at the tip. Their short bristly manes stood up straight and stiff. Their ears were like rabbits' ears. Those long ears stood up above their long, gaunt faces, and while Almanzo stared, one of the creatures pointed its ears at him and stretched out its neck.
> Close to Almanzo's bulging eyes, its nose wrinkled and its lips curled back from long, yellow teeth. Almanzo couldn't move. Slowly the creature opened its long, fanged mouth, and out of its throat came a squawking roar.
> 'Eeeeeee, aw! Heeeeeee, Haw!'
> Almanzo yelled, and he turned and butted and clawed and fought through the crowd towards Father. The next thing he knew, he reached Father, and everybody was laughing at him.

This is an experience of shame probably familiar to those of us who can remember very much about our childhood. But the next sentence of the story is the most important of all. It reads: 'Only Father did not laugh.'[4] What a difference it made that Father did not laugh! This is a faint shadow of

God's acceptance of us in our shame. God does not ridicule his children or laugh at them, even though as he only knows, we are all ridiculous enough.

In the letter to the Hebrews it says that God 'is not ashamed to call them brethren' (Heb. 2:11). This shows the measure of his acceptance. He is not ashamed to have us numbered with him, as part of his family, to let the world know that we are identified with him and he with us. Think of how easy it is to be ashamed of people in your family. Children can easily be ashamed of their parents because they seem so hopelessly out of touch. Brothers and sisters are often ashamed of each other. Parents sometimes get ashamed of the public bad behavior of their children – especially when friends who also have children are part of the audience. You see, it is no small thing that God is not ashamed to call us brethren. He actually takes us into his family as children by adoption. There is no greater degree of acceptance.

Jesus teaches the same message in his parable of the prodigal son (Lk. 15:11–32). A son takes his inheritance and squanders it far from home. It was only when he was faced with starvation that he 'came to himself' and went back ashamed but humbled, to his father. The son's escapades had clearly not improved the father's public reputation (think of the gossip), nor the solvency of his estate. Nevertheless the father did not reject the son, ridicule him or lay guilt on him. The father's response is the response of God himself. He had been looking for his son; when he saw him coming at a distance he raced out the door and down the road to meet him. He threw his arms around him and kissed him. He brought him back in honor, put the best robe on him, a ring on his finger to show that he was reinstated as a son, shoes on his feet, and then laid out a banquet to celebrate his return, 'for this my son was dead, and is alive again; he was lost, and is found' (v. 24). Do you see how far this surpasses perfunctory forgiveness? God accepts us lovingly and joyfully even as we come to him in our guilt, petty shame, and pseudo-heroism. He comes to us to embrace us because he loves us.

The Bible says of Jesus that 'for the joy that was set before him endured the cross, despising the shame' (Heb. 12:2). What was this joy that was set before him that enabled him to endure the cross and despise the shame of crucifixion? Literally the only thing that Jesus had to gain by coming to the earth to die was to secure our salvation. He didn't do it for his own good. He didn't do it under the compulsion of God the Father. The only thing that he would receive as a result would be a redeemed relationship with us. Any other joy would have already been part of his experience before he even came to earth. It is hard to believe that someone would do so much for the shining reward of knowing you and me, and especially when that someone is God the Son himself, come in the flesh. Yet, that is exactly what the Bible says. The joy that was set before him was the joy of knowing us, his people, those who trust in him.

This then is the first step to resolve shame – to realize that God, through Jesus Christ, accepts you. Your adopting Father joyfully receives you with all your vanity, sin, and contradictions. God accepts the Christian whether the Christian accepts him or herself or not. Then one day he will replace our shame with its opposite – true glory and honor. The hope of the Christian is that he or she will pass through death and its shame (there is nothing less heroic than being dead) and go into the presence of God, to share something of the very glory of God himself. This will not be the fleeting, empty glory of popular heroism, but the true eternal glory of God.

God's solution to the problem of morals and models is the foundation of the self-acceptance of the Christian. I do not accept myself just because it is easier, the psychologically healthy thing to do, or because everybody says it is a good idea. I can accept myself because God has forgiven and accepted me, because he loves me and wants to spend time with me. This is my basis of personal value and worth. In crude terms of economics, a thing is worth what someone is willing to pay for it. In the cross of Jesus Christ, we have a full picture of what God was willing to give for the life of the Christian. There is no higher mark of value imaginable. Self-acceptance is built on the foundation of a growing understanding and appreciation of the forgiveness and acceptance of God.[5]

## Taking God at His Word

Some Christians have claimed that this solution to our problems of identity is so wonderful that it resolves all questions of self-acceptance on the spot. The gospel is wonderful, but it is not an automatic solution. Christians, because of the sin and confusion left in their head and heart, must sometimes struggle to grasp or retain an awareness of this acceptance and their own consequent worth. Much of the teaching on the Christian life in the New Testament is aimed at helping Christians keep a grip on the earthshaking truths of the love of God for them. It is a question of taking God at his word, whatever else might pass through their consciousness.

We are prone to self-deception as the prophets knew well. When Jeremiah confronted the people with the seriousness of their sin, the people usually replied, 'No, we know better.' People have always had a hard time accepting unfavorable evaluations of themselves even though the evaluation is justified. We don't like to be called sinners. We don't like to need anyone's mercy or to change our ways. This is under-standable, though not necessarily commendable. But there is another side of self-deception that is more difficult to fathom. This is the fact that when God says something comforting to us, we secretly disbelieve that too! The perversity of human nature is such that when God says 'I forgive you,' 'I accept you' or 'I love you,' again we are apt to say, 'No, I know better.' It seems that whatever God says we tend to say, 'No, I know better.'

Sooner or later we must make up our minds whose verdict we are going to accept – our own verdict, the verdict of others, or God's verdict. Most of us at one time or another receive criticism. The apostle Paul did also – very severe criticism, casting doubt on his spiritual integrity and his life's work. We can learn something from his response to that criticism:

> With me it is a very small thing that I should be judged by you or by any human court. I do not even judge myself, I am not aware of anything against myself, but I am not thereby acquitted. It is the Lord who judges me. (1 Cor. 4:3–4)

Paul's answer is clear. He counts it a small thing that any other human being should pass a verdict on him. But he has no illusions that his own conscience is infallible either; rather he looks to God who is the true judge. Paul's strength in these verses is not arrogance, but is his confidence in the overriding importance of God's verdict. It is finally not what you or I might think that matters, but what God thinks and

At his temptation Jesus himself was under attack at precisely the point of certainty of his own identity (Mt. 4:1–11). Two of the three temptations began with: 'If you are *really* the Son of God . . .' He *was* the Son of God and had been for eternity, but the devil still tried to wedge his way into Jesus' mind through casting doubt on his self-understanding. Jesus answered by turning to the word of

God. If we are to believe God, we need to believe what he says about us also. He has spoken his verdict very clearly. He forgives and accepts the believer in Christ, having already judged that believer's sin on the cross of Christ. By his grace and love he accepts the Christian unconditionally. He then helps us to overcome the power of sin in our lives, sometimes a faltering and slow process, but one in which there is substantial progress nonetheless. If we are to accept God's verdict, it means that our attitude toward ourselves must be the same as his attitude toward us. If the God of all creation says that he loves you, that you are forgiven and accepted, then who are *you* to deny it? On what authority do you say 'No, I know better'? On the authority of your scruples, inadequacies, and petty comparisons with others? It is only with false humility that Christians deny their own affirmation by God.

God wants the Christian to start with the confidence of being accepted by the Creator of the universe. This does not mean that Christians can lie down and wait until going to heaven or sin without conscience; it does mean that they can throw themselves into serving God without crippling fears that God might abandon and condemn them if they do not do well enough. The Christian can be gratefully certain of God's love and encouragement.

## The Danger of Regression

It is possible to believe God's word, but then for any number of reasons end up denying it. In the church in Galatia Paul called this beginning with the spirit and ending with the flesh (Gal. 3:3). There is a perverse resident in our nature called pride. Pride keeps people from accepting the grace of God in the first place. Pride does not like to be at anybody's mercy, does not like to receive anything unearned, or to feel obligation to anyone. It is pride that says, 'I am and there is none beside me.' Pride is vicious and self-destructive. It could make the orphan in the parable refuse to receive the gift of the judge and stubbornly take his punishment. To receive mercy from another would seem too degrading. Pride can reject the gospel because it is too humiliating and can make the Christian lose sight of the radical and overwhelming truths of God's grace.

If you know that you are a Christian, you can still let your mind drift back to the notion that your acceptability before God depends on your own sincerity, effort, or performance. Perhaps in searching for a greater level of confidence in the fact of God's love for you, you can look for some inner reason *why* God should love you. If only you could point to something within yourself that was clearly deserving of love, then it would be easier to trust that God in fact does love you. It would all seem so much more tangible and certain.

This line of thought, so understandable and attractive, ends up making all the difference in the world. Our foundation for confidence and security no longer lies in the death of Christ and the character of God, but rests on something within ourselves that we think will make us loveable and acceptable to God. It is an unconscious step from solid rock to quicksand. We cannot locate this loveable quality within ourselves because there *is nothing* within us so good that it makes us deserving of God's love. To search for it is fruitless, and risks plunging us into introspective self-doubt. Indeed, any attempt to find a compelling reason why God *must* love us is an evasion of the most basic truth of the gospel – that our acceptability to God depends on what Jesus Christ has done for us, not on what we have done for ourselves. We can only accept his acceptance as a free gift; we can add nothing to it. Every Christian needs to live under the humbling words of Moses to the Israelites to whom God had promised a land of their own.

> For you are a people holy to the Lord your God; the Lord your God has chosen you to be a people for his own possession, out of all the peoples that are on the face of the earth. It was not because you were more in number than any other people that the Lord set his love upon you and chose you, for you were the fewest of all people; but it is because the Lord *loves you* and is keeping the oath which he swore to your fathers. (Dt. 7:6–8)

> Know therefore, that the Lord your God is not giving you this land to possess because of your righteousness; for you are a stubborn people. (Dt. 9:6)

The clear application of this teaching to Christian experience is that God loves you because he loves you, and that's that. The direction of faith therefore is not inward, but outward, trusting in the objective promises of God.

Because this habit of looking to ourselves for the basis for confidence is so widespread and so destructive, let us break it down further. In my experience there are three main ways that Christians slip into it: in their view of their own level of religious experience, their victory over sin, and in their fulfillment in life.

Christians may sometimes look within themselves to see if their experience of God measures up to what they think they should experience if God really loves them. They will undoubtedly compare themselves to others and discover that their experience of God falls short of what they think others are experiencing. They may reason in this way: 'If God *really* is at work in me I would certainly experience him more deeply, have more of my prayers answered, speak in tongues, have much more meaningful experiences of worship,' and so on. They may not doubt their ultimate salvation, but doubt that God really cares about them now. They enter themselves in God's blacklist.

The second area where Christians might try to find confidence is in their struggle to turn away from sins. They would concede that a clear improvement in getting rid of besetting sins is evidence that God is actually at work in them now. But it seldom works out that way. Even the apostle Paul admitted that 'the evil I do not want is what I do' (Rom. 7:19). A long struggle against a besetting sin hardly means that God has forgotten us. Yet Christians reason in this way: 'If God were really at work in me then I would have been able to hold my temper for at least five minutes after praying for patience.' As Christians fail (as they will), they apply this convincing logic to their own situation and conclude that God could not be with them. They exclude themselves from God's present care.

The third area of false confidence is in the Christian's level of fulfillment in life. They know that knowing Christ makes their lives meaningful and that salvation is something that should make them a light to the world. But if Christians do not feel that their life's work is meaningful, they are apt to exclude themselves from that group that they think God is especially interested in. They say, 'God is working with them, not with me. If God really cared about me, I would surely be more fulfilled than I am.' They too conclude that God has forgotten them.

Of course our experience of God, our success in turning from sin, and meaningful work can give us encouragement and greater confidence in the truth of the gospel. But these factors lie within ourselves. If we let our confidence of God's acceptance rest within ourselves, then we are in for trouble. God has no blacklist and does not forget us, but we will too easily conclude that he has if we put our confidence in anything but him. God's visible work in us is a cause for rejoicing, but it cannot take the place of the cross and resurrection of Christ as the main foundation of Christian confidence. If you are a Christian, God has accepted and forgiven you knowing full well that you had no reason for security within yourself. That is why Jesus had to come and die in the first place.

This pattern of false confidence twists the Christian life out of shape. It becomes sickly and introverted. Rather than simply praying, worshipping, looking to God and living our lives to his glory, our minds are dominated by crippling, in-turned questions. We monitor ourselves constantly. Rather than just praying, we ask 'How am I feeling as I am praying? Am I getting through to God?' Rather than simply worshipping God we ask, 'What sort of experience of worship am I having? Do I experience real communion with God as I take the Lord's Supper?' It can easily get to the point that the main task in a Christian's life is taking one's spiritual temperature. Either religious experience or Christian growth can actually become an idol in that they can have a larger place in a person's life than God himself. Progress, or lack of it, becomes the final point of integration. Instead of getting on with life confident in God's promises, we ask 'Am I growing?', 'Am I improving?', 'Am I growing fast enough?' Of course this ruins the very growth that is sought for. C.S. Lewis described this practice. It is like pulling a plant up each day to check the roots just to be sure that it is progressing properly. So it is with us. If we really are to grow we need to turn off this self-monitoring system as it searches for internal grounds for confidence. Then we will at least give ourselves a chance to know God and to grow. Let us learn from the apostle Paul whose faith was not inward-turned, but outward-turned, 'For to me to live is Christ' (Phil. 1:21). It is only when confidence in our salvation and in God's present love for us is securely rooted in the cross and resurrection of Christ that we can examine ourselves fruitfully.

This whole process of introversion and self-exclusion is spurred on by rear-view-mirrorism. The phrase was coined by Marshall McLuhan in quite a different context. I use it to mean spending more time looking in the rear view mirror to check and compare ourselves to ourselves and others than looking where we are going. It only leads to pompous self-satisfaction if we compare well, and feelings of inadequacy and inferiority if we do not.

I have belabored the theme of taking God at his word when he says that he loves you because it is no simple thing. It is against our natural inclinations to trust in him when there are contrary feelings and messages in and around us. Although we become Christians at a point in time through justification and adoption, the significance of these acts of God does not automatically dominate our minds. Francis Schaeffer points out the importance of applying the present meaning of the work of Christ for us not just once but moment by moment throughout our lives. [6]

## Guilt and Shame Untangled

We have spoken of God's answer to guilt and shame being forgiveness and acceptance respectively. Then we tried to touch on some of the difficulties in taking God at his word and really experiencing his love and acceptance. Another obstacle to living in these promises of God comes from a confusion of guilt and shame. Often it is not necessary to identify exactly what is going on in us, but there are times when it is very important. Have you ever said or heard someone say, 'God may forgive me, but I can't forgive myself'? Sometimes we can feel so awful and are so far from being able to forgive ourselves that we conclude that God must have abandoned or given up on us. At this point any head-knowledge of God's forgiveness becomes technical and remote. This can often come from mistaking shame for guilt.

As Christians we often have sins we commit that we become accustomed to. We get used to doing them and they become almost 'permissible' sins in our minds (though not in God's). When we do them we do not go into agonies of regret, but say 'Oh well, I did it again.' It is as if we have a perimeter of respectable sin drawn in a circle around us within which our sin is not all that bad. But then we commit sins from time to time which are outside our perimeter of respectability. They shock us. We are not the sort of person who would do *that* . . . and yet then again, we just did! It is often this kind of experience that turns into the self-hatred of 'I can't forgive myself.'

If you have been following the discussion you will realize that this is not an experience of guilt so much as it is of shame. First of all, God does not distinguish between re-spectable and unrespectable sins. For him sin is sin, any perimeter dividing them is only in our minds. This sort of experience shows that we are not so much bothered by breaking God's laws as we are of breaking our little china models of ourselves. We are not terribly bothered by being guilty (nobody is perfect after all), but when faced with having acted unheroically, the end of the world seems upon us. This suffering of shame therefore is more a fall from ourselves, a blow to our pride in our own heroism than it is a fall from obedience to God. In this situation we need to talk very straight with ourselves. God has forgiven and accepted us in our sin and shame. This is a fact. To say, 'I can't forgive myself' is a confusion. What it usually means is 'I am ashamed of myself. I have violated my models and acted unheroically.' We need to admit that all we have done when we feel this way is to hurt our own pride. We are sinners, not respectable sinners, but real sinners, we always were and always will be (until we were joined with Christ).

There are no respectable sinners in the sight of God. But there are shameful sinners who are accepted and forgiven through Jesus Christ, whether they accept themselves or not. We should regret all sin and turn away from it, but then go on to claim forgiveness and acceptance. God not only wants us to be forgiven and accepted. He wants us to know it and live in its reality, and in the power of that knowledge.

## Free to Face Failure

Many people who follow trends in modern psychological thinking assume that mental health requires them to believe in their heart of hearts that they are good, nice people who would never be cruel or have feelings of envy, lust, hatred, or despair. They resist anything that would threaten that public and private image. Many popular therapies reinforce this tendency by encouraging uncritical self-approval. Different generations in different cultures have felt guilty for different things. This has always been true. But we are one of the first generations to produce people who feel guilty for feeling guilty about anything. We are told to surround ourselves with the glow of self-acceptance – no matter what our lives are like.

If we are to take the biblical view of humankind seriously, we find ourselves inevitably in tension with some schools of psychological thought. Many would say that to point out a person's guilt to them is to attack their identity directly and to undermine their sense of worth as a person. Jesus did not seem to recognize this kind of constraint but with great love carried on a ministry that often involved direct personal confrontation. The Bible in many instances sees the exposure of guilt as the necessary first step to relief and freedom from it. Think of the warnings against false prophets who say only what people like to hear:

> Your prophets have seen for you false and deceptive visions;
> they have not exposed your iniquity to restore your fortunes,
> but have seen for you oracles false and misleading. (Lam. 2:14)

Notice that the prophets' failure to expose sin was wrong not only because it involved deception, but also because it failed to open the door to repentance and restoration. It allowed the people to remain complacently in their sin without hope of reconciliation. In the last chapter we discussed the destructive effects of the fear of honesty. Now let us look at the other side – the blessing and freedom of honesty.

Christians have less excuse than anyone to be unrealistic about their own failings. Yet how often it is that Christians are so shocked to discover the ugliness of deep selfishness, resentment, or jealousy in their own hearts that they try to deny the existence of these feelings. If we believe the Bible, we know for certain that we will sin seriously, painfully, destructively, and despite our better intentions. God has forewarned us. We are to hope that we can increasingly have victory over sin, through God's Spirit working in us, but we know this work will never be complete in this life. One of the ways God helps us to have victory over sin is to teach us how to respond to it when it does happen.

A particularly helpful insight is found in the book of Proverbs: 'for a righteous man falls seven times and rises again; but the wicked are overthrown by calamity' (Prov. 24:16). Both the righteous and the wicked sin. The difference between them is not in the righteous person's freedom from failure. The difference is that when they fail they simply admit it, get up, and go on. By contrast, the wicked person is one to whom failure is so unthinkable that when it comes, it shatters himor her. Although we should enlist God's help in making every effort to avoid sin, we should learn how to cope with it so that it does no more damage than necessary. We must learn how to learn from sin.

If you are a Christian you have already accepted the fact that you are personally a sinner. Despite all this, you may not find it easy to admit specific sins, especially in the present or recent past. As we saw in the last chapter, David is a good example of the destructive aspects of fear of honesty. As long as he was blind to his guilt, not openly recognizing it, David punished himself with a self-hatred that he also projected on others. After Nathan's rebuke there was remarkable change in David. When he had seen and accepted God's view of him, he was free from the whole syndrome of self-deception and hatred. David's own words are the best explanation.

> When I declared not my sin, my body wasted away through all my groaning all day long.
> For day and night thy hand was heavy upon me; my strength was dried up as by the heat of summer. (Ps. 32:3–4)

This psalm was probably describing the events around the encounter with Nathan and tells of great internal suffering including physiological complications and a sense of aliena-tion from God. The reason seems to be that David's sin was undeclared. It was the hiding of sin that brought on all this suffering. But then David continues:

> I acknowledged my sin to thee, and I did not hide my iniquity; I said, 'I will confess my transgressions to the Lord'; then thou didst forgive the guilt of my sin.
> Therefore let every one who is godly offer prayer to thee; at a time of distress, in the rush of great waters, they shall not reach him.
> Thou art a hiding place for me, thou preservest me from trouble; thou dost encompass me with deliverance. (Ps. 32:5–7)

Suddenly David has confidence in God's love and even in his own ability to instruct others about how to find it. He did not get there by some process of psychological white-washing, a new self-affirmation gained at the price of a moral sell-out. David did not suddenly see himself as a wonderful person who had never intended to harm anyone, but rather accepted himself in a new way despite his sin. He had honestly faced it before God and God had forgiven him. By no longer hiding his sin from God (v. 5) he was able to find a *hiding place* in God (v. 7). When he hid his sin from God, God seemed an enemy. When he acknowledged his sin, God became the one in whom he could hide from the trouble in the world. David's peace with himself and God was dependent on his honest recognition of what he had done. Self-acceptance and repentance are not in conflict, but are dependent on each other. This high level of honesty before God seems for a moment to risk our psychological safety, but brings with it the deeper peace that only integrity with God can yield.

This attitude is integral to Christian faith itself, if that faith is to withstand the failures and self-doubts that are common to most of us. George MacDonald wrote, 'That man is perfect in faith who can come to God in the utter dearth of his feelings and desires, without a glow or an aspiration, wandering forgetfulness, and say to Him, "Thou art my refuge." '[7]

The same pattern is evident in the very different personality of Paul. Paul sometimes used very derogatory language about himself. This was never in the form of self-flagellation or self-pitying invitations to sympathy, but usually referred to specific events in his life about which he grieved. He called himself a 'miscarriage of an apostle' and the 'chief of sinners.' About his ability to carry out his good intentions he said, 'For I do not do the good that I want, but the evil I do not want is what I do' (Rom. 7:19).

These are the kinds of things someone on the edge of despair might say about him or herself. However, the same man made some of the strongest affirmations in all of literature. He wrote, 'I can do all things in him who strengthens me' (Phil. 4:13), 'If God is for us, who is against us?' (Rom. 8:31), and 'By the grace of God I am what I am' (1 Cor. 15:10). How can these two kinds of thoughts go together in the same person? How can some-one have such a very negative view of oneself and the next minute a very positive one?

The answer is that repentance leads to the right kind of self-acceptance. If I openly recognize my sin, I can then reject it and even hate it. Repentance allows me to achieve a certain distance from it. I have objectified it as something that I have either done, felt, or said, but which is an 'it.' It is not 'me,' though of course I am responsible for it. I am not my feelings, my words, my thoughts, or my actions. I am an image of God and child of God. My sin is mine, but is not me. I have a power of sin working within me for which I am responsible, but which does not define me or exhaustively sum me up. Paul makes this point clearly:

> For I delight in the law of God, in my inmost self, but I see in my members another law at war with the law of my mind and making me captive to the law of sin which dwells in my members. (Rom. 7:22–3)

In short, even though sin has a firm hold on us, our inmost selves are able to stand back from it, be separate from it, and condemn or reject it.[8]

As we accept responsibility for sin and turn away from it, we can hate the sin and accept ourselves. This is precisely God's attitude toward us. He loves us and accepts us, but hates our sin having condemned it already in Jesus Christ's suffering in place of the believer. This is exactly the freedom and self-acceptance we see at work in David and Paul. For David, peace with himself and God came only when he openly faced and confessed the truth. Only then could he accept himself. So it was with Paul whose brutal honesty about his sin in Romans 7 was part of the foundation of his confidence in Romans 8. In both men's lives, their great strength was not inconsistent with their awareness of sin, but depended on it.

If your self-acceptance rests on maintaining an image of yourself as a nice, good person who never did anything wrong on purpose, then you cannot afford to allow much truth into your field of vision. True self-acceptance is in stark contrast to this self-delusion. Self-acceptance does not *survive* honesty; it rests on it. Integrity thus is one of the main paths to identity. The Christians are not people who are so brave or thick-skinned that they can face the truth about themselves unafraid; rather they are sinners who can face their sin because they have confidence that God has forgiven and accepted them in spite of it. The acceptance of God is the basis of self-worth.

Being open with God and ourselves about our sin frees us from the power that our sin would otherwise have over us. Think of the time, energy, and anxiety it takes to keep sin hidden. Sartre once wrote that a person 'struggles with all his strength against the crushing view that his mistakes constitute his destiny.' This view is not half so crushing as the one, also common today, which would hold that one's parents' mistakes constitute one's destiny. But if we are free enough to face our mistakes we can minimize the degree to which they control our destinies. We need not suffer the vulnerability that blameshifting and hypocrisy bring on us. It is a foolish conspiracy of pride, promising to protect, but in fact destroying.

To summarize, the Christian's security is immense and exciting. We know that we are exhaustively known by God and yet completely accepted. God says, 'I, the Lord search the mind and try the heart . . .' (Jer. 17:10). God knows our hopes, our fears, our every motivation and memory through and through; we are completely naked before God. But because we are in Christ, the Christian does not shrink back in terror at being known by God but shouts for joy. God has always known exactly what we were like and loved and accepted us anyway. This is why the Christian message has revolutionary psychological implications. We can be brutally honest with ourselves and still not be crushed by what our honesty reveals because it is within the psychological safety of the love and acceptance of God. At the same time, living before a holy God pushes one to live with greater and greater integrity.

We began this book by speaking of the two sides to a sense of identity – self-acceptance and internal coherence. In this chapter we have seen how self-acceptance is rooted in a reconciled relationship to the One who is beyond our identity. Self-acceptance is not achieved at the price of loss of coherence and integration. A self-acceptance that is not based on such honesty has excluded a great deal of truth. This causes inner division and tension since there are parts of you that you dare not face. By contrast, self-acceptance rooted in God's acceptance includes an honesty and open-ness that contributes to inner coherence. Both David and Paul knew this well.

David wrote, 'Blessed is he whose transgression is for-given, whose sin is covered' (Ps. 32:1). The sin was covered by God, not by David. It was God whose love for David was as great as the heavens are high above the earth, and who separated his transgressions from him as far as the east is from the west (Ps. 103:11–12).

Paul also was a man who had done a great deal that he was not proud of. As he reflected on the suffering he had inflicted on innocent people, he said:

For I am the least of the apostles, unfit to be called an apostle, because I persecuted the church of God. But by the grace of God I am what I am, and his grace toward me was not in vain. On the contrary, I worked harder than any of them, though it was not I but the grace of God which is with me. (1 Cor. 15:9–10)

Wretched as Paul's past had been, he did not need to hide it from himself or others. Being the object of God's grace and love simply overshadowed all else and overwhelmed him. It was at the core of his identity, dominating his thoughts and feelings about himself. But God's grace did not make him lazy, indifferent, or inactive. Quite the contrary, it motivated him to serve God with an extraordinary energy and creativity out of thankfulness for what he had received.

The Christian's reason for self-acceptance lies in God's attitude toward us. If you are a Christian, your final environment is a world whose Creator forgives, accepts, and loves you in all your uniqueness. God not only loves you in this way, but he wants you to be always aware of it. He wants you to have that confidence and to live in it.

# FOUR

# Identity Found: A Restored Reflection

*... people try to be what they cannot be, pretend to be other than they are, overlook their own best strengths in imitation of someone else's story.*[1] (Michael Novak)

*Self-centeredness is not self-discovery. This says something very valuable about the nature of the self. It is not germane to its nature to be egocentric. This is only to choke itself to death. The self can only be exhumed from its egocentric burial ground by hitching itself to something outside of itself.*[2] (John Fitch)

In the last chapter we spoke of our true identity being found in a healed relationship with the God who made us. When we come to him in humility and ask forgiveness, putting our lives in his hands, he forgives and accepts us because he loves us. This is the bedrock foundation of the Christian life; we are to build our house on it, never losing our grip on it. This affirmation from our Maker is also the basis for our self-acceptance and self-confidence in a world filled with danger and confusion.

Although it is impossible to separate self-acceptance from a sense of self-coherence, this chapter will emphasize the latter – those teachings of the Bible that, as they are embraced, bring a unity, fullness, and coherence to lives otherwise fragmented and constricted. We have seen how God's image is twisted through humankind's sin. People do not cast a true reflection of the original image; it is distorted, as your image is radically distorted in a carnival mirror. God's salvation restores men and women to the true image of God, the original. Here we will discuss both the negative side of this task – God's warnings to not be conformed to the world – and the positive side – self-coherence in our internal or imaginative reality and then in our outward actions.

## Do Not Be Conformed

When they dealt with growth into the image of God, the apostles often began with the negative side. They tell us what we have to put off before telling us what to put on. Both Peter and Paul used similar language to outline the direction of Christian growth. Peter wrote, 'As obedient children, do not be conformed to the passions of your former ignorance' (1 Pet. 1:14). He is telling us not to let ourselves get stuck in our earlier ignorant passions which hem us in and lead to destruction. Paul wrote in the same vein: 'Do not be con-formed to this world' (Rom. 12:2), or as translated by J.B. Phillips, 'Do not let the world squeeze you into its mold.' Being conformed to something less than the image of God is wrong for two reasons. First it is wrong because the old mold is rebellion against God and involves a refusal to obey him. Second, no other mold is big enough or rich enough to allow your individuality to grow within it. All other molds are smaller than the one you were made for. Only God the Creator is great enough to be our final point of integration, the one whose character we can shape ourselves around.

The biblical language suggests that we are like some malleable substance that is beaten around or poured into a mold, thereby taking on the shape of the mold ourselves. Let us look at some of the molds our society offers.

## The Image of Other People

We have seen how easily a person with a weak sense of identity can let his or her personality be formed in the image of others' opinions. This is a tyrannical force during adoles - cence and early adulthood, but it never entirely leaves us. 'I belong, therefore I am' has always been one of the quickest shortcuts to temporary feelings of adequacy. Cults often rely heavily on one's need for peer-group approval to provide a pre-packaged identity for the unsuspecting. If other people are the source of our identity, we take shape only as we discover ourselves reflected in their faces. The actual compass by which we steer is not so much what they really think, but what we think that they think of us – an exceptionally erratic source of direction. Arthur Miller's Willy Loman takes this to its tragic extreme by deriving his security from anticipating the multitudes who would come to his funeral. He might be a nobody now, but then they would know:

> Ben, that funeral will be massive! They'll come from Maine, Massachusetts, Vermont and New Hampshire! All the old timers with strange license plates – that boy will be thunder-struck, Ben, because he never realized – I am known! Rhode Island, New York, New Jersey – I am known, Ben, and he'll see what *I am*, Ben! He's in for a shock, that boy![3]

People seeking their identity through other people, whether it be from a particular group or the mass of humanity, are trapped in unreality. They will agonize over their image, their speech, their personal appearance, all the while hating themselves for caring so much about what everybody else thinks.

It is especially easy to let oneself be cast in the image of another person within marriage. If one partner derives his or her whole sense of identity from the other, a very unhelpful dependence can arise that strangles love. The current mythology which still sees marriage as the be-all-and-end-all of human existence intensifies this problem. It encourages both partners to believe that all problems will be easily overcome once they are married because their inadequacies as individuals will be compensated for once they complement each other as husband and wife. Gail Sheehy describes the destructiveness of the 'piggyback principle' where one partner attaches to the other with the unspoken desire of 'complete me.'[4] This mythology of marriage has a reverse side in its effect on single people. The single person often sees his or her identity as defined by the absence of a partner. One often hears the implicit complaint, 'How can I be expected to be a whole person? I'm not married!'

We can also root our sense of identity in others by identifying ourselves without reservation with some wider group of people – for example, with our race, economic group, or sex. All of these qualities must be part of our identity, but if they define it they confine our imageness of God and unnecessarily isolate us from others. They make us see ourselves more in terms of the color of our skin or the size of our salary than of membership in the human race. All of these constricted identities limit our horizons, making it too easy to fall into simplistic and destructive solutions to our life's problems.

## The Image of Things

I never understood how we build our sense of self around our possessions until I was inducted into the U.S. Army. Within a very few hours I was with hundreds of other men who were separated from their cars, clothes, and hair. This created insecurity way beyond what I had imagined. Some compensated by telling stories about themselves that no-body ever believed. Others just withdrew in anxiety. Possessions can differentiate us from one another and establish our sense of individuality and thereby our value. When they are taken away we are left without a real part of ourselves.

Chekhov's play *The Cherry Orchard* catches the same pattern. The loss of the family estate causes a deep loss of identity for the members of the family. 'I am what I own' sounds too crude to our ears, but also may be too true for us to dare to take seriously. How quick some are to let everyone know that they have money – or at least that they used to. The listener understands that the speaker is telling who he is.

## The Image of Achievements

We can mold ourselves around our positive and negative achievements. We can picture ourselves being made up of our accomplishments. 'I am a self-made person,' 'I am a university graduate,' 'I used to be an athletic prodigy,' 'I am a good violinist,' are all perfectly legitimate thoughts to have. However, they can also define and limit one's notion of who one is. We can do the same thing with our negative achievements – our sins or failures. How often one hears 'I am a failure,' 'I am an ex-con,' 'I am no good' as a person's full self-description. Likewise, 'I am an alcoholic' or 'I am a homosexual' can be one's dominating self-concept. Instead, we should see ourselves first as a person in God's image, then as one who has a particular problem in a particular area. If one's identity is too much rooted in achievements, whether positive or negative, one's identity becomes foreclosed, and there is little room to move.

### The Image of a Label

Many labels can dominate one's sense of identity. I will mention only two of the more popular ones. An astrological sign can become part of a person's identity in such a way that it controls his life as a self-fulfilling prophecy. Psychiatric labels are also too easy to incorporate into one's fundamental concept of self. 'I am a schizophrenic,' 'I am a manic depressive,' or, if one has failed to respond to psychiatric treatment, 'I am an inadequate personality' are all labels which in themselves can have a great formative effect on the course of a person's life. The expert imputes an identity to the patient.

### The Image of Models

Many people have no conscious philosophy of life, but have models – heroes and heroines – that define them to the extent that they see the world through the model's eyes. Think of the writings of Ernest Hemingway. They articulate no systematic philosophy but rather present a coherent hero-system, a certain kind of macho model, that has molded many lives. Similarly the elitist, esoteric heroes of Herman Hesse's writings, so superior to other people in every way, have gripped the lives of thousands of people who might well have balked at the same ideas presented in philosophical discourse.

Most of these social factors are legitimate aspects of a person's identity, but none of them is sufficient to carry the weight of a whole human being. They confine people to a shape smaller than that for which they were made. Each of these things becomes an idol if given the central place in one's identity. It will constrict one's life and growth and isolate one unnecessarily from other people.

To grow into the image of God, we must grow out of the many things that we put in God's place. The two main passages in the Bible dealing with growth into the image of God make this clear.

> Put off your old nature which belongs to your former manner of life and is corrupt through deceitful lusts, and be renewed in the spirit of your minds, and put on the new nature, created after the likeness of God in true righteousness and holiness. (Eph. 4:22–4)

> Do not lie to one another, seeing that you have put off the old nature with its practices and have put on the new nature, which is being renewed in knowledge after the image of its creator. (Col. 3:9–10)

We cannot simply *put on* the image of God without first taking a great deal *off*. Our lives are a process of taking off and putting on, reorganizing and consolidating. Whatever stands in the way of the image of God must be put off – whether it be a habit, an attitude, an idea, or any of the social molds we have just mentioned. To grow as a Christian we must be weaned from the things which are less than God which have come to take the place of God for us.

Most discussions of identity quite rightly point out that a child's sense of self is very largely established by the attitudes and responses they receive from their parents. The child's most important information about him or herself comes from their smiles, frowns, attention, or neglect. As children grow, they have more and more sources of information, and begin to believe things because *they* believe them, not just because their parents do. Finally, when they are adults we assume that they have some real measure of independence. But what kind of independence is this? Overstreet writes, 'From birth to death we build our self-confidence out of the responses we win from others and particularly from some few who are part of our daily life.'[5] Does growing in 'independence' mean merely that we free ourselves from the authority of our parents only to have the same authority taken over by our peers? It does not need to be. Jesus' call to discipleship challenges this assumption. He told those who would be his disciples to loosen their grip on everything else in their lives. They would have to be willing to break human relationships built on deep psychological bonds in their pasts (Lk. 14:25–33). Jesus expected fully grown people to have weaned themselves from dependence on constant human approval. He offered them the assured approval of God which he explained might well cause them to be rejected by their own closest friends and family. Jesus' call to discipleship is an invitation to be free from final dependence on everything in the world apart from himself.

This may involve a conscious act of disidentification, of separating oneself from parts of one's world that would otherwise be too important. The Italian psychotherapist Roberto Assagioli has made this an integral part of his view of therapy encouraging his clients to deliberately say, 'I have a body but I am not my body,' 'I have emotions but I am not my emotions,' and so on. We might well want to add other disidentifications: 'I have possessions but I am not my possessions,' 'I have friends but I am not my friends.'[6]

Jesus disidentified himself from his glory and status as God as he joined the human race on the first Christmas. He 'did not count equality with God a thing to be grasped, but emptied himself taking the form of a servant, being born in the likeness of men' (Phil. 2:6–7). It is with him then that we must finally identify ourselves. He is not some brutal taskmaster, but is the one who has sacrificed himself for us. It is to our positive identification with him that we now turn.

## New Models

In the last chapter we considered part of God's answer to the shame we feel when we violate our models. We saw that he accepts us personally in the midst of it. But there is a second side to God's solution: he wants us to change our models. This challenges our imaginations. Both the recovery of dominion and of love begin, as so many of our actions begin, in our thought life. Our models exert tremendous control over our lives, often more than our morals do. They must be examined and redeemed.

Paul prays that the Christians at Philippi would 'approve what is excellent' (Phil. 1:10). We are to recognize true excellence when we see it. In a world where we are tempted to let Hollywood construct our models for us, we are not to be torn by a tension between morals and models, or put in the crossfire between guilt and shame. David's wonderful prayer ought to be ours, 'unite my heart to serve your name' (Ps. 86:11).

In an age of cynicism about heroes, the Christian gospel has a titanic answer. The hero to end all heroes is Jesus Christ. The Greek word *archegos* is used of him.[7] It denotes the relationship of the goddess Athena to the city of Athens. She was its founder and represented all the virtues that the city aspired to. She was its heroine. The author of Hebrews applies this word to Jesus as he calls him the 'hero and perfecter of our faith' (Heb. 12:2). He is all that a human being was ever intended to be. He is the image of God in perfect focus. Look at him and you will see the commandments of God acted out in flesh and blood. There will never be a conflict between your morals and models if Christ is your model and his teaching constitutes your moral framework. Morality and heroism will be in perfect focus and there will be no false shame or guilt.

## The Imitation of Christ

The imitation of Christ is a teaching largely ignored in Protestant circles but which nonetheless appears prominently in the New Testament. In the gospel narratives Jesus repeatedly invites his disciples to treat him as their model. In the epistles the notion of the imitation of Christ seems to take over where the term 'disciple' is dropped.

Because the idea of imitating Christ has been both misused and disused we must first point out what it does *not* mean. First, it does not mean that we imitate Christ in order to be good enough to be accepted by God. Jesus teaches that we are saved by grace, not in any sense by accumulating merit or acceptability in the sight of God by our own righteousness. Neither is Christ on some high and remote point of ground, far above us, as if by a joyless moral effort we struggle to live up to his example but always fall far short. Second, the imitation of Christ does not mean the imitation of his outward actions or circumstances of his life. Some Christians do this. I heard of a boy who started a forty day fast in the desert in southern California in imitation of Jesus. He died of dehydration before the forty days were up. An evangelist carried a heavy wooden cross around the countryside. He gained publicity, but did not do what Jesus meant by telling us to 'take up your cross.' In a South American tribe a boy is crucified every two years. He is taken down before he dies, but it is the high point of a religious festival in which the Easter story is re-enacted.

Others try to imitate the conditions of Jesus' life – for example the fact that he had no home, he was not married and he quit regular employment – saying that these things are holy in themselves because Jesus did them. The New Testament does not teach this. It says that God might ask any of his disciples to do these things to serve him, but they are not holy just because Jesus did them. An extreme and rather humorous example of this tendency is found in a passage from Islamic literature. The writer points out that Mohammed ate watermelons, but notes that it is not certain whether the prophet ate the seeds or spat them out. The writer concludes that Muslims should not eat watermelons at all to avoid the risk of doing what Mohammed had not done with the seeds.

What, then, *is* the imitation of Christ? It is the imitation of his quality of life, the simple excellence of the way he lived. Our worldly models are easy and superficial; we ape the way someone speaks, walks, dresses, or their style of success. Jesus offers himself to us as a hero on a much more profound level. He stretches and expands us in our very core. Let us consider some of the ways he challenges us, areas that are explicitly taught in the New Testament:

## Love

Jesus said, 'This is my commandment, that you love one another as I have loved you' (Jn. 15:12). It was not just a command to love, but to love *as Jesus loved*. To do this, we must watch him carefully. By loving as he loved, all people will know Jesus' disciples (Jn. 13:35).

## Forgiveness

The apostle Paul wrote that you should be 'kind to one another, tenderhearted, forgiving one another, as God in Christ forgave you' (Eph. 4:32). Again we are not just to forgive, but to forgive in the particular way that we were forgiven in Christ – out of love and kindness and with no strings attached.

### Suffering unjustly

One of the teachings that grates hardest against twentieth-century attitudes is found in the words of Peter. He wrote,

> For one is approved if, mindful of God, he endures pain while suffering unjustly. For what credit is it, if when you do wrong and are beaten for it you take it patiently? But if when you do right and suffer for it you take it patiently, you have God's approval. For to this you have been called, because Christ also suffered for you leaving you an example, that you should follow in his steps. (1 Pet. 2:19–21)

What might seem unthinkable to us, we see demonstrated before our eyes. Who else would we ever listen to with such a teaching?

### Generosity

In one of the most concise summaries of the work of Christ, Paul said:

> For you know the grace of our Lord Jesus Christ, that though he was rich, yet for your sake he became poor, so that by his poverty you might become rich. (2 Cor. 8:9)

Paul immediately makes the application to the Corinthians that they should complete their gift for other poorer Christians. The proper way to imitate Christ's generosity to us is to do the same in our relationships with one another.

### Humility

In a closely related passage Paul wrote:

> Have this mind among yourselves, which you have in Christ Jesus, who, though he was in the form of God, did not count equality with God a thing to be grasped, but emptied himself, taking the form of a servant, being born in the likeness of men. And being found in human form he humbled himself and became obedient unto death, even death on a cross. (Phil. 2:5–8)

Jesus stepped down to earth and even to the cross. You, if you are a Christian, have his mind in you; therefore you too can afford to be humble with one another. This is our way to imitate the incarnation.

### Service

The idea of being a servant in the first-century Roman world was a lowly thing indeed, but through Jesus' life and teaching it became the highest calling:

> . . . whoever would be great among you must be your servant, and whoever would be first among you must be slave of all. For the son of man came not to be served but to serve, and to give his life as a ransom for many. (Mk. 10:43–5)

> If I then, your Lord and Teacher, have washed your feet, you also ought to wash one another's feet. For I have given you an example, that you also should do as I have done to you. (Jn. 13:14–15)

How could Jesus hope to subvert and reverse such a deeply imbedded natural and cultural tendency to want to *be* served? Only by his example.

The point is clear. Jesus put himself before us as a model. He shows us true heroism. Let us not reduce this heroism to a series of commands such as 'you ought to love,' 'you ought to be generous,' etc. Such commands are true, but they lose the dynamism of a flesh and blood person living in a heroic way in our own history. To reduce the imitation of Christ to a dozen or so moral assertions misses his appeal to our imaginations and our sense of aspiration. Instead let us study his life and meditate on it. Let us find his quality of life on the pages of the New Testament, and make it our goal.

The imitation of Christ means that we are asked to imitate not just anything Christ has done, but what he has done for us. Who are those whom he has loved, forgiven, suffered injustice for, been generous to, been humiliated for, and served? It was us. The imitation of Christ is a thankful worshipful response to the way Christ has dealt with us. He is not far off; he is beside us. Remember that he is the one who is not ashamed to call us part of his family. Imitating him is imitating an older brother who is walking beside us through life. It is not like an orphan hoping to impress prospective parents so that he might be adopted. It is rather the orphan, having been adopted, responding out of gratitude to parents and brothers and sisters.

## The Imitation of Those Who Are Christ-like

The New Testament also tells us to imitate those who imitate Christ. Other people can be our models in a limited way. The apostle Paul wrote 'Be imitators of me as I am of Christ' (1 Cor. 11:1). Paul put himself forward as a model, but he carefully qualified himself. He did not just say, 'Be imitators of me' but added, '*as I am of Christ.*' Christ is still the model, but we can imitate Paul *in so far* as he is Christ-like. We are to look for Christ-likeness in the lives of those around us (Heb. 6:12). But how are we to avoid the kind of hero worship which immobilizes and discourages us when our hero is someone radically different from us?

The writer of Hebrews had some very shrewd advice. He wrote,

> Remember your leaders, those who spoke to you the word of God; consider the outcome of their life and imitate their faith. (Heb. 13:7)

The genius of what he said is this: we are to look to those who have been helpful influences in our lives, reflect on the fruit that their lives have borne, and then imitate their *faith*, not their lives. This leads us to identify with others' trust in God, their courage in following him, and their peace in resting on his promises. In other words, we are to imitate their *Christ-likeness*. We are not to imitate the specific way they lead their lives, their calling, their gifts, their opportunities, their mannerisms, or vocabulary. Such imitation inevitably fails. When Paul told the Corinthians, 'Be imitators of me,' he did not want them all to become missionaries (no one would have been left in the churches that he started), tentmakers, Roman citizens or to wear the kind of clothes he did. He wanted them to imitate his 'ways in Christ' (1 Cor. 4:16–17) which he taught wherever he went.

This heroism is accessible to us. It is not like the heroism of the pop stars and celebrities of the media world who are beyond our reach. True heroism is in the realm of the possible for each one of us who is willing to walk humbly with God and be challenged by the life of his son.

The Bible itself is a gold-mine of models for us – not the cardboard and plastic one-dimensional models of Hollywood, but real people presented in a real way. Think of Moses, David, Job, Peter, and Paul – people who were sinners for sure, but people in whose lives we see a strong hint of the glory of God. The eleventh chapter of Hebrews is a list of the heroes of faith, written with the intention that they be models for us. They were all men and women who stepped out following the Lord, not knowing where they would end up.

Three of my favorite heroes are Shadrach, Meshach, and Abednego (Dan. 3). Too often their lives have been trivialized by bouncy Sunday School songs and stories. They are heroic because of three words they said when they refused to worship an idol built by Nebuchadnezzar, the king of Babylon. When threatened with being incinerated in a furnace as punishment, they answered:

> O Nebuchadnezzar, we have no need to answer you in this matter. If it be so, our God whom we serve is able to deliver us from the burning fiery furnace; and he will deliver us out of your hand, O king. *But if not*, be it known to you, O king, that we will not serve your gods or worship the golden image which you have set up. (Dan. 3:16–18)

These three were among the most promising young men in their whole country. They were not ready to shuffle off and die, nor were they people who had nothing to live for. They were the Rhodes and Fulbright scholars of Israel. They did not know whether they would be saved from the fire or not. They had no advance knowledge; they had not read the Sunday School literature to find out; their future on earth was a question mark. They knew that God was great enough to get them out, but they did not know that he would, so they said these three wonderful words, 'But if not.' They were willing to lose their lives rather than worship the idol. Here is faith that has its analogy in countless smaller places in our lives.

## Despising the Shame

We have seen how we can feel shame for things that are not shameful at all. This feeling of shame points to no real dishonor, but only to the fact that our models are less than Jesus Christ, and that these models have been violated. We have Jesus' reaction to such shame in the continuation of Hebrews 12:2, 'looking to Jesus the hero and perfecter of our faith, who for the joy that was set before him endured the cross, despising the shame, and is seated at the right hand of the throne of God.' Jesus despised the shame of the cross. The cross was without doubt the most shameful way to die in Jesus' time. Cicero had initiated legislation that no Roman citizen would ever have to die on a cross. Often it would take days to die, and the bodies would be left exposed for weeks as examples to others.

Jesus despised the shame of the cross because in it he saw not shame but glory. In God's sight the cross was the greatest manifestation of his glory and the focal point of all of human history. Pointing forward to the cross, Jesus told his disciples, 'Now is the Son of man glorified; if God is glorified in him, God will also glorify him in himself and glorify him at once' (Jn. 13:31–2). Notice the emphasis on glory. Jesus had not forgotten the agony that was to come, but the cross was glory because it would show the character of God displayed and magnified. Here they would see the extent of his love for men and women demonstrated the way it had never been demonstrated before.

The source of God's glory can be humankind's shame. The magnificent eleventh chapter of Hebrews, the list of heroes of faith, is not a list of great kings who prospered and reigned happily ever after. It ends like this,

> Some were tortured, refusing to accept release, that they might rise again to a better life. Others suffered mocking and

scourging, and even chains and imprisonment. They were stoned, they were sawn in two, they were killed with the sword; they went about in skins of sheep and goats, destitute, afflicted, ill-treated – of whom the world was not worthy – wandering over deserts and mountains, and in dens and caves of the earth. (Heb. 11:35–8)

How different this heroism is from the glory of power, money, and visible success. Here were people wearing animal skins and living in holes in the ground of whom the world was not worthy! The world in all its finery, power, money, rockets, and skyscrapers is not worthy of these men and women who lived in holes in the ground. Their names are forgotten to all but God. We should never associate true glory with riches or shame with poverty. If we do, we are way out of step with the God of the Bible (cf. Jer. 9:23–4).

Perhaps we, like the prophets of the Old Testament, need to consciously debunk the false heroes of our time. We could share Isaiah's scorn for 'those who are heroes at drinking wine, and valiant men in mixing strong drink' (Is. 5:22). Think also of the ladies of Samaria's high society who, in the time of Amos, were waited on hand and foot and were doubtless models to many. Amos called them 'cows of Bashan' and promised that they would be carried away with hooks (Amos 4:1–2). The writer of Proverbs describes the Don Juan hero who has promiscuous sex as 'an ox that goes to the slaughter' (Prov. 7:22).

We have before us a huge task if we are to reintroduce something of true heroism into the popular mind. Unhappily, the church has not done well. Far too many of God's people have used God's money to buy into the crass heroism of the consumer economy. Hear the voice of one from outside the church,

Today religionists wonder why youth has abandoned the churches, not wanting to realize that it is precisely because organized religion openly subscribes to a commercial-industrial hero-system that is almost openly defunct; it so obviously denies reality, builds war machines against death, and banishes sacredness with bureaucratic dedication. Men are treated as things and the world is pulled down to their size. The churches subscribe to this empty heroics of possession, display, manipulation. I think that today Christianity is in trouble not because its myths are dead, but because it does not offer its ideal of heroic sainthood as an immediate personal one to be lived by all believers. In a perverse way, the churches have turned their backs both on the miraculousness of creation and the need to do something heroic in this world.[8]

The redemption of your imagination in this area of models is no small thing. It is a lifelong task, but it is an important part of the development of your relationship with the one who is the author of life itself. We are to imitate Christ as he walks beside us as an older brother until he will one day turn our shame to glory.

God is interested in more than our imaginations. If he wanted only to change our minds, we would only need to be good daydreamers. A very down-to-earth lady that I knew in England used to tell those who seemed to be chronically and passively unemployed, 'You need to put your backbone where your wishbone is.' This is an entirely Christian sentiment. The Christian life is an active life. It cannot be lived just inside one's head; it must be lived out in the world.

## Choices

Biblical teaching gives a very important place to the mind and the choices that it makes. Our mind has been given to us by God and he expects it to be used. The apostle Peter told his readers, 'gird up your minds.' The image is a helpful one. At the time, men commonly wore long robes. Before they would get up to walk anywhere or do any work they would gird themselves up by putting a belt around their middle to keep the robe from getting in the way. This same idea was applied to the mind. To gird up our minds is to prepare for work. We must not let our thoughts wander loosely. We must be mentally disciplined and sharp. The mind has a very active role.

The biblical writers address commands directly to our minds. We are expected to control and direct our minds. We do not need to be passive about the contents of our conscious mind. Our control over our thoughts can never be complete, but we can usually decide to think about one thing rather than another. We are often told to set our minds on God and on his truth. For example, Paul tells us to 'Set your minds on things that are above' (Col. 3:2) and to 'think about these things' (Phil. 4:8). Finally, we are told that we are not to think of our minds as static, but that we can be renewed in the spirit of our minds (Eph. 4:23) so that we become more truly the image of God.

The German psychologist Grodeck wrote that 'we are lived by our subconscious.' Freud was said to have given this statement his stamp of approval. Although the statement is in no sense a fair summary of Freud's thinking, people often naively credit this idea with Freud's authority. The idea is well known. It is said that our real decisions are made in a warfare that goes on beneath the surface of our consciousness. Our conscious ego is said to be quite passive despite its feelings to the contrary. Therefore, since the real decisions are made by the unconscious mind, the measure of one's integration as a person is said to be the degree to which he is in touch with, or has insight into, his unconscious. Rollo May complained of this syndrome, 'People go to therapists to find substitutes for their lost will: to learn how to get the "unconscious" to direct their lives.'[9]

We must say with emphasis that the battles of the conscious mind are real battles, the choices real choices. There is the crude notion that the unconscious mind is to our selves as the smoke-filled room is to a political convention. It is a remote, inaccessible, and carefully guarded place where all the important policies are made by people motivated only by self-interest. Their decisions surface mysteriously into the outside puppet world where a show is made of justifying them on more respectable grounds. The whole world view of the Bible would push us in a very different direction.

Other psychologists would reduce all of human behavior to the categories of a machine, in which input causes output according to well-defined rules. That is to say that the stimuli which come to us completely account for all the responses we make.[10] The biblical viewpoint is again very different. We can investigate, analyze, and evaluate the stimuli. Our 'I am' can mediate between the stimuli and the responses. We can use our minds to understand the 'futile ways inherited from his fathers' (1 Pet. 1:18) and respond in a host of different ways toward them, few of which are inevitable.

The eighteenth chapter of Ezekiel is instructive at this point. Ezekiel speaks of God's absolute fairness in judging each person on his or her own right and not for the life led by their fathers. He tells of three successive generations. The first man was righteous and walked with God in every way. His son was an outright rebel and did everything to grieve God. Then the grandson grew up, saw the mess that his father had made of everything, and lived a righteous life as his grandfather had done. Many conditioning factors, both positive and negative, worked in these generations. However, each son was the image of God, able to make his own decisions in the midst of powerful influences on him.

Of course the degree of self-awareness and freedom varies widely among individuals. Some people are severely restricted in these areas for a host of reasons. This, however, does not mean that we need to abandon the biblical teaching on the reality of human's choice. It is rather a reason to be flexible in our application of this teaching to each individual.

## Active Obedience

I have emphasized the reality of choice because many in today's intellectual climate deny that our choices are real. But choice leads to action. Peter wrote that we should live 'no longer by human passions but by the will of God' (1 Pet. 4:2). Living by our passions will not lead us to reflect the likeness of God. Only active obedience to the law of God in his word will begin to restore something of our original image as well as our intended dominion over the earth.

This raises the question of the law of God. Many today regard God's law as backward, arbitrary, and restrictive. But the apostle James had a very different notion; he called it the law of liberty, and wrote:

> He who looks into the perfect law, the law of liberty and perseveres, being no hearer that forgets but a doer that acts, he shall be blessed in his doing. (Jas. 1:25)

God's law is to be obeyed not just contemplated. It is a law of liberty because the commands of God are not arbitrary or burdensome, but designed for our fulfillment. They are rooted in the character of God. We become more our true selves when we obey them.

However, the Christian cannot be passive. The Bible teaches clearly that we must exert an effort to obey God.

Sin is still a very real force in the life of every Christian while they are on earth. We must wrestle against it with every ounce of strength that God provides. The Bible commands us to combat sin with all our mind and will. Active obedi - ence involves a daily battle to choose and to act on the basis of God's law and against the counterdemands of sin. It is no accident that there is so much military imagery in the New Testament vocabulary.[11]

The life of Abraham illustrates both the struggle and the rewards of obedience. God tested Abraham but also gave him strength. Taking his son Isaac to be sacrificed was certainly the most difficult thing Abraham ever had to do. He did not feel like doing it, yet he was willing to obey God even to the point of sacrificing his son. The one to benefit from this testing was undoubtedly Abraham. Imagine what it would have been like for Abraham to *know* that he was willing to withhold absolutely nothing from God. Think of the confi - dence he would have had in God's ability to work through him. He was not puffed up by the experience, saying, 'Lucky me! I have passed God's test.' Instead he was overwhelmed with the conviction that 'The Lord will provide' (Gn. 22:14). Abraham, with Moses, Jeremiah, Elijah, and many others after him, obeyed God under the most extreme conditions and received strength from him in their obedience. In his obedience, Abraham quite literally was an image of God in his willingness to sacrifice his only son. In him, we get a glimpse of the mystery of God's provision of his own Son.

There is a solidity and reliability about a person who believes in the ways of God and lives them out with consis - tency even in the midst of difficulty. Here we are dealing with words that do not often find their way into psychological discourse, such as 'character.' The psalmist is saying the same thing when he says of the righteous, 'He is like a tree planted by streams of water, that yields its fruit in its season, and its leaf does not wither.' This is contrasted to the wicked, who are 'like chaff which the wind drives away.' (Ps. 1:3–4) There is something solid and substantial about a person who really honors God in an uncompromising way. In another psalm David makes a similar point, 'He who walks blamelessly, and does what is right, and speaks the truth from his heart . . . who swears to his own hurt and does not change, . . . He who does these things shall not be moved.' (Ps. 15:2–5) Notice the phrase, 'who swears to his own hurt and does not change.' This is some one who enters an agreement, then later discovers that it will hurt in some way to fulfill their side of the bargain – but sticks to the bargain nonetheless. That is, they do not budge, even though it causes them discomfort, cost, or hardship. He or she then becomes a person who will 'never be moved.' The person who lives this way develops strength of character and is not blown around like chaff in the wind. He or she is the opposite of the righteous one who 'gives way before the wicked' and who is described as being like a 'muddied spring or a polluted fountain' (Prov. 25:26). What is described here is integrity of personality, continuity of character in a changing, unpredictable, and painful world.

By obeying God, we begin to re-establish the dominion over the earth we were intended to have. Obedience gives us a measure of self-mastery and also the ability to act in our environment. I see this growth in dominion and mastery in the concern with gifts in the church today. Some of this concern about gifts is ingrown, but on the whole it is a legitimate desire to see one's gifts used. We were made to be creative in the world as God was the Creator of the world. We do this by using the gifts God gave us to express our mastery over our little piece of the earth for God's glory. All of us have gifts. It might be the gift of building a building, nurturing a relationship, healing a body, or teaching a class. Our gifts extend across the whole range of human culture. We need to know what we are and are not good at. Here the church can be a great help by challenging people to see the diversity of their gifts and helping them to express them both within the church and in the culture at large.

In all this, of course, we must not forget the danger of rooting our identity in gifts, job, achievements, or role in society. God is at the center. Our identity is in him. We must throw ourselves into serving him with all the gifts that we have.

As we imitate Christ and actively follow his law, we are led closer to God and therefore closer to reflecting his image – our true nature. We are not cramped by a model too small for us, but we are moving toward our fullest potential as human beings. Human dominion over the earth was radically restricted and spoiled by the Fall. We are enslaved by things and forces which God had meant humans to control. Obedience to God through Christ moves us closer to our God-given task and purpose. Our obedience is ruled by nothing less than God; therefore, it restores in some small way the dominion that was our original task.

## The Recovery of Love

Recall our discussion in chapter two of Paul's exposure of the person without love (1 Cor. 13:1–3) who could only say, 'I am nothing, I gain nothing I just make noise' – a picture of one who is almost less than human. Let us look at Paul's next statement.

> Love is patient and kind; love is not jealous or boastful; it is not irritable or resentful; it does not rejoice at wrong, but rejoices in the truth. Love bears all things, hopes all things, endures all things. (1 Cor. 13:4–7)

This is a picture of a person who loves. It is not a theoretical definition, but rather a description of what love does.

The tone of this passage parallels the qualities of Jesus' life that he taught us to imitate. The person who loves can only be humble, ready to serve others, not demanding service for oneself, not holding a grudge. Some scholars think that Paul is here consciously giving us a description of Jesus himself.

Many of Paul's qualities of love have to do with its duration. It is easier to love someone for a few minutes than it is to do what love demands day after day, year after year. When we mistakenly grab a hot platter off the stove, we can usually hold it for a few moments until we can find a safe place to put it down. But all of us have a limit. If the pain is too great we will drop the platter as a sheer reflex. Our love is often similar. We can love up to a certain point. If our love is not returned or is frustrated, we drop it. What a powerful thing Paul is describing! It is a love that 'bears all things, hopes all things, endures all things.'

Our image of someone who lives this way is probably that of a person who gets hurt, walked on, and ignored. But people who love are not weak. They are so strong that they do not need to meet criticism or insult with a cutting remark. Their self-esteem is so secure that they do not need to constantly defend it. They are not threatened when people laugh at them. They do not need to always get their own way by manipulation, intimidation, or marathon argument. Their love does not turn to exasperation if it is not quickly returned. They give and give and keep on giving. They are free in the midst of internal and external pressures, free to be themselves. To be fully human has little to do with always being the center of attention, getting your way and having all your ambitions met. To be fully human is to be like Christ, to 'count others better than yourselves' (Phil. 2:3). This is not a groveling debasing of the self in false and obsequious humility. It is a response to our highest call. It takes rare strength to treat others as more important than yourself.

In the same way, some of Jesus' teaching which might seem to negate the self, actually has the opposite meaning. For example, his invitation, 'If any man would come after me, let him take up his cross and follow me' (Mt. 16:24) calls us not to deny the self, but to deny the self's lust for less important things – for personal gain, greed, pride, and security in this world. It is a call to be what you were meant to be. The self-denial which Jesus calls us to is a repudiation of selfishness and an affirmation of the highest value to which we can aspire – love. It is a call to relinquish something of lesser worth to gain something of greater worth. In God's economy, even our physical lives can be a lesser value: 'whoever loses his life for my sake will find it' (Mt. 16:25). Take Jesus' commandment that he gives to his disciples:

> This is my commandment, that you love one another as I have loved you. Greater love has no man than this, that a man lay down his life for his friends. (Jn. 15:12–13)

Even martyrdom – physical death – is not a negation of the self. It is the response of the self to the high calling of God. It shows that humankind, the image of God, cannot be bought from serving God by physical comforts and security, or even threats to life itself.

Loving another person is one of the many kinds of dominion that we have. But in certain relationships there can seem to be a tension between love and dominion that needs to be worked out with great care and courage.

Love does not mean fulfilling all of the expectations someone has of you. The person who loves is not always at everyone's beck and call. In fact love of another person may require you to rebuke them or to refuse to do something they want. If love means being under other people's control, we lose our own dominion and ability to direct our lives to follow God's direction. If their demands are unrealistic or unfair, we must tell them so out of concern for them and ourselves. On the other hand, we often face demands that are not unrealistic or unfair, but simply go beyond the limits of our own gifts, resources, time, and energy. We can never do as much as we would like to do. We can only be in one place at a time. We can only go just so long without sleep. We have just so much money to give away. We must simply make very difficult choices.

There are no rules that others can set for our limits. Because each of us has an extraordinary capacity for self-deception, we must have the highest level of integrity before God so that we can be guided by him. One can only say that there are obvious extremes to be avoided. On the one extreme there are those who are so concerned to protect themselves and their property that they are like the priest and the Levite who pass by on the other side of the road as a man lies dying. On the other extreme there are those who so expend themselves that they collapse and become a problem for some one else, not the solution. There is a lot of space between these two extremes, plenty of room to move. We need to look to God each day ourselves, not assuming that someone else's place is where we should be, or that yesterday's pattern will be tomorrow's rule.

## Identity and Christian Growth

It is time to explain Jesus' command 'love your neighbor as yourself.' We can understand it best in the context of what we have seen about love.

Just what is self-love? Is it legitimate or inevitably conceited and pompous?

Some say that self-love is intrinsically selfish and always involves pride.[12] They point to places in the Bible which see self-love as clearly evil. Paul predicts that people 'will be lovers of self, lovers of money . . .' (2 Tim. 3:2) in times of decadence. Jesus warned, 'He who loves his life loses it . . .' (Jn. 12:25). If you love your life in the sense of being concerned only for yourself and your own interests then you will lose everything.

Others take the opposite view – that self-love or self-acceptance must precede all other aspects of growth. This view is widely held among Christians who have been influ-enced by the Humanistic Psychology movement. I call this approach to self the four-commandment view. The first commandment is that you must first find someone else to love you unconditionally. Only when another person accepts you in this unconditional way can you be expected to love and accept yourself. Once this person has been found, you can go on to the second commandment – to love yourself for who you are. Then you can love your neighbor. (You cannot love your neighbor if you do not first love yourself because your own self-esteem would be too low, your ego too weak.) In the same way, the love of your neighbor is the precondition to being able to love, honor, and obey God. You can only relate to God in a non-neurotic way after you have learned to establish human relationships, especially with those who are authority figures in your life.

There is enough truth in this theory to make it sound plausible. It is perfectly true that it is easier to accept ourselves when others accept us, easier to love others when we are at peace about ourselves, and easier to love God when we have loved people. However, feelings of inade-quacy do not *force* us to be unloving. I might want to cut someone down, manipulate, or exalt myself over them when I am feeling insecure and unloved, but it is not *inevitable* that I do so. I still have a wide range of responses available to me. In the same way, it is dubious to suggest that one's self-acceptance depends so completely on unconditional acceptance by another human being.

I would suggest that the inevitability of the four-commandment view – the notion that these four commands can be approached only in sequence – encourages helplessness, self-pity, and blame shifting. This framework makes it too easy to attribute one's feelings of inadequacy to the failure of other people to give unconditional love. Everything depends on the action of another person, not on anything that you can do, and you may have noticed that people who love unconditionally do not grow on trees.

However, the most profound objection to the four-commandment view is that it relegates God to a subordinate role in the last step of a process which he in fact initiates, sustains, and completes. He alone accepts us unconditionally. Because he accepts us, we can have a personal relationship with him that helps us to accept and love ourselves and to love others. The four-commandment view turns the gospel upside down and becomes salvation by psychology.[13] It would have us come to God only after we are psychologically scrubbed and clean, sufficiently integrated to cope with such a complex relationship. The Christ who came to save sinners, to seek and save the lost, the God who meets us whoever we are wherever we are, is obscured. The underlying assumption of this four-commandment view is that self-love is the highest goal, the fulfillment of our human potential, and our final obligation. A relationship with God becomes an optional extra available only for the well-integrated personality.

If we seek self-love and self-acceptance as our primary goal, our identity becomes a cult of self-worship. Identity sought in this way is like the pot of gold at the end of the rainbow; when you get there to collect it, it has always moved on. There is a self-love that is neither proud nor complacent, but is an integral part of our sense of identity before God. But the Bible never tells us to look for it, because we were never meant to pursue it directly. Jesus never exhorted his disciples to have self-esteem, he just told them to have faith in him. The Bible gives two great commandments. The first is 'you shall love the Lord your God with all your heart, and with all your soul, and with all your mind and with all your strength.' The second is 'you shall love your neighbor as yourself' (Mk. 12:30–1). The phrase 'as yourself' simply qualifies the love that we are to have for our neighbor. It tells us how much love we are to have for *him*. It is not a command in itself at all. The right kind of self-love comes as a by-product of Christian living rather than as a conscious goal in itself. It is not the highest good, but comes to us from the side, as it were, when we are aiming at a higher one.

All this might seem like a psychological 'Catch-22': loving others is easier if we are at peace with ourselves, but loving others is also one of the ways of finding peace with yourself. How do we get into this circle if we are not already in it? The truth is that this circle is really a spiral in which growth follows and encourages growth. Our strength of identity is both the parent and the child of our own growth. Identity is the parent because it gives us the security and confidence to step out in greater trust in God. It is the child because growth in faith and in grace gives us a stronger sense of identity. An example is Paul's advice to the husband: the man 'who loves his wife loves himself' (Eph. 5:28). The man enters a spiral of growth: as he loves her, he benefits. Love has this reflexive character. The more he loves her the stronger he becomes. The stronger he becomes the more he is able to love her.

We are never to sit passively expecting others to build us up or to supply us with security so that we will then be able to reach out in love. Jesus made this abundantly clear in his new commandment. The old commandment was to 'love your neighbor as yourself.' The new commandment went further: we are to love one another 'as I have loved you.'

Note two things. First, we are expected to love others not as much as, but more than, ourselves. Our standard is Jesus' sacrifice of his life for us. Second, our starting point in loving others is not in ourselves, but is in knowing that God has unconditionally loved us. He loved us in a very costly way, and we are eminently unworthy of that love.

## Growth in Wisdom and the Mind of Christ

Individuals usually grow in spiritual wisdom in an erratic pattern. Even the heroes of the faith in the Bible often went three steps forward and two back. All of us are tested and tried. We fall down, lurch in wrong directions, often get discouraged and want to give up. Throughout this battle, God is at work within us, bringing us into conformity with his image. One of the words used in the Old Testament to describe the goal of this growth is 'wisdom.' Wisdom brings security and confidence, God 'stores up sound wisdom for the upright; he is a shield to those who walk in integrity' (Prov. 2:7). One of the most helpful of the many New Testament images for spiritual growth is the command that we are to have increasingly the mind of Christ about every situation in which we find ourselves (Phil. 2:5). In fact Paul says that the Christian already has the mind of Christ; we must put it to work.

Wisdom and the mind of Christ both hold humans to be a unity. They refer to a kind of organic growth from the inside to the outside. Our spontaneous feelings, responses, and decisions gradually become closer to those of God. The self that we are is gradually integrated with the self that we ought to be. We do not grow by suppressing our recalcitrant emotions, but by allowing God to gradually free our better feelings and attributes, gradually starving out those that are destructive. This is a life-long work of God. It takes struggle and effort, and includes times of agony and doubt. It is not completed in this life, but God gives us solid hope for growth that is substantial.

Ironically, if we seek spontaneity and freedom as ends in themselves, we rarely find them. If we give our emotions free rein to determine our behavior they usually constrict us, to shrivel us up instead of freeing us. Again the word of God gives extraordinarily practical wisdom: 'A tranquil mind gives life to the flesh, but passion makes the bones rot' (Prov. 14:30). How true this is. I know a woman who rushed into life trying to feel as many strong feelings as she could, hoping her feelings would establish integration within. She soon described herself as 'a non-person. I have no feelings left.' Or consider the man who did his best to gratify every sexual desire and whim; he was shocked when he eventually realized that he could no longer feel anything, not even anger at someone who had seriously wronged him. Apathy was his defense against overstimulation of the feelings.[14] There is sober truth in the words of Newman and Berkowitz:

> People say they want to 'let go.' What they need is to take hold. Only when you are really in charge of yourself can you afford to 'let go,' to be spontaneous and expect good to come out of it.[15]

A similar irony is that, in a psychological society such as our own, with such expectations of self-awareness, self-esteem, and self-actualization, a great self-consciousness is created about our psychological health and integration. Rather than producing greater psychological freedom, it crushes spontaneity in infinite regressions of psychological calculations. William Kilpatrick complains that the whole attempt is counter-productive. There is a deep 'psychological seriousness' in which the self has become a new kind of burden. The serious pursuit of happiness becomes an unhappy project.[16]

When Jesus was on earth he promised to give abundant life to those who would follow him. This means that the character of God himself will form the framework within which the Christian's whole being is expressed. As we give our lives more fully to him, we do not thereby warp our personalities, but become like the prodigal son who finally 'came to himself' (Lk. 15:11–32). Like him, we find ourselves in God's image.

It's time to summarize the ground that we have covered so far. We have traced some of the dynamics of the losing and finding of our sense of identity. Two of the most important factors were a sense of self-acceptance and a sense of coherence. We have then tried to show that the true foundation for both of these is in a right relationship to God. We are able to accept ourselves because God loves, forgives, accepts, and adopts us as his children. We are able to grow in our internal coherence because we can grow in the image of God with new models and new actions built around the nature of God himself. His character becomes the connect-ing thread that runs through ours. God's acceptance and his challenge to a new life are entirely intertwined. Without the grace, love, and forgiveness of God, Christianity would be another ugly and brutal moralism offering only condemna-tion to our consciences. At the same time, without the demand for new thoughts and actions, the Christian faith would be a dead letter and the worst kind of apathetic hypocrisy. Through it all, God himself is there nurturing us as a Father nurtures his children when he wants them to grow.

Sometimes everything else is taken away from us and God himself is all that we have. Dietrich Bonhoeffer found himself in just this situation when he was in a German prison in World War II. He was executed in prison, but left

us a number of writings including a short poem entitled
'Who am I?'

Who am I? They often tell me
I would step from my cell's confinement
Calmly, cheerfully, firmly
Like a squire from his country house.
Who am I? They often tell me
I used to speak to my warders
Freely and friendly and clearly,
As though it were mine to command.
Who am I? They also tell me
I bore the day's misfortune
Equably, smilingly, proudly,
Like one accustomed to win.
Am I then really all that which other men tell of?
Or am I only what I myself know of myself,
Restless and longing and sick, like a bird in a cage,
Struggling for breath, as though hands were compressing my
    throat,
Yearning for colors, for flowers, for the voices of birds,
Thirsting for words of kindness, for neighborliness, tossing in
    expectation of great events,
Powerlessly trembling for friends at infinite distance,
Weary and empty at praying, at thinking, at making,
Faint, and ready to say farewell to it all?
Who am I? This or the other?
Am I one person today and tomorrow another?
Am I both at once? A hypocrite before others,
And before myself a contemptibly woe-begone weakling?
Or is something within me still like a beaten army,
Fleeing in disorder from victory already achieved?
Who am I? They mock me, these lonely questions of mine,
Whoever I am, thou knowest, O God, I am thine![17]

Notice that Bonhoeffer did not say that 'my faith pulled me through it and everything was fine.' He did not even take solace in his knowledge of God. The crucial thing, cutting through his confusion, was that God knew *him*.

Perfect integration of feelings, thoughts, and actions is not possible in this world. It is at best a romantic dream; at worst, it is a dangerous utopian idol. The world is filled with conflict. We are called not to withdraw from it, but to be involved in it to such an extent that our sense of selfhood will sometimes be strained to the limit. Yet God is with us. His Spirit is our comforter. He not only sustains us, but gives us positive growth.

We have spoken of an innermost self or heart that is radically 'me.' Our sense of identity is not found by an effort of self-integration, by trying to relate all our roles, feelings, attitudes and relationships *to* this central self. It is *from* this self or heart that God intends us to have total confidence in him and in our status as his children. Our sense of identity is found by looking first to God from our innermost selves and letting all our roles, feelings, attitudes, and relationships find their place in relation to him.

# FIVE

# Reconciliation:
# Toward a Higher Honesty

*I set it down as a fact that if all men knew what each said of the other, there would not be four friends in the world.* [1]
(Blaise Pascal)

*. . . speaking the truth in love, we are to grow up in every way into him who is the head, into Christ* (Eph. 4:15).

The hinge pin of the Christian's identity is our reconciliation to God. The Christian is a reconciled child, welcomed into God's family by the love of the Father, the sacrificial death of the Son, and the work of the Holy Spirit within us. Our identity, however, is also being shaped in continual interaction with others. An important aspect of the Christian's calling is to reflect the reconciliation we have with God into our relationships with other people. We will have many opportunities to offer others the reconciliation we have received from God. Just as our relationship to God is always marred by our sin, so our human relationships will be marked by conflict. God calls us to be committed to bringing reconciliation wherever and whenever we can. This is what being honest to God commits us to. The apostle Paul says it in this way: 'If possible, so far as it depends upon you, live peaceably with all' (Rom. 12:18). Honesty to God demands that we take this seriously.

What does reconciliation actually involve? It requires that we not be content with leaving conflict and sin unfaced in our relationships with one another. The easiest course is often to simply ignore conflict. This is of course impossible where there is open battle, but the more familiar pattern is increasing distrust, coldness, and alienation justified by: 'I can't be best friends with everybody can I?' We settle for less and less. The world is littered with unresolved relation-ships. Lifelong 'friends' do not know where they stand with one another because they have never faced or dealt with conflict between them. This grieves God. Reconciliation calls for tying up these loose ends and resolving conflicts as much as possible in a broken society.

We all develop certain patterns to cope with conflicts. Whether we are aware of it or not, these patterns have a great influence on our life and personality. For example, what do you do when you have hurt someone? There are many choices. You can avoid them, get angry at them, try to forget it and carry on as usual, or a combination of these responses and more. Or, what do you do when someone hurts you? You can withdraw, explode at them, gossip about them to others, or plot revenge. What is your response when someone close to you does something seriously wrong and does not seem to be aware of it or care about it? You might first tell the minister or the neighbors, you might let someone else handle it (after all it does not seem to be *your* problem). Or, on the other hand, you might march up and shout them down. Your ways of coping with such situations fall into certain patterns. These patterns shape your identity over the years. They are often strategies of which we are unaware, that vary according to whom the conflict is with, and which may originate with the example of our parents.

But they are important enough to our future that they are worth examining.

Since God wants us to be committed to reconciliation, let us look at three ways that he has given us to achieve it: confession, forgiveness, and restoring one another. As we discuss them and consider their use ourselves, our own strategies of coping with conflict will come to mind.

## Confession

I use confession in this sense not to mean confession of one's faith, but the confession of wrong done to another. It means to make known, acknowledge, or admit to a wrong that you have done to that person.

Confession is very out of fashion today. This has something to do with today's values and life style, but at a deeper level confession has never been in fashion. It is always hard to do. There has to be a good reason for doing something that is as painful as confessing our sin to God or each other. Why then is confession necessary?

Sin opens a chasm between you and another. You may experience it as outrage, pain, or disappointment, but you are in some way alienated from each other. All sin brings with it alienation from God. When sin entered human life, our first parents' response was to hide from God. God's response was to pronounce his judgment over the earth (Gn. 3). Jesus experienced alienation when he died to bear the punishment for sin. As he took the judgment for sin on himself he was separated from his Father and cried out 'My God, my God, why have you forsaken me?' (Mt. 27:46).

John in his gospel pictures sin as darkness:

> Men loved darkness rather than light, because their deeds were evil. For every one who does evil hates the light, and does not

come to the light, lest his deeds should be exposed. (Jn. 3:19–20)

Sin hides in the darkness. It wants to avoid detection. It drives us to self-justification and blameshifting. This in turn produces greater isolation, and further erodes self-respect and integrity. Our sins are like mushrooms; they grow best in the dark.

The remedy for such alienation is to openly admit our sin and ask for forgiveness. When we have wronged someone, we should deliberately take sin out of the darkness of our own private fear-ridden world and put it into the glaring light of another's awareness – as an apology. This accomplishes two things. First, the power of sin over you is broken. You are no longer afraid of exposure or loss of face since all has been exposed and there is no face left to lose. Confession brings great internal freedom. Secondly, confession closes your half of the chasm that exists between you. Even if the one you have hurt chooses not to forgive you, you have done all you can to make peace.

In the end, confession is necessary because God says to do it. God wants you to experience the reconciliation that he offers. God pleaded with Israel through the prophet Jeremiah, 'Only acknowledge your guilt, that you rebelled against the Lord your God' (Jer. 3:13). He does not ask us to do anything bizarre, strange, or inordinately heroic, but just to admit the truth. Whether we confess sin to God or to another human being whom we have wronged, the act is essentially the same. The prodigal son did both at once as he returned to his father. He said, 'Father, I have sinned against heaven and before you' (Lk. 15:18). He confessed his sin to both God and his father because he had wronged both. For the same reason we are told to confess our sins to God (1 Jn. 1:9) and also to one another (Jas. 5:16).

## Why Is Confession So Hard?

Our mechanisms of self-defense and face-saving are so powerful that someone who thinks they are apologizing often ends up doing no such thing. What does it mean to ask forgiveness and why is it so hard?

We have a tendency to weaken the meaning of asking forgiveness. C.S. Lewis points out the radical difference between being excused and being forgiven.[2] We can ask another to excuse us if there are extenuating circumstances for our actions. Suppose you keep someone waiting for several hours after the time you had set for an appointment. The reason was that you had been involved in a car accident. You could then quite properly offer the accident as an excuse. It was not your fault, and you would hope to be excused for being late even though it might have caused the other person considerable inconvenience.

However, let us suppose that you were late because you did not get out of bed on time. Traffic might have been heavy too, but not enough to account for your lateness. If you try to excuse your lateness because of the bad traffic, you would be avoiding the real issue – your laziness and lack of consideration. You were at fault this time. To be honest, you should admit your wrong was inexcusable and ask forgiveness. Forgiveness begins where excuses leave off. Asking forgiveness means confessing what you did as sin. If there is to be reconciliation, the offended party will have to decide not to hold it against you.

In the first instance, no forgiveness was needed; in the second, no excuse was sufficient. The apostle Paul says that we are without excuse before God (Rom. 1:20; 2:1), but that being inexcusable does not mean being unforgivable. On the contrary, God, through Christ, joyfully forgives those who are without excuse but who ask him for forgiveness (Rom. 3:21–6).

Trouble comes when we get the two ideas confused in our minds. How often we think we are asking forgiveness when we are only offering excuses. We roll out our excuses to convince ourselves and others that we need no forgiveness. Is it any wonder then that such feigned confession of sin brings no reconciliation? Confession of sin is never easy on our pride, and there is no way of making it so.

Confession is also difficult because it is often misused. A disastrous experience of confession leads people to say 'never again.' Here are five ways in which confession can be misused. The list is not exhaustive, but all of these misfire because they miss the purpose of confession-reconciliation.

Confession can be primarily a catharsis – a painful experience that relieves one of guilt feelings. Some people confess sins constantly to get attention or to lure others to join them in their self-pity. Cathartic confession is trivialized by self-indulgence. It soon loses any credibility as a tool for reconciliation.

Confession can also become a mechanical exercise. We make an apology for the sake of form, but do it in a way that preserves our pride. One of the best ways of doing this is by being light-hearted about confession, communicating that though I might be technically to blame, I certainly do not take my guilt very seriously. I might say 'Sorry for smashing up your car; it's a good thing we don't have treasure on earth, isn't it!' This reduces confession to a clever little ritual whose function is to get me off. Needless to say light-hearted confession is likely to anger the offended person more than silence.

Exhibitionism is another way of destroying confession. This could be called 'spiritual streaking.' We apologize in order to publicly display our piety and sensitivity of conscience to all who might be impressed. This is done by confessing acts that are either trivial or not sins at all, while carefully avoiding reference to those things that really ought to be apologized for.

Confession can also be an act of cowardice. Suppose I suggest that you have done something wrong and you explode in an outraged reply. If I am afraid of you I may beat a hasty retreat and apologize for ever having thought such a thing. Thus I confess something as sin that I know perfectly well was not wrong at all. This kind of confession is likely to cause additional resentment.

The most destructive perversion of confession is the use of confession as a veiled attack. Its goal is the very opposite of reconciliation. Its purpose is to put the other person down or at very least establish one's own blamelessness. A man once came to our home in London to apologize for having stolen money from us on a previous visit. To our naive amazement, we discovered after he left that he had again stolen more money and several possessions which we had foolishly left visible. We can do with words what this man did with his hands. Have you ever heard someone say contritely, 'I'm so sorry for making you lose your temper!' or, 'I'm sorry for resenting you when you ignored me or lost your temper at me'? It is very common to hear someone say, 'I'm sorry *if* I wronged you.' 'If' is a very big word in this case – it speaks volumes. It can express a legitimate doubt about whether I have done wrong. As such it is an inquiry more than an apology. But it can also be saying, 'there is a remote possibility that I have been at fault (but it is very unlikely) and I am sorry for this possibility.' Or, somewhat more cynically, 'I am sorry that your feelings are so sensitive that you seem to have been hurt by what I did, because I did nothing that would harm an adequate person.' We may need to ask questions about what the consequences of our action have been. But when we come to confession of sin, it must finally be without 'ifs' or 'buts.'

All these examples of confession fail because they do not serve the purpose of reconciliation. Instead they are self-serving, face-saving, or self-indulgent. They crush any possibility of true reconciliation.

There is something about confession that people want to avoid. We fear it will make us lose self-respect, betray ourselves, and ruin our public image. Often it is harder to confess to other people than it is to God.

Some of this fear is unnecessary. For example, to confess a specific sin does not mean we are summing up our whole identity and saying, 'I am no good,' 'a total failure,' or 'malicious person.' But sometimes we wrongly feel this way. But the main fear of confession comes from old-fashioned pride. Pride can bring us into the same sort of fear that would make us prepared to go down with a sinking ship rather than be seen unable to swim well. We can know that confession stems from honesty and brings freedom, know that as we confess a sin we do not associate our entire identity with the sin, and still resist the act of confession.

## Getting On With It

After surveying all the pitfalls and risks, there is simply no substitute for going and asking the forgiveness of whomever we have sinned against. We do not need to grovel on the ground and say what awful people we are, but we do need to state what we have done without 'ifs,' 'buts,' or efforts at saving face. The sooner we do it the better, because we give our own sin less time to do its work on us and less time for mistrust to build in the relationship.

Questions and objections inevitably arise. 'But what if they have wronged me too?' (Another's offense always seems more serious and less excusable than yours.) 'It would be so much easier if he or she confessed to me first.' Again and again we have to remember that each one of us will ultimately have to give account of our own lives to God. He is interested in your life, but much less in your account of someone else's life. Our place is to deal with our own sin as God would have us do it, irrespective of what was done to us. If we know we have done something that needs to be confessed, then the first move is ours.

Consider the wisdom of Proverbs 23:13: 'He who conceals his transgression will not prosper, but he who confesses and forsakes them will obtain mercy.' If reconciliation is the goal that we pursue in honesty to God, then we must make every attempt to forsake the thing that we are confessing as sin. We seldom accomplish this by merely trying harder next time. We must carefully examine exactly what we did as well as the situation that gave rise to it. We must change our attitude, behavior, and our environment which can help us forsake the sin. Sometimes a solution can be insultingly simple as in the case of the man's advice to his son to stay away from a prostitute. He said: 'Keep your way far from her, and do not go near the door of her house.' This simply required him to walk home by a different street out of respect for his own weakness of motivation.

'Blessed is he whose transgression is forgiven,' said David after much personal experience (Ps. 32:1). If you confess your sin, you have, with God's help, overcome the power that would otherwise have controlled your relationship. There is blessedness and freedom in honesty to God. Our sense of identity is closely tied to how we live out our values. If you confess wrong that you have done, you have taken a costly stand and acted on the values that you affirm. You have not compromised yourself or God, but have honored God and strengthened your own identity. You have also radically increased the likelihood that there will be reconciliation. Imagine if the prodigal son had apologized only to God and not to his father, if he had sauntered into his father's house without a word about his sin and gone straight to the refrigerator to get some supper. Think of the tension in that home! God had been wronged, but so had the father. Confession had to be made to both if there was to be reconciliation of conflict. The parable in fact shows just this in the father's welcome and the banquet for all who could rejoice in the wonder of reconciliation. It shows God's promise to invariably forgive those who come to him in humility and honesty about their sin. Even though people might not receive our confession, we have the promise of God that 'If we confess our sins, he is faithful and just, and will forgive our sins and cleanse us from all unrighteousness' (1 Jn. 1:9).

## God Freely Forgives

Hannah Arendt once wrote: 'Forgiveness is the key to action and freedom. Without it life is governed by an endless cycle of resentment and retaliation.' Forgiveness is a necessary link in the chain of reconciliation – without it reconciliation never happens, whether between parent and child, husband and wife, brother and sister, Arab and Jew, Catholic and Protestant, or black and white. Without forgiveness we are locked into an endless war, each party requiring the last word, the last bullet, or the last bomb. Retaliation follows violence like a dog chasing its tail, but with far greater persistence. Forgiveness can break this vicious circle from one side. Either antagonist can agree to not hold the wrong against the other, to forego vengeance.

Forgiveness can never be taken for granted because it does not always happen. But God wants it to happen. He wants us to reflect the forgiveness that he has given us himself. He wants us to be free from the bondage to our own pettiness and resentment. We will start where the Bible starts: by looking first at the forgiveness of God.

The entire Christian religion hinges on this pivot point: God freely forgives all who come to him in faith. Without God's forgiveness there would be no such religion. There might be high moral teaching, but there would be no salvation by a holy God.

Many of the words in the Bible that refer to forgiveness point to something that is done to sin. 'Atonement' means that sin is covered. 'Remission' means sin is lifted off or sent away from us. God acts against our sin because he is merciful to us. The Bible speaks of God having 'victory' over our sins: 'he will tread our iniquities under foot. Thou wilt cast all our sins into the depths of the sea' (Mi. 7:19). Or, in the words of Isaiah 'you cast all my sins behind your back' (Is. 38:17). God himself says, 'I, I am He who blots out your transgressions for my sake, and I will not remember your sins' (Is. 43:25). And finally, in the well-known words of David, 'as far as the east is from the west, so far does he remove our transgressions from us' (Ps. 103:12). God puts our sin away, out of arm's reach, so that it does not stand between us and him.

The forgiveness of God knows no limits. Nothing is beyond his forgiveness. No sin can disqualify us from God's forgiveness as long as we come and ask God for it in humility. Many of the same people who had a hand in crucifying Jesus were forgiven by God on the day of Pente-cost. Men and women who scorn God's salvation for years are welcomed by God as they turn to him and ask for forgiveness, even if they do so as a last resort.

God does not need to forgive anyone. It is not his duty or obligation. Behind his forgiveness is his love. One of the best known verses in the Bible says, 'For God so loved the world that he gave his only Son, that whoever believes in him should not perish but have eternal life' (Jn. 3:16). What God did with our sin was to put it on Jesus so that its wages would be paid off in his death (Rom. 6:23). Jesus was willing to do this. Referring to his own life he said: 'No one takes it from me, but I lay it down of my own accord' (Jn. 10:18). When wrong is done, someone must absorb the loss if there is to be reconciliation. Otherwise there will be a stalemate or endless cycle of retaliation and revenge. Jesus has absorbed the loss for our sin, taking our punishment on himself. This is not because of anything excusable in us, but simply because he has loved us enough to forgive us.

We have looked at the parable of the prodigal son (Lk. 15:11–32) from the perspective of the son. Let us look at it from the father's side as well. How might the father have received his son's apology? The pain of love rejected can make people cruel beyond words. The father could have barred the door and refused to let his son in at all. He could have inflicted a punishment on the son – some equivalent to 'go to your room!' to make sure the son would feel sufficient guilt for his sin. He could have made him pay back the money he squandered. The father in the parable did none of these things. He had obviously been watching the road and saw his son while he was still far off. He got up and ran out to meet him in compassion and joy and embraced him. Not only was he reinstated in the family and forgiven, but he was forgiven with joy, celebration, and feasting because 'this my son was dead, and is alive again; he was lost and is found' (Lk. 15:24). God in his forgiveness is not reluctant or begrudging, but like this father, welcomes reconciliation with joy.

## Forgive One Another

If you are a Christian, your identity is as an image of God, forgiven and therefore reconciled to your Father. An important expression of this derived identity is to forgive others as God has forgiven you. In fact, you are to imitate God himself. The apostle Paul sees our forgiving each other in exactly these terms.

> . . . and be kind to one another, tenderhearted, forgiving one another, as God in Christ forgave you. Therefore be imitators of God as beloved children. (Eph. 4:32–5:1)

Forgiveness like confession is something which does not come easily or naturally to us. Christians can be quite willing to have God forgive them and others, but refuse to grant forgiveness themselves. Let me give you an extreme example from Luis Bunuel's film 'The Discreet Charm of the Bourgeoisie.' One of the characters in the film was a bishop in France who had been orphaned as a young child when both of his parents had been poisoned. The murderer had never been caught. Many years later, the middle-aged bishop was called to the death-bed of a nearby gamekeeper to hear his confession and to administer the last rites. As he knelt by the dying man's bed the bishop listened without change of expression while the gamekeeper confessed that as a young boy he had poisoned the man and woman who had employed his father. He had felt the couple had been unjust to his father and he had taken revenge. The bishop realized that the dying man had killed his own parents. The bishop, still without show of emotion pronounced absolu- tion, assuring the man that God would forgive him. He then walked over to the corner of the room, picked up the gamekeeper's loaded shotgun and shot the dying man full in the face with both barrels.

It is all too easy to believe that forgiveness is God's job, he is good at it, after all – while we staunchly reserve our own right to a pound of flesh and a life-time of resentment. However, this denies the Christian's identity as one who first receives God's gift, and then imitates God by giving it to others.

Two of Jesus' parables are helpful here. Jesus tells the parable of the unforgiving servant (Mt. 18:23–35) in response to Peter's question, 'Lord, how often shall my brother sin against me, and I forgive him? As many as seven times?' Jesus' reply was not what he had expected: 'I do not say to you seven times, but seventy times seven' (Mt. 18:21–2). In the parable, Jesus tells of a man who was forgiven a vast debt by a king. On leaving the king he met a man who owed him a small amount of money. He flew into a rage and threw him into prison when the man was unable to pay. When word of this got back to the king, he withdrew his forgiveness of the servant, saying, 'You wicked servant! I forgave you all the debt because you besought me; and should you not have had mercy on your fellow servant as I had mercy on you?' The king then put the man in jail until everything could be paid. Jesus unsparingly applies the parable to us at its conclusion as he says: 'So also my heavenly Father will do to every one of you, if you do not forgive your brother from your heart.'

The point of the parable is clear: We have been forgiven so much more by God than we will ever be expected to forgive in another that we ought to be able to forgive as a response. If we refuse to forgive the debts against us, we jeopardize our own forgiveness with God.

Jesus obviously went over and over this point with his disciples during his three-year ministry. On another occasion he said to them:

> Take heed to yourselves; if your brother sins, rebuke him, and if he repents forgive him; and if he sins against you seven times in the day, and turns to you seven times, and says, 'I repent,' you must forgive him. (Lk. 17:3–4)

Jay Adams offers a helpful insight into these verses by showing their relationship to the dialogue that follows.[3] The verses just quoted demanded what to the disciples seemed

an impossible level of faith. Imagine trying to forgive someone seven times in the same day, possibly for doing the same
thing against you each of the seven times. That means
forgiving on an average of every two hours and twenty
minutes of your waking day if we were to take the number
seven literally. Bear in mind that a person who apologizes
to you seven times in the same day is probably more difficult
to forgive than one who does not apologize at all because
they are making a mockery of confession, perhaps even
goading you with it. The disciples respond understandably
with helplessness, 'Increase our faith!' They thought that if
they had more faith they might be able to obey what seemed
quite impossible. Jesus had little sympathy with them,
pointing out that their problem was not lack of faith because
even a mustard seed of faith can move mountains (vv. 5–6).
  Then Jesus told them a parable (vv. 7–10):

> Will any one of you, who has a servant plowing or keeping
> sheep, say to him when he has come in from the field, 'Come
> at once and sit down at table?' Will he not rather say to him,
> 'Prepare supper for me, and gird yourself and serve me, till I
> eat and drink; and afterward you shall eat and drink? Does he
> thank the servant because he did what was commanded? So
> you also when you have done all that is commanded you say,
> 'we are unworthy servants; we have only done what was our
> duty.'

The parable seems very harsh, but Jesus is saying that the
disciples' problem is not a shortage of faith, but rather a
shortage of obedience. They need to put into action the faith
that they already have. Forgiveness, like the work of this
servant, is a thankless task but it is simply our duty. It is not
something for the spiritual elite, nor is it something for
which you can expect a medal. If you are a Christian,
forgiveness is required of you.[4]

Forgiving one another is such an integral part of the Christian life that Jesus simply assumed it in giving us the Lord's prayer. We are to pray, 'Forgive us our trespasses as we forgive those who trespass against us' (Mt. 6:12). This is a prayer we must be very careful not to pray if we do not forgive those who have sinned against us. To make doubly sure that we do not miss this point, Jesus adds immediately after the prayer:

> For if you forgive men their trespasses, your heavenly Father also will forgive you; but if you do not forgive men their trespasses, neither will your Father forgive your trespasses. (Mt. 6:14–15)

There are few matters about which Jesus gives us such stern and uncompromising warnings.

How, then, do we forgive? If forgiveness is so important and often so difficult, we need to learn how to do it. C.S. Lewis wrote:

> Real forgiveness means looking steadily at the sin, the sin that is left over without any excuse, after all allowances have been made, and seeing it in all its horror, dirt, meanness and malice, and nevertheless being wholly reconciled to the man who has done it. That, and only that, is forgiveness; and that we can always have from God if we ask for it.[5]

Sin causes a chasm between two people. If I betray a commitment to you, I experience it as guilt and fear while you experience it as pain and outrage. Forgiveness is the decision that the wrong done against you will not count or cause a separation. It is to say 'I will make every effort in my inward and outward life to live as if this thing had never happened.' The requirement of forgiveness does not apply only to the nuisances of this world such as the missed appointments, the snubs, and the petty thefts. It applies also to the life-jarring agonies – divorces, large-scale dishonesty, and long-term cruelty. The task of forgiving must be a match for the magnitude of the pain involved.

We must be clear that the statement 'I forgive you' is not necessarily a statement about your emotions. It is a decision – a commitment to an inward and outward course of action. If our feelings support this commitment so much the better, but forgiving feelings are not a prerequisite for us to forgive. A verse that is very helpful in making this concrete is Proverbs 17:9: 'He who forgives an offense seeks love, but he who repeats a matter alienates a friend.' This verse sets a choice before us. Whenever we are wronged, we can choose out of a desire for love to forgive. Or, out of a desire to alienate, we can repeat the matter.

The choice to forgive becomes a commitment of your action and attitude in many areas. You choose to never repeat the wrong again to the person who hurt you, to a third party in the form of gossip, or to yourself (to the best of your ability) in the form of self-pity and righteous indignation. Forgiving is a big decision that should never be made lightly. The person who replies to an apology, 'No I will not forgive you,' may understand more about true forgiveness than the neighbor who says with a smile 'Oh, don't mention it' but then spreads the news. The one who refused to forgive cannot be commended for their refusal, but they at least understand that forgiveness requires a serious commitment of their future. To forgive is to decide to relinquish the right to whole arsenals of overt and covert retaliation. If I forgive you I deny myself the right to hold the offense over you in any form – even the subtle reminder at a later time that you have been forgiven.

Another way to make the act of forgiveness more con-crete is to follow up Jesus' image of forgiving being like cancelling a debt. Forgiving might be a cancelling of a literal debt, but more often we deal with a felt indebtedness. My expectations of you – for reliability and loyalty – were shattered when you spread false rumors about me to my friends. I felt that you owed me a certain minimal level of honesty. When this expectation was violated, I experienced it as a painful reneging on an obligation, therefore a debt incurred. Forgiving involves being aware of what my broken expectations were, and then choosing to cancel the debt that stood against those expectations.

A common misconception often keeps people from forgiving. They think that if they forgive, they have to reach the conclusion that what was done against them was not really so bad after all. On that basis they would forgive. This goes back to the confusion of forgiving and excusing. If it was not that serious or if there were extenuating circumstances, then it was excusable, and didn't need to be forgiven in the first place. In forgiving, you don't decide that you have not been wronged, you decide that though you were wronged, you are setting it aside, cancelling that debt. You were wronged but you forgave. It therefore involves no minimizing or whitewashing of what was done against you.

The relief and freedom of forgiving can take a great weight off our backs. An unforgiving heart holds resentment and so carries with it resentment's poisonous side effects. How often forgiving a neighbor or friend or member of the family can be a gigantic breakthrough in one's relationship also with God.

Forgiveness is a tool in the service of reconciliation – the essential first step in building a new and reconciled relationship. We cannot do without it.

Have you ever tried to develop a free and open relationship with someone you resented? You cannot even start without forgiveness.

Forgiveness ends conflict, but it is nevertheless only a beginning. It leaves us with a bare foundation upon which we must build a new building. This is the continuing task of reconciliation. We must not say after forgiving, 'now I can end the relationship in peace and good conscience.' Of course some relationships are impossible and others unwise to continue, but our usual course should be the full biblical pattern: putting on love, kindness, and thoughtfulness as we put off resentment and retaliation. Building a reconciled relationship is the best way to prevent further sin and need for repeated forgiveness. It also helps us to forget the wrong done to us and enables us to leave it behind.

Once we have forgiven someone, we need to consider the apostle Paul's teaching on having the mind of Christ. He wrote to the Philippians:

> Complete my joy by being of the same mind, having the same love, being in full accord and of one mind. Do nothing from selfishness or conceit, but in humility count others better than yourselves. Let each of you look not only to his own interests, but also to the interests of others. (Phil. 2:2–4)

In doing this we imitate God. God does not stop at forgiveness, but takes us into his family and builds a relationship with us. Jesus taught not only that we should forgive, but that we should go beyond that to love and pray for those who have been our enemies.

> But I say to you, love your enemies and pray for those who persecute you, so that you may be sons of your Father who is in heaven; for he makes his sun to rise on the evil and on the good. (Mt. 6:44–45)

Once again, the Bible ties the demands of the Christian life into our identity as imaging God our Creator. God's pattern for our lives is not arbitrary, but reflects who we are and who we are to become.

Let us never forget that God forgives joyfully and without reservation all those who ask him. He asks those who have been forgiven to treat their fellow human beings the same way they have been treated by him. If you are a Christian, God requires you to forgive always and to forgive every-thing without exception. However, he will also give you the power to do it, a power that does not reside in you naturally. Ask for this power, meditate on God's joy in forgiving you, and commit yourself to the difficult task of forgiving one another as God in Christ forgave you.[6]

## Restoring One Another

If someone is doing something seriously wrong and seems either ignorant or unconcerned about it, the Christian is not free to simply ignore the situation. Depending of course on the measure of one's involvement with the person and the seriousness of the wrong done, the Christian may need to go to the other and try to help him or her be restored in fellowship with others and with God. It is easy, but often wrong, to sit back and say, 'It's their problem, let them worry about it,' or to mumble 'Isn't it awful' to our friends. The difficulty is that the task of restoring another person very often involves reproof or rebuke.

Confession and forgiveness form two halves of the proc-ess of reconciliation. Confession is for the offender and forgiveness is for the offended. They are a pair and they must work together. Restoring one another is not exactly parallel to these two acts, but it is also an integral part of the ongoing process of reconciliation in any group of people.

Its importance is twofold. First, the one doing wrong needs help. In fact this person needs help more than at other times. Even the apostle Peter needed to be confronted by Paul. He was presumably grateful for it since Paul's rebuke kept him and others faithful to the integrity of the gospel (Gal. 2:11ff). Secondly, doing what is necessary to restore another is an active attack against sin in the world. The Christian life is not to be lived lying down; we are not doormats for everybody's muddy feet. Christians are to be the salt of the earth and the light of the world. We cannot do that from the prone position, never standing up against wrongs done. We are in a world where God wants to see 'justice roll down like waters, and righteousness like an ever-flowing stream' (Amos 5:24). The Christian cannot foster justice without being willing to speak of the righteousness of God to those who are not doing it.

Rightly understood, restoring one another is as impor-tant to the functioning of Christian community and to the reconciling of relationships as confession and forgiveness. Let us first look at what 'restoring one another' means. Then we will examine some of the difficulties in going about it and finally look at ways to overcome these difficulties.

## Walking in the Spirit

The idea of 'restoring' another person comes from the last chapter of Paul's letter to the church of Galatia. Paul contrasts fruit of the Spirit to the fruit of the flesh. He then goes on:

> If we live by the Spirit, let us also walk by the Spirit. Let us have no self-conceit, no provoking of one another, no envy of one another.
>
> Brethren, if a man is overtaken in any trespass, you who are spiritual should restore him in a spirit of gentleness. Look to yourself, lest you too be tempted. Bear one another's burdens, and so fulfill the law of Christ. (Gal. 5:25–6:2)

Paul closely connects the task of restoring one another to our life in the Spirit. The Christian is to live out the fruit of the Spirit by walking in the Spirit. This has a lot to do with our attitude to one another. If a brother or sister is over-taken in any trespass, you who are spiritual should restore him in a spirit of gentleness.

The verb 'to restore' means to carefully repair or mend something. It is used of the disciples mending their fishing nets on the shore of the Lake of Galilee. Those who restore do so carefully and lovingly. It is a spiritual process, done by men and women, motivated by the Spirit of God. Paul prayed 'Let the word of Christ dwell in you richly, as you teach and admonish one another in all wisdom' (Col. 3:16). Restoring one another will tax our spiritual integrity to the utmost. It must be inspired by the Christian's attitude of love, joy, peace, patience, kindness, and goodness. If we act out of a spirit of self-conceit, desire to provoke or of envy, the result will not be reconciliation.

Restoring another person may involve direct rebuke. A suggestion or a hint that something might be wrong often does not make the point. Jesus tells us what to do when someone sins against us. First we are to go to the person privately and tell them their fault. If that fails, we are to take one or two other people with us as witnesses. As a last resort, we can take the matter to the church (Mt 18:15–17). At each step we must give the person the benefit of the doubt. We must make great allowance for bad communication. We may have misunderstood the whole affair completely.

The emphasis on gentleness is crucial. The purpose of rebuke is reconciliation, and rebuke without gentleness asks too much of the one rebuked. We are committed to the ultimate welfare of the other person. Thus the command to restore someone overtaken in sin is immediately linked to a personal warning and to a further command to bear one another's burdens. Restoring another person is not like fixing a broken appliance that will run after being kicked a few times. We may have to rebuke someone, but we are then called to get down and help bear the other's burden. This is costly; it may mean hours and hours of our time.

## Why Rebuke Is Difficult

We can deliver a rebuke in the right spirit only when we acknowledge the difficulties and face our own weaknesses. There are three main problems that make reproof difficult.

The first problem is fear. All of us want to be accepted and loved by everybody else. When you reprove someone, this approval is threatened. The other person may turn against you. Rebuke is therefore much riskier than gossip. The person who is gossiped about is not meant to hear it so it ideally does not find its way back to you. However, failure to rebuke is also risky. Eli, the priest in the Old Testament, like many parents after him, was afraid to confront his own sons in their sin (1 Sam. 2:25; 3:13). The result was destruction for all of them.

Our fear of rebuking someone can also be unfair because it prejudges the other person's reaction. It assumes that they will respond out of pride and self-defense and will retaliate inwardly if not openly. Your fear can rest more on how *you* respond to rebuke than on how the other person will respond. As such it is a projection of your own vanity onto another.

Rebuke also opens you up to moral inspection. By rebuk-ing another, you set yourself up as a target for rebuke in the future. There are few things that people enjoy so much as catching someone in hypocrisy. Once caught, the hypocrite receives no quarter. (Think of how teenage children work to catch their parents in this way.) If you try to restore other people, others are apt to keep a special eye on you to see how you measure up, and to call you on it if you don't. Perhaps King David ignored his son Amnon's rape of Tamar because he was unwilling to have his own sexual sin dragged up again. We all fear the rejoinder 'And who are *you* to talk?'

A third difficulty is past experience. If you have unsuccessfully reproved someone in the past, you are not likely to want to try it again if your efforts only led to further anger and mistrust on all sides.

Because of these difficulties, we are apt to put reproof off much too long. We will admonish another only when our anger is so great that it overrides our fears and inhibitions. We have the courage to confront only when we are so mad that we have lost control. Rebuke in these circumstances is for our benefit instead of the other person's. We release our own emotional time bomb with all the pomp, bluster, and self-righteousness of an inflated ego. Disaster is almost inevitable because we tend to load on the gripes of past decades.

Rebuke is among the most delicate of tasks. Both the giving and the receiving of rebuke touches the hair-trigger of human pride at its most sensitive point.

## Rebuke in the Spirit

No technique or system of rebuke can cover all cases. It is best to get all such ideas of spiritual technology out of our minds. The difficulties are so profound and complex that any such attempt would be bound to cause more damage than it heals. I suggest only directions toward restoring one another based on some of the underlying dynamics of human pride and the work of God's Spirit.

One of the most basic issues we must grapple with is the well-known admonition to hate the sin but love the sinner.

Unless we possess this attitude we are not qualified to try
to restore another to fellowship with God and humanity.
Let us look in some depth at two passages from God's word.

One of the most searching passages in the Bible on this
subject is from Jesus' sermon on the mount:

> Why do you see the speck that is in your brother's eye, but do
> not notice the log that is in your own eye? Or how can you say
> to your brother, 'let me take the speck out of your eye' when
> there is the log in your own eye? You hypocrite, first take the
> log out of your own eye, and then you will see clearly to take
> the speck out of your brother's eye. (Mt. 7:3–5)

This passage makes us realize just how far we fall short of
the goal of loving the sinner and hating the sin.[7] We do not
miss the mark by a narrow margin, but rather tend to get it
completely backwards. We end up hating the sinner and
loving the sin.

Jesus makes several perceptive points in this passage. First,
hard as it may be to admit, we can enjoy finding faults in
others and pointing them out. We can get a perverse satisfaction out of this. It takes our attention from our own inadequacies and also makes us feel superior. Second, for all our
concern with unrighteousness in other people's lives, we can
be curiously indifferent to it in our own. We always seem to
be excused by exceptions and circumstances beyond our
control. The point is that we are not hating the sin at all if we
are more upset at sin in another person's life than in our own.
The only sin that you can do anything about directly is the
sin in your own life. If you really hate sin, that is where it will
show. Unfortunately, we are more apt to enjoy putting the
sinner down and accepting the sin – the exact reverse of the
attitude needed to restore a brother or sister.

Jesus' solution to this is, first, to look at yourself. Not
only is it hypocrisy to be worried about a speck in someone

else's eye when you have a log in your own, but it is also a very good way to make a mess out of the other person's eye. The eye is an extremely delicate thing; with a log in your eye, you will only damage the other person's eye. Martyn Lloyd-Jones points out that this is far worse than the blind leading the blind; it is a picture of a blind oculist. [8] The solution is to forget all about the other person for a time. Get your own eye cleaned out first. Look first to your own sin; then you have hated sin where it matters most – in your own life. Then and only then can you begin to see the other person clearly

If you take this admonition seriously, you will often find that there is no need for rebuke at all. Perhaps you yourself needed to confess sin to the very person you were about to rebuke. Jesus teaches that our perception of another's problems is radically inaccurate when we have not dealt with sin in our own lives, especially when our sin is against that same person. I have often heard people say that their attitude toward someone they were about to rebuke was marvelously changed after they worked out their own sin. In fact, the other person had not changed at all; the change was all in the attitude toward them. Many is the time that I have had to call off a planned reproof because I realized that my own motivation was not for their own good.

After you have taken your own sin to God, searched your heart before him, and found that you still need to reprove someone, you can act in the Spirit if you are motivated by a concern for the other's welfare and by God's glory. This does not mean that your rebuke will be received and heeded, but it changes the tone of the whole encounter. There is a good example of this from the life of Moses. Korah and two hundred and fifty influential men of the nation challenged Moses' authority to govern Israel. They said he was setting himself up over God's people, exalting himself at the expense of the rest who were just as holy as he was. Moses' reply was memorable. He did not argue, but said that tomorrow morning the Lord himself would decide who was his and who was holy. He did not shout this challenge as an outraged prophet. Some of us can imagine Charlton Heston or Burt Lancaster in the role of Moses doing that from a high point of ground to the masses beneath him. In fact, when Moses heard their accusation he fell on his face in the sand. He seems to have given his rebuke from that position. The point is clear. Moses was not defending himself or trying to put Korah down. He was horrified at their rebellion against God. If we gave rebukes in this spirit, then we would bring more reconciliation than we do.

In the face of the modern creeds of 'you do your thing and I'll do mine,' all the talk about rebuke and reproof can seem like a return to the Inquisition. In fact it is no such thing. But it does involve taking a stand against the moral indifference of our time and looking to something far better. Remember that I have a log in my eye and you have a speck in yours. Do we each stumble along doing our own thing, me with my log and you with your speck? Jesus wants something far better for both of us. He wants me to take my log out and wants me or someone else to help you remove your speck. Note that Jesus' solution is not that both of us should learn to accept each other as we are. He wants us both to change, to grow and to be able to see each other as well. This mutual growth is the grace of God in action.

A second passage of the Bible shows us the responsibility we have for one another:

> You shall not hate your brother in your heart, but you shall rebuke your neighbor, lest you bear sin because of him. You shall not take vengeance or bear any grudge against the sons of your own people, but you shall love your neighbor as yourself. (Lev. 19:17–18)

This passage shows that there are two ways to express hatred of your brother or sister. One is by taking vengeance; the other is by bearing a grudge against them. We can eliminate both if we forgive. Both ways of hatred also endanger us: we risk bearing sin on the account of one whom we should have warned but did not.

The way to love your neighbor, to love them as yourself, is to warn them about the seriousness of what they are doing. So often we use love as a reason for not rebuking one who is close. We say 'I love him so I don't want to hurt him.' This more accurately means 'I love my own feelings about him so much that I don't want to risk losing them!' A sentiment that seems altruistic is really egocentric. We are meant to love our own welfare enough to 'pluck out the eye that offends' (Mt. 5:27–30). If we are to love another as ourselves, we need to be willing to inflict a small amount of pain in order to eliminate a far larger danger.

Love requires that you care enough about another's welfare that you be willing to have that person reject you, even hate you, for telling them the truth about themselves. If you are not willing to do this, you are willing to be well thought of at their expense. This is not only cruel but foolish. We usually respect those who have the courage to rebuke us and we welcome the security of knowing that close friends would rebuke us when we needed it. Dietrich Bonhoeffer spoke of this responsibility.

> Reproof is unavoidable. God's word demands it when a brother falls into sin. The practice of discipline in the congregation begins in the smallest circles. Where defection from God's word in doctrine or life imperils the family fellowship and with it the whole congregation, the word of admonition and rebuke must be ventured. Nothing can be more cruel than the tenderness that consigns another to his sin. Nothing can be

more compassionate than the severe rebuke that calls a brother
back from the path of sin.[9]

We should reprove in such a way that if offense is taken,
the reason for it is the offense of the truth of God. Our pride
gets in the way here but is not the only obstacle to reconciliation. Just plain clumsiness can also sabotage our efforts
to warn a friend. I will not try to give prescriptions to cover
every eventuality, but will mention a few general ideas to
encourage you to apply biblical principles in situations you
might face.

First of all, beware of your natural inclinations. Be careful
of your first impulse. It is not always wrong, but it is not a
reliable guide. Correcting another may come far too easily
for you; you might love an opportunity to straighten someone else out. Are you grieved as Jesus was when he encoun-
tered sin, or are you filled with an only partially secret joy
at scoring points off another? Or you may have the opposite
problem. To rebuke anyone would be unthinkable: 'I
couldn't possibly say that to someone!' In this case you need
less sensitivity to yourself and a greater love for the person
who is in the wrong. Both of these inclinations have as much
to do with temperament as they do with righteousness. We
need to know our weaknesses and compensate for them.

Another important point is the question of timing. Here
there is no substitute for sensitivity and graciousness. It is
true that some matters must be brought up quickly and
firmly, as, for example, when Jesus confronted the Pharisees. But we must be very wary of quick confrontations,
especially when they are in public. It is extremely easy to
storm in so bluntly that you actually frustrate your own
efforts to restore someone.

You need to be careful not to try to force a person to
choose in thirty seconds to abandon views and attitudes that
they have held for years. You can easily demand the kind

of volte-face that you are virtually never prepared to make yourself, even when you suspect that you might be wrong. Once again, the book of Proverbs has a helpful warning: 'For pressing milk produces curds, pressing the nose produces blood, and pressing anger produces strife' (Prov. 30:33). If you rebuke people at a time when they are angry already, you are foolish indeed unless there is no other option. Remember that our goal is not to discharge some formal responsibility, but to bring about reconciliation. Paul mentions another caution in his advice to Timothy, 'Do not rebuke an older man but exhort him as you would a father' (1 Tim. 5:1). It is particularly hard to be rebuked by someone who is much younger than you are. Your attempts to restore someone older should be more in the form of suggestion and exhortation. Sensitivity involves being attuned to how another person perceives you.

A danger in discussing each tool for reconciliation separately as we have done is that we may easily lose sight of the wider picture. Love requires that we be willing to correct another if our goal is integrity and obedience to God. But it would be quite wrong to give the impression that reproof is the central part or the essence of love. We are not little moral police officers overseeing one another. Love is infinitely wide and rich. Our relationships should include affection, acceptance, giving, sharing, encouragement, prayer, and just simply relaxing and enjoying one another. Without this richness, love becomes sterile, formal and rigid.

I once knew a couple who vowed their marriage would be different from others they had seen where disagreements had been papered over and differences never settled. They set out to inform each other whenever they thought anything was wrong, no matter how small or great. Of course this brought disaster of the sort that one might expect when two blind oculists try to improve one another's vision. They then agreed to take a time of making no corrections at all, but simply praying for each other. This eventually led to a better balance. Paul beautifully describes such balance in his ministry in a letter to the church in Thessalonica:

> We speak, not to please men, but to please God who tests our hearts. For we never used either words of flattery, as you know, or a cloak for greed, as God is witness; nor did we seek glory from men, whether from you or from others, though we might have made demands as apostles of Christ. But we were gentle among you, like a nurse taking care of her children. So, being affectionately desirous of you, we were ready to share with you not only the gospel of God but also our own selves, because you had become very dear to us. (1 Thess. 2:4–8)

Paul was not bound by what any person might think, but spoke what he felt God wanted him to say. Yet at the same time he did not do it from behind a shell of self-righteous-ness or authoritative distance, but with the warmest and most affectionate relationship to his hearers. At another time he said, 'I did not cease night or day to admonish every one with tears' (Acts 20:31).

## The Challenge of Reconciliation

We have discussed three tools for achieving reconciliation. Because all three are involved with conflict of some kind, we find ourselves in the midst of raw sin in ourselves and others. If we have understood what is at stake we will be driven to God – to seek his face for ourselves and to pray to him for those whose lives we touch.

We began the chapter referring to Paul's command, 'If possible, so far as it depends upon you, live peaceably with all' (Rom. 12:18). This does not mean that we should live peacefully with all if we can find the time. It means that we ought to 'seek peace and pursue it' (Ps. 34:14) with all the energy and ability that is available to us. However, we must realize that the Bible never promises perfect peace in this world. Sometimes we do our best and still there is no reconciliation. Even the leaders of the New Testament church experienced this kind of stalemate. There was once a 'sharp contention' between Paul and Barnabas as they were planning their second missionary journey in Antioch. It was a powder-keg situation involving the complications of family loyalties and theological principles. Barnabas wanted to bring his cousin Mark; Paul refused because Mark had abandoned them on the previous journey. They were unable to resolve the matter and Paul and Barnabas went their separate ways. Only years later did it seem that there was full reconciliation. Paul revealed in his letter to the Colossians that Mark was there with him as a helper (Acts 15:36–41; Col. 4:10). He and Barnabas had had to agree to disagree for a time, hoping to work it out later. So we too must not panic if reconciliation seems impossible. We must wait, pray, and keep trying.

Confession is both a commandment and a provision from God to give us freedom from living in two different worlds – one of pretense and the other of fear and guilt. It enables us, with God's help, to rise above the power that our past sin has over us. As we confess our sins to God and our fellow human beings, we grow in openness and reaffirm our identity in God's image.

By forgiving one another, we can in a small way imitate the wonder of God's grace toward us and break the endless cycle of resentment and retaliation. As we forgive and keep on forgiving, forgiveness becomes a habit. We can change from being a touchy and resentful person to being a forgiving person. This too is growth into being the image of God who throws our sins behind his back and abounds in steadfast love.

We also reflect the one in whose image we are cast in trying to restore one another to fellowship with God and humankind. Jesus is willing to rebuke us, but also to weep for us and to even die for us, taking our place under the anger of God against our sin. As we restore one another and bear one another's burdens, we help to create a community that brings strength to men and women and glory to God.

Sin and conflict are inevitable in this world. Reconciliation is not inevitable but it is possible. We must be committed to work for it. God has given us confession, forgiveness, and restoring one another to accomplish it. Let us use them well. If we do, honesty is established. This is a higher honesty than broadcasting our feelings; it is living in honesty to God, as he wants us to live, and showing ourselves as he sees us. Jesus taught, 'Blessed are the peace-makers, for they shall be called sons of God' (Mt. 5:9).

# SIX

# Anger

*Anger for most people is an alternative to fading away.* [1]
(Ernest Becker)

*Good sense makes a man slow to anger, and it is his glory to overlook an offense.* (Prov. 19:11)

*Woe to those who are at ease in Zion, and to those who feel secure on the mountain of Samaria . . .* (Amos 6:1a)

Anger is both attractive and terrifying at many levels of our existence. Our personal futures rest on how we and our fellow humans cope with it in international relations, national politics, work, the fellowship of the church, our families, and inside our own heads. In anger we have a tool for almost unlimited destruction on all these levels, but also a source of formidable motivation for constructive change. We will look briefly at some of the different views of anger that are widespread in our society, focusing on the anger of the individual, not that of groups. Then we will draw together some of the teaching of the Bible to look for solutions that will not simply hold anger at bay, but lead to positive growth.

It is impossible to discuss anger honestly without starting at home – that is, in your own life. Few feelings grip us so completely and are so easy to identify with in others. When people talk of being angry we all know what they mean. Everybody gets angry. Not everybody realizes it and fewer still show it, but everybody gets angry. I have even seen people get angry when they hear a Christian perspective on anger, so perhaps the reading of this chapter will be a good place to begin for you.

I will make no attempt to give a comprehensive survey of the different theories about anger. My intention is to help us visualize a Christian viewpoint toward anger in the midst of today's popular discussion.

## Anger in Popular Psychology

The discussion of the nature of anger itself suffers from the kind of squabbles that are common in psychology. Where is the origin of anger? Is it instinctual to humankind and therefore biologically integral to our nature? Or does anger come from our environment, a result of early childhood frustrations and deprivations or patterns of learning? There is also disagreement over the remedy for anger. One opinion holds that since we now 'understand it,' we can learn to sublimate and ventilate it harmlessly by doing things like kicking empty tins, engaging in competitive sports, and conducting the Olympic games. This was a suggestion made by Konrad Lorenz, needless to say some years prior to the 1972 Munich Olympic games where the Arab-Israeli conflict was carried right into the games themselves and resulted in the death of Israeli athletes.[2] Others argue persuasively that anger is such a serious problem that we all teeter on the edge of self- annihilation. Some feel that nothing short of total behavioral engineering or the universal administration of calming drugs afford hope of controlling anger. Our purpose is not to become embroiled in these larger discussions, but rather to point to a polarization in the very practical area of how each of us should understand and handle our anger as individuals. Most views cluster around one of two poles, that of the ventilationists on the one hand and those who argue for the control of anger on the other.

## Ventilationists

Ventilationists feel that the over-control of anger is one of the major causes of psychological problems. It plays an important part in stifling one's whole emotional life. Because anger is especially unsettling and difficult to reconcile with one's self-image as a 'nice person,' we tend to deny its existence to ourselves and certainly to others. It then crops up in painful but more socially respectable places such as in headaches, insomnia, depression, overeating, or inconsiderate driving. Anger expressed is said to function as an emotional laxative; it is healthy and therapeutic, it lets out bad feelings which would otherwise be turned loose inside of us. Ventilationists give numbers of case histories in which repressed or suppressed anger led to a host of painful physical and psychological symptoms. There is a lot to be said for their argument up to this point. The power of unacknowledged anger to cause psychological havoc is beyond doubt. It can be disguised and hidden behind all kinds of justifications, and is therefore all the more destructive in the long term.

At the same time ventilationists do discourage physical violence and other ways of 'playing dirty.' They are therefore not as completely against control as one might think from their writings. For example, Theodore Rubin in his celebrated *The Angry Book* asked provocative questions such as:

Have you ever experienced the good, clean feel that comes after expressing anger, as well as the increased self-esteem and the feel of real peace with one's self and others?[3]

This is tempered, however, by words of caution:

> Strong language is the poetry of anger, and we should expect
> poetry. But poetry does not include sarcastic biting, tearing,
> and stabbing . . . All expressions of warm anger will be short,
> finite; they will not go on and on and become chronic.[4]

One might well wonder about the realism of this advice,
knowing that our discernment between what is and what is
not poetry can become blurred at such times. Anger that is
expressed only briefly and without sarcasm or destructive
words is anger that to a large measure *is* controlled. There
may be a considerable gap between the ventilationist's
rhetoric and their actual advice to a person consumed with
malice and desire for revenge.

There are many variations within this overall viewpoint,
from George Bach who said, 'Anger cannot be dishonest' to
Fritz Perls and many of his followers who have encouraged
people to imagine biting the flesh of the person with whom
they are angry. This group suggests many techniques enabling someone to express his anger and thereby defuse it in a
relatively harmless way. Although Rollo May should not be
classed with these more extreme ventilationists, nevertheless
he sees the expression of anger as important to one's emotional survival at times when freedom is taken from a person:

> Hating or resenting is often the person's only way to keep from
> committing psychological or spiritual suicide. It has the func-
> tion of preserving some dignity, some feeling of his own
> identity, as though the person – or persons, in the case of
> nations – were to be saying silently to their conquerors, 'You
> have conquered me, but I reserve the right to hate you.' . . .
> Such contempt for the conquerors keeps the person still an
> identity in his own right even though outward conditions deny
> him the essential rights of the human being.[5]

May also sees clearly the destructive side of anger and concedes that violence is an 'expression of impotence.'[6]

### Advocates of Control

This group seems to be less vocal, but more experimentally based.[7] They concede the point that the ventilation of anger brings quick emotional release and relief, but add that it also tends to make the person more aggressive in the future. They argue that while the expression of anger does release bad feelings, it commits the person to anger as a habit, as a way of getting their way. The expression of anger as a practice seems to plow anger more deeply into our personality. They point out that the human personality is more complex than a pressure-cooker which must be allowed to let off steam occasionally to maintain equilibrium. Leonard Berkowitz cites the example of a letter to a newspaper counselor on personal problems:

> I was shocked at your advice to the mother whose three-year old had temper tantrums. You suggested that the child be taught to kick the furniture and 'get the anger out of his system.'
> . . . My younger brother used to kick the furniture when he got mad. Well he's thirty-two years old now and still kicking the furniture – what's left of it, that is. He is also kicking his wife, the cat, the kids, and anything else that gets in his way. Last October he threw the T.V. set out the window when his favorite team failed to score and lost the game. (The window was closed at the time.)[8]

There is something to be said for advocates of both ventilating and controlling our anger. While the ventilationists tend to confuse *any* control with suppression rooted in fear of anger, the advocates of control are often unhelpful in showing ways of actually identifying anger and dealing with it. Both suffer for lack of a wider philosophical framework for human nature and ethics within which our anger can be understood and directed positively.

## A Christian View of Anger

Anger is never right or wrong, good or bad in itself. The Christian must learn to distinguish righteous from unrighteous anger. This is seldom easy to do, both because our anger almost always feels righteous while we are angry, and also because the ethical issues themselves often turn out to be quite complex even when we reflect on them in the cool of the day. Nevertheless we are given some helpful criteria by which to evaluate anger. We must not be afraid of grey areas or feel that we need to account for every eventuality. The world is not a neat and tidy place to live, and human anger is one of the most chaotic and confusing things we have to deal with here.

It is clear from the Bible that God is sometimes angry. His anger burns hot, he has controversies with his people, and vengeance belongs to him. The biblical references to the anger of God show that anger is too closely tied to God's character to be dismissed as a reflection on a primitive concept of divinity. Anger is therefore not intrinsically wrong. Outrage is the right response when cruelty, betrayal, and injustice have been done. In fact, it is sometimes seen as morally reprehensible when people are *not* angry – a mark less of humility than of moral apathy (Amos 6:1–6). Praise was given by Jesus to peace makers, not just to anyone who feels peaceful. The important question then becomes how we distinguish legitimate from illegitimate anger.

In order to make this distinction, we need to separate three aspects of anger. They are the cause, the quality of the anger and the expression of it. If anger is to be legitimate in the sight of God it must honor him in all three areas. The cause of anger is the thing that 'makes' you angry, the occasion for it. The quality is the nature of the feeling, what it is saying. The expression is whatever you choose to do with it once you are angry. We must evaluate anger on each of these three counts.

If the cause of anger is not legitimate, then no expression of it can be legitimate (apart from trying to get rid of it). For example, if I am angry at someone because I am jealous of his success, no direct expression of this anger will be pleasing to God. Such anger is unrighteous because of its cause. On the other hand, if the cause of my anger is injustice or wrong done to some standard more important than my own pride, then I may have a legitimate reason for anger.

Jesus was angry in the synagogue at Capernaum when the Pharisees silently censured him for thinking of healing a man on the Sabbath. 'And he looked around at them with anger, grieved at their hardness of heart, and said to the man, "Stretch out your hand." He stretched it out, and his hand was restored.' (Mk. 3:5)

Jesus was angry because the Pharisees lacked compassion for the man, they were content to let him continue life with a withered hand. That Jesus' anger was unselfish is made clear by the way it was accompanied by grief. He was angry when he threw the money changers out of the temple. The house of God had been made into a den of thieves. Jesus' anger was not that of self-protection or self-advancement, but it came when moral wrong was done, particularly when moral wrong was surrounded with hypocrisy.

It becomes very difficult to distinguish legitimate from illegitimate anger when the injustice that causes the anger is an injustice done to me or someone close to me. In this case it is terribly easy to confuse hurt pride with injustice, or vice versa. Caution is necessary, but if the injustice done is serious, our anger may be legitimate. Paul said, '*Be angry, but do not sin . . .*' (Eph. 4:26). The question is how to be angry without sin. I will offer some tentative suggestions.

When a wrong is done to us, we must ask whether the wrong is serious enough to warrant anger, or whether our love should cover it. The apostle Peter tells us that love covers a multitude of sins (1 Pet. 4:8). The implication is that the greater our love, the more sins our love will cover. We do not always need to rise to our own defense each time our piece of cake is thinner than our neighbor's or our job seems more difficult than theirs. Those who are angry whenever any injustice is done to them are far more miserable than they need to be. A wise saying in Proverbs observes that 'Good sense makes a man slow to anger, and it is his glory to overlook an offense' (Prov. 19:11).

However, sometimes injustice is so great and serious that anger is called for. Think of the example of the apostle Paul. He was beaten and imprisoned without trial in Philippi, and when the magistrates decided to let him go quietly the next day Paul showed real anger at their violations of their own laws. He spoke with heat, 'They have beaten us publicly, uncondemned, men who are Roman citizens, and have thrown us into prison; and do they now cast us out secretly? No! Let them come themselves and take us out' (Acts 16:37). Others had been wronged too, but Paul was angry at least partly because *he* had suffered.

Determining the cause of anger is our first task. What then about other aspects of anger – its quality and expression?

Anger is not a precise or narrowly limited feeling, but encompasses many different feelings and attitudes. Some are appropriate; some are not. Distinctions among types of anger may seem unduly pedantic when we are angry, but these differences are nevertheless significant. We use many words to describe anger: rage, outrage, indignation, malice, bitterness, desire for revenge, fury, animosity, meanness, and resentment. From all these kinds of anger we must distinguish between the anger that Paul commands in 'Be angry . . .' and the malice, five verses later, that he wants us to 'put away.' In other words, anger with a legitimate cause can have a quality that makes it illegitimate. For example, there is a difference between being outraged at evil done and thirsting for revenge on those who have done the evil. Vengeance is God's business, not ours. That is not to say that he will avenge everything that we would like to see avenged, but that he is the final judge. When ultimate and perfect justice is done, he will be the one to do it. We impose the punishment that justice might require only when we are in an official capacity to enforce the law of the state.[9] Otherwise, our job is to trust his judgment and leave punishment to him. Here again Jesus was an example for us. As Peter wrote, 'When he was reviled, he did not revile in return; when he suffered, he did not threaten; but trusted to him who judges justly' (1 Pet. 2:23).

The quality of legitimate anger must focus on the wrongness of the evil done rather than on the destruction of the person who did it. It is an indignation that pushes for change, not a malice that hungers for revenge. Our judgments on this point are inescapably subjective. There is no check-list that will instantly separate legitimate from illegitimate anger. But this obvious problem does not erase God's principles. Just because there is grey in the world does not mean that there is no black and white. We have broad guidelines from God's revelation and we need to have deep personal integrity as we apply them to our lives.

How then do we express anger? How should it come out into the open? Jesus' anger is a good place to begin.

Jesus' anger was hot and powerful, but it was not uncontrolled rage. Some suggest that when he cleaned out the temple he was possessed by an irrational fury. I doubt this. Although he was clearly very angry, he knew exactly what he was doing. In fact a straightforward reading of all four gospels seems to show that Jesus cleaned out the temple twice – once at the beginning and once at the end of his public ministry (Jn. 2:14–17; Mt. 21:12–13). This suggests that he had a definite plan in his mind all along, rather than a sudden flare-up of anger. The first time he did it, he took the time to sit down and make himself a whip of cords. Anger, then, must not be expressed uncontrollably. If it is, too many of the wrong people get hurt in its path, and those who need to hear it most are either hurt by it unnecessarily or enabled to dismiss it as fanatical and unbalanced. We are unlikely to be able to honor God with chaotic rage.

At the same time we need to avoid the opposite danger: that we will stifle and smother righteous anger out of the fear that expressing it will rock the boat or appear unrespectable. Remember we are to 'Be angry . . .' but not sin. Sometimes others need to hear and feel that anger, even though it might shock them.

How long should we be angry? Not long, according to the Bible. Paul says we are not to let the sun go down on our anger. Anger against another person held for a long time is resentment and collides with Jesus' uncompromising teaching about forgiveness. Perhaps what this means is that a day is time enough to separate the sin from the sinner in our minds and forgive the sinner. Stephen was able to forgive those who were in the very act of stoning him to the extent at least that he prayed for God to forgive them (Acts 7:60). Anger against another person, if it is to be legitimate in the sight of God, must be short-lived. Otherwise it is a failure to forgive. However, righteous anger can and should last far longer when it is directed not against individuals but against evil, injustice, and prejudice. In this case, righteous anger is not just a flare-up of temper, but is a steady burning fire against wrongs done. There is a clear difference between being angry at injustice and wanting a pound of flesh from the those who did it, wrong though they were.

This is a place where Jesus' teaching was and still is too radical for most of us to hear. He said, 'Love your enemies and pray for those who persecute you.' (Mt. 5:44). We are to turn the other cheek and not respond in kind to attacks on us. Here the sin is separated in our minds from the sinner. The sin is hated, but the sinner is not only forgiven, but loved.

Another characteristic of legitimate anger is that it leads to corrective action. It seeks not resentment or revenge, but what actually can be done to change wrongs. For Jesus, corrective action meant that he was willing to pay the ultimate price to do away with the things that provoked his anger – human pride and sin which brought alienation between God and humankind. Angered by our rebellion and hardness of heart, he went to his own execution to take away the penalty and guilt for the sins of those who would trust in him. Having risen from the dead, he sent the Holy Spirit to work in those same people. He can counsel us to pray for those who persecute us because he did that – and more.

Paul's anger at his mistreatment in Philippi illustrates anger leading to constructive action. He did not accept his release quietly, but nor did he plot revenge against the magistrates. Rather he told them to come down personally to make an open apology. This not only cleared the gospel of unnecessary stigma, but did something to deter the magistrates' future carelessness with others.

These restrictions on righteous anger do not give it the 'death of a thousand qualifications,' for all practical pur-poses eliminating righteous anger from human life. The biblical writers to be sure, gave many warnings about anger because it so easily deceives us and can do such great damage. But we are left with the command to 'be angry but do not sin . . . ,' and the example of Jesus himself.

The world is a better place today because Christians in the past have been outraged by sin and evil. The Christian view of God and humanity has at times in the history of the church given Christians a powerful vision to change society, not as an alternative to spreading the gospel but as an expression of the gospel itself. It has motivated Christians to fight for justice and fairness even when their own individual interests were not immediately at risk, but those of others were. Righteous anger of this sort becomes inseparable from courage and compassion. It is not so much legitimate as commanded. This is the kind of anger that we need far more of. It is not much in evidence in the church today. It would make our lives less comfortable and predictable, but we would make a greater contribution to the kingdom of God. It is not in the scope of this book to outline issues that ought to make a Christian angry today. However, we would do well to reflect deeply on Jesus' anger, and then imagine him turned loose in the modern world.

## Unrighteous Anger

If all we had to cope with was righteous anger, we would be very different people and the world a different place. Unfortunately a large proportion of our anger is unrighteous. Too often our anger begins with someone thoughtlessly walking in the flower garden of our pride, damaging some aspect of our self-image, and our anger is expressed without thought or control and followed by resentment. It is a sobering fact that in most cases when the Bible mentions human anger God remains unimpressed. James warned: 'Let every man be quick to hear, slow to speak, slow to anger, for the anger of man does not work the righteousness of God' (Jas. 1:19–20). We should remember James' warning when we think we are about to show God's righteousness by our anger. How easy it is to think that God's cause is at stake when it is only our pride that is endangered. When God's compassion on Nineveh threatened Jonah's racial pride and reputation as a prophet, 'it displeased Jonah exceedingly, and he was angry.' God then very gently asked Jonah a question which speaks volumes, 'Do you do well to be angry?' (Jonah 4:1,4).

Human anger is one of the well-developed themes in the wisdom literature of the Bible. Anger in general is said to be destructive in many ways, 'Wrath is cruel, anger is overwhelming' (Prov. 27:4). However, the main theme is that the angry person, especially the one who expresses anger quickly, is a fool and does not know the way to live. Here are some examples:

1. The fool is a person who is quick to lose their temper:

The vexation of a fool is known at once, but the prudent man ignores an insult. (Prov. 12:16)

A man of quick temper acts foolishly, but a man of discretion is patient. (Prov. 14:17)

He who is slow to anger is better than the mighty, and he who rules his spirit than he who takes a city. (Prov. 16:32)

Notice that the angry fool is not a self-directed person; they do not rule their own spirits, though they might rule a city. They are not secure enough to ignore an insult, but must leap to do battle in their own defense.

2. The fool is one who holds nothing back once angry:

A fool gives full vent to his anger, but a wise man quietly holds it back. (Prov. 29:11)

Again fools are not their own masters; they are controlled by feelings of anger. Their anger is always at full throttle regardless of who or what might be in the way.

3. The fool is also a person who cannot get rid of anger:

Be not quick to anger, for anger lodges in the bosom of fools. (Eccl. 7:9)

Fools seem to be passive with respect to their own anger. It is lodged in the center of them, and is there to stay.

4. Finally, the angry fool is a good person to stay away from:

A man of wrath stirs up strife, and a man given to anger causes much transgression. (Prov. 29:22)

Make no friendship with a man given to anger, nor go with a wrathful man, lest you learn his ways and entangle yourself in a snare. (Prov. 22:24–5)

Angry people never just act for themselves, but inevitably drag others into the fray. However, they are not apt to be aware of that, so it is best to steer a wide path around them.

The wisdom literature makes it abundantly clear that the wise person and the angry person are as different as they can be. The way of wisdom is the way of one who has a strong sense of their own identity. The wise person is patient, and prudent. They have discretion and are able to be quiet when others are on their feet shouting, throwing things, or swinging their fists.

Although they give a very negative picture of anger, the biblical writers are not shocked by it. They do not give a little gasp of horror and then tell us to avoid anger because it is indecent, or because others will no longer think that we are sweet and nice. They approach the matter with a quiet calmness and teach us that our anger does us and others a lot of damage, and therefore we are not to be fools by letting it have its way.

We are also to avoid unrighteous anger because it stunts our growth in the Christian life. Anger seems like such a 'human' failing, and has a certain charm about it. However, the Bible does not regard anger as charming at all. In a number of ways our anger puts roadblocks between us and our ability to serve God. I will mention five areas.

## Prayer

'I desire that in every place the men should pray, lifting holy hands without anger or quarreling' (1 Tim. 2:8). If we pray with anger in our hearts, we are not praying as we should. Paul does not say that God will never hear us, but implies that we have no right to expect him to.

## Giving

'So if you are offering your gift at the altar, and there remember that your brother has something against you, leave your gift there before the altar and go; first be reconciled to your brother, and then come and offer your gift' (Mt. 5:23–4). In this case the problem is not your anger but someone else's. An attempt at reconciliation is more important to God than receiving your gift.

## Christian Leadership

'For a bishop, as God's steward, must be blameless; he must not be arrogant or be quick-tempered or a drunkard or violent or greedy for gain' (Tit. 1:7). The easily angered person or the person who is violent are both disqualified from Christian leadership in the office of bishop or elder.

*Beyond Identity*

### Guidance

'He who loves his brother abides in the light, and in it there
is no cause for stumbling. But he who hates his brother is
in the darkness and walks in the darkness, and does not
know where he is going, because the darkness has blinded
his eyes' (1 Jn. 2:10–11). This statement is very strong
indeed. It seems that if we hold hatred in our heart for a
fellow Christian, God does not guide us because we have
put ourselves into the darkness. As with prayer, this does
not mean that God never will guide us if we hate another,
but we have no business expecting him to.

### Assurance

'Any one who hates his brother is a murderer, and you know
that no murderer has eternal life abiding in him' (1 Jn. 3:15).
Here continued hatred for a brother or sister is cause for us
to question our salvation itself.

These examples are enough to show that unrighteous
anger has an utterly crippling effect on the Christian life,
sabotaging our prayer, giving, leadership, guidance and
confidence of salvation, not to mention grieving the Holy
Spirit of God (Eph. 4:30–1).

## Anger and the Self

Anger is no small or insignificant emotion. Our feelings of
anger can involve the totality of our being the way few other
emotions do, bringing instant and profound physiological
changes with them.

Unrighteous anger may be the mark of the fool, but we
must not think that we are just being stupid when we get
angry. Anger usually makes sense to us. As Overstreet

points out: 'People always do what makes sense to them in terms of what they see. They do not do things which, from their point of view, in the moment of action, are stupid and uncalled-for.'[10] That is to say, there is always some internal rationale for human actions, however misguided, flimsy, selfish, and irrational it might be. To rid ourselves of unrighteous anger, we must understand its inner logic or rationale. The fact is that anger is a widespread phenomenon because it often gives certain short-term psychological benefits, however disastrous the long-term results might be.

Sometimes anger is undeniably satisfying. There is a curious twist in the story of Jacob and Esau. After Jacob had swindled his brother out of his birthright and his rightful blessing, Esau was enraged and plotted to kill Jacob. Their mother heard of his threats and told Jacob of it in this way: 'Behold, your brother Esau *comforts himself* by planning to kill you' (Gn. 27:42). What kind of 'comfort' could this be that comes from plans to murder your twin-brother? A strange kind of comfort indeed, and yet maybe not so strange if we reflect on times when we have ourselves been wronged seriously by someone we ought to have been able to trust. What are these satisfactions?

First, expressed anger gives a sense of relief from feelings of anxiety and inadequacy. Anger changes a mouse into a Napoleon in a matter of seconds. It can give relief to a painfully weak identity, and reaffirm a threatened sense of self. Whatever kind of pain we feel about ourselves – guilt, fear, helplessness, jealousy, humiliation or frustration – anger seems to offer a momentary respite. Esau, already indignant about Jacob's dishonesty, had also been made a fool of, Jacob had made him look and feel guilty and dumb. These are all very uncomfortable things to feel about yourself. The inner logic of anger is clear. To kill Jacob would have taught Jacob a lesson, accomplished justice, and transformed the clumsy and dull-witted hunter who had been

conned, into a righteous judge and executioner. No wonder
Esau was comforted by his anger. As with the fool (Prov.
12:16) whose anger is immediately known to all when they
are insulted, anger gives relief from the humiliation of
insult. It is our turn to do some insulting.

Many have pointed out the relationship between anxiety
and anger. Harry Stack Sullivan saw it in this way:

> Anger is much more pleasant to experience than anxiety. The
> brute facts are that it is much more comfortable to feel angry
> than anxious. Admitting that neither is too delightful, there is
> everything in favor of anger. Anger often leaves one sort of
> worn out . . . and very often makes things worse in the long
> run, but there is a curious feeling of power when one is angry.[11]

This is echoed by the words of Caryl Chessman, the controversial death-row author who was finally electrocuted
for first-degree murder: 'There is nothing that sustains a
man like hate; it is better to be anything than afraid.' Again,
the role of anger in this case is to displace a feeling that is
more threatening to our sense of identity.

Anger also offers relief from feelings of helplessness and
impotence. We are fallen creatures, created to have dominion over the earth but frustrated and curtailed in that
attempt. Anger and often violence are the result. Rollo
May, in a similar vein, suggests that the experience of
powerlessness is one of the main sources of violence in
Western society.[12] All of us need to feel that we matter and
have some significance. People try to derive this sense of
significance from many different things. Some of us feel
that we matter as we order the most expensive meal on a
restaurant menu, daydream of doing great exploits, or
drive our car dangerously fast. But others feel important
only when they shout at their spouse, shoot a public figure,
or hijack an airplane.

The second benefit of anger is that you get results from it. Anger often commands a certain respect, but respect along with isolation from others. If you have a reputation for anger, people are less likely to cross you, and might allow you to have your way more often. If you happen to measure strength by power over others, then being angry is a good way to make people afraid of you and therefore step more quickly at your command.

The third source of satisfaction that we derive from anger is both more unsettling and also more difficult to describe. It goes beyond providing momentary strength to a weakened sense of self. A particularly passionate expression of anger, especially if it involves physical violence, can have the psychological result of giving a person a sense of intense total involvement. They might experience an integration of their personality that they seldom find at other times. For this reason, some have compared violent anger to sexual and religious experiences of ecstasy. Rollo May points to a self-transcendence and total absorption that lies at the heart of many acts of violence and also explains the wider fascination with violence that most of us feel.[13] Uncontrolled anger is satisfying precisely because it is uncontrolled. The controlling center of the self is bypassed, the person is no longer able to reflect on himself, evaluate or make a decision, but the anger is carried along by a force all its own. This can provide not just relief from painful self-scrutiny and self-condemnation, but also a positive sense of exhilaration in powerful self-assertion.

Anger has its own rationales. It tends to carry more weight in the heat of the moment than it does when we are more free to reflect on our situation, but it will not be belittled or ignored.

We turn now to the ways anger interacts with other emotions. An important question is, 'Is anger always a "secondary response"?' Does it have an independent status all its own in our lives, or is it always the result of some deeper complex of emotions and attitudes? This is a very real question to anyone who has grappled with the problems of understanding and coping with anger. Some would take the remarks of Caryl Chessman to be a paradigm for all anger. That is, all anger is to be seen as an outward expression of inward pain in the form of guilt and especially anxiety or fear. The question is important because it affects how we deal with anger. If it is always a cover-up for some underlying loss of self-esteem, we should pay more attention to the underlying problem than to the anger itself. However, if anger has a life of its own, we need to deal with the anger directly. There are two issues that need to be clarified.

First, both daily experience and the Bible often link anger with other emotions. Sometimes anger does clearly seem to be a result of a deeper cause as with the person who is afraid of losing their job and 'being a failure,' and who beats up their spouse over a trivial quarrel. Anger can be related to fear, guilt, frustration, tiredness, depression, physical pain, and low self-esteem. All these and other emotions are sometimes at least partial causes for anger. The Bible gives numerous instances of anger flowing from denied guilt. We have discussed one instance in David's rage against 'the man' in Nathan's parable. Soon after the confrontation with Nathan, David's son Amnon loved his half sister Tamar so much that he was making himself sick. But when he raped her, suddenly he 'hated her with very great hatred; so that the hatred with which he hated her was greater than the love with which he had loved her' (2 Sam. 13:15). A third example of anger covering up guilt is in Jesus' parable of the unforgiving servant (Mt. 18:23–5). A servant who had been forgiven for having squandered a vast amount of money was instantly infuriated on encountering one of his fellow servants who owed him a pittance. Such anger is not only triggered by another feeling but seems to be rooted at a deeper level. To this degree then, anger can be considered a secondary response in the sense that it can spring from a more primary emotional struggle.

But there is a second issue. Anger can result from other feelings, but that does not mean that it always does, that anger's nature is inevitably secondary. One recent tendency in popular psychology is to say anger is always a symptom of a deeper problem and that we therefore need not take it seriously in itself, but rather spend our time worrying about underlying anxiety or lack of self-esteem. However, this approach rests more on a humanistic presupposition that humankind is almost perfectible than it does on an honest wrestling with our well-attested capacity for deliberate destructiveness and cruelty.

The biblical writers seem to treat anger as a secondary response at times, but as a problem in itself at other times. Often the Bible sees anger not as merely a symptom of some need, but as a sufficiently basic problem to be confronted in its own right. Humankind is a very complex unity. Different feelings, attitudes and actions are intermeshed with one another in a whirlwind of interrelationships. Anger can be at least partially caused by guilt, fear, or other emotions, but anger itself *causes* guilt, fear, anxiety, depression, tiredness, low self-esteem, physical pain, and more anger. The causal relationship works both ways. There are times when fear, anxiety, and guilt are secondary to anger. No one feeling, instinct, drive, or need is absolutely prior and basic. Often psychologists attempt to make one drive primary because they have no wider philosophical frame-work to account for the complexity of human nature, and therefore need to take one thing as a starting point or foundation to which all else is reduced. The Bible itself is refreshingly free from such reductionism. It teaches us to take each emotion or need seriously in itself, but also to expect interactions with many other feelings and needs. Anger is therefore confronted directly (see Eph. 4:26), but never as if it stood alone in isolation from other areas of a person's life. For example, in the verse just mentioned (to which we will soon turn) advice on anger is given as one of several important aspects of putting off the old person and putting on the new. The danger in isolating one problem area as I am doing in this chapter is that we will lose sight of the way that each of us acts and feels as a whole person. This wholeness is made up of a magnificently intricate system of interrelationships within every person. Let us then not be afraid to call anger anger, and yet at the same time not be foolish and expect it to exist in a hermetically sealed container neatly separable from the rest of our lives.

## Dealing with Unrighteous Anger

Much of our anger is unrighteous anger. It is not selflessly motivated, free from vengeance, controlled in its expression, or followed by constructive action. Often it is a supreme expression of pride, whether it be from frustration in creating or protecting our public image, impatience or loss to ourselves. There are two steps in dealing with unrighteous anger. We must recognize it for what it is and then get rid of it. Both of these steps are difficult, requiring more humility than comes naturally to any of us.

When told that the first step is to recognize anger, you might reply, 'that's easy, I can recognize it a mile away.' Unfortunately we often cannot. Of course anyone can recognize in oneself or others a red face, clenched fists, and a loud voice. However, anger comes in many disguises, sometimes as a wolf in sheep's clothing.

## Why Anger Is Disguised

Many people feel that anger is childish, undignified, un-christian, and destructive. Thus it undermines our image of ourselves to admit anger. We like to think that we have given up childish ways, that we are mature and secure enough not to be infuriated by all the petty and trifling things that do in fact make us angry. Petty anger from hurt pride in no way corresponds to the nice, reasonable person that we would like to see when we look in the mirror. While it is considered perfectly respectable to be angry at rank injustice and oppression, it is humiliating to realize that we are angry at being snubbed, criticized, or ignored. To admit that some of these affronts anger us exposes us as arrogant and fragile people, delicately sensitive to our reputations and selfish interests. This is very far from the kind of Christian character that is put before us as a goal in the Bible and by our own consciences. Therefore to admit that this sort of anger is our own is to admit substantial failure. For many this is too painful an admission. We deny the anger, but life increasingly takes on the character of pretense, maintaining an acceptable public and private image.

Another closely related motivation for disguising anger is the fact that many of us feel insecure in any situation involv-ing conflict between people. The person afraid of conflict is apt to be committed to peace at any price. They have in each relationship a mental dossier of sensitive subjects that are to be avoided in conversation. They range from the traditional subjects of religion and politics to domestic questions such as who should take out the garbage or what clothes are appropriate for a party. When conflict avoidance becomes a long-standing pattern, we can create a superficial sense of peace for ourselves that camouflages rising resentment. Usu-ally this sort of peace is interrupted by occasional explosions which quickly subside and then the old pattern is resumed.

These patterns and many others hide anger. Maintaining peace at any price inevitably involves lying to others about what is really going on in one's head. This becomes part of a far-reaching emotional isolation from others, but just as inevitably includes isolation from one's self. We all at least half believe our own lies.

In the lives of Christians this syndrome usually comes from the fatal confusion of Christianity with respectability. To be angry seems to violate Christian propriety, ruining our witness. Christians, knowing God's loving acceptance of failures, ought to be able to admit every sort of short-coming freely. But by confusing spirituality with respect-ability, they can in fact end up denying ever feeling angry to themselves and everyone else.

A very different cause for the disguising of anger is seen in the person who has been dominated by parents or other powerful and authoritative people. Every expression of their own individuality, especially when they felt angry, has been stamped on and not allowed a voice. Perhaps they have been either ignored or severely punished for ever expressing an opinion contrary to the party line. Their anger has been so unacceptable, a cause of such fear and pain, that it has been pushed down out of sight and never recognized. Outwardly they may have the attitude of indifference and apathy, but this is a thin paper covering over a deep source of potential violence.

How is anger disguised? Consider a few of the typical ways that anger is euphemized in our conversations. Has a spouse, child, or close friend ever asked you: 'Are you angry with me?' Perhaps you have a standard reply. A very well-used one is, 'Of course not.' Another is 'of COURSE not!' The idea is that it is unthinkable that a nice person like me should ever be angry with a nice person like you. It is impossible in principle; therefore it is not true in fact.

A variation is, 'No, why should I be angry?' Again this reveals a naive assumption: namely, that the absence of a *rational cause* for anger makes the presence of anger out of the question. Take jealous anger for example. I might be infuriated with someone out of jealousy, even though they have done nothing to hurt me. In fact I might be jealous of someone I do not even know because they have something that I want and cannot have. It can be so humiliating to recognize such irrational anger in ourselves that we simply deny that we are angry.

Another mask is the notion that because anger is fruitless, I am obviously not angry. How often we say or hear: 'No, I'm not angry, it doesn't do any good to get angry, does it?' A nice, decent, reasonable, practical person like myself can hardly indulge in such a useless feeling as anger.

Still another way to disguise anger is to clothe it in weakness. We say, 'No, I'm just depressed,' 'fed up,' 'tired,' 'discouraged,' or with a quick twist of the knife, 'I'm only disappointed in you.' You have accounted for your obvious displeasure by pleading weakness in yourself, not the one with whom you are angry. Since everyone feels down or tired at times, such an admission does not threaten you, and at the same time saves you the embarrassment of admitting that you are angry.

In all these ways and more we avoid admitting to ourselves that we are angry.

### Recognize What Anger Is Saying

Recognizing that you are angry is only the first step. You must often go beyond the specific thing that triggered the anger to recognize what anger is saying. Anger seems to come from expectations that are not met. To recognize anger, you must learn to identify what these frustrated expectations are. They are as diverse as life itself. People should remember to say thank you and apologize when they hurt you. They should not be late for an appointment and keep you waiting. They should not leave their clothes all over the floor for you to pick up, their cigarette butts in the ash tray, or have the radio turned on loudly when you are trying to sleep. We have deeper expectations than these, expectations touching directly on our sense of identity itself. People ought to listen to you and take you seriously, recognizing that you are of value. They should not try to control your life or treat you as if your time and effort were of no importance. They ought to appreciate you and not take you for granted. At the same time, they should not expect too much from you. When expectations like these are not fulfilled, the frustration can lead to anger. We feel that the wrong done is so serious that it needs to be punished outright or at least the offender hung in effigy inside our own head.

These feelings may be righteous or unrighteous. First, we must try to see where they come from. As we do this we find that some of our expectations are absurd. Other expectations, perhaps less ridiculous, were never made explicit to the one who frustrated them. Once we have seen where our anger comes from we are then in a position to think of doing something about it.

And we need to do something about it. It is no recent discovery that anger will not stay hidden. The Bible itself is filled with stories of delayed grudges exploding. Once again the book of Proverbs has a special incisive wisdom:

> Like the glaze covering an earthen vessel are smooth lips with an evil heart.
>
> He who hates, dissembles with his lips and harbors deceit in his heart;
>
> When he speaks graciously, believe him not, for there are seven abominations in his heart;

Though his hatred be covered with guile, his wickedness will
be exposed in the assembly. (Prov. 26:23–6)

A person's anger will find its way to expression no matter
how respectable and tranquil appearances might be. The
seven abominations in the heart will be exposed eventually.
Medical research has shown that virtually every system of
our body can be affected adversely by anger. Unresolved
anger can cause headaches, asthma, and even heart disease.
Doctors trace many skin diseases, forms of arthritis, and
disorders of the digestive tract to hidden resentment.[14] If
unresolved anger brings organic symptoms with it, the
psychological results are legion as well. Anxiety, guilt, and
depression all thrive on resentment.

Recognizing the existence and the message of anger is still
not the whole solution. After honestly admitting the anger,
we must seek God's help and the help of people close to us
to get rid of it.

## Getting Rid of Anger – Today

One of the best known pieces of advice about anger is the
one we have already mentioned – Ephesians 4:26. The
whole verse runs like this: 'Be angry, but do not sin; do not
let the sun go down on your anger, and give no opportunity
to the devil' (Eph. 4:26).

Paul does not prohibit all anger. He knows that some of
our anger is righteous anger. His main concern is that we
not sin; he does not focus on our feelings as much as on
what we *do* with our feelings. If our anger is righteous, then
it should fuel constructive action. If it is not righteous anger,
then we are not to let it control us, but we are to get rid of
it as soon as possible. If we do not get rid of it, but instead
sleep on it, we then grow resentful. Paul intended that we

take him quite literally and not allow the day to end with anger in our hearts. This is not easy. If the sun is sinking and your heart is raging, what do you do? Without trying to make a program or system, let us see how the apostle Paul would have us begin to resolve the problem.

Occasionally God wants us to do the very thing we feel least like doing. For many of us, keeping quiet when we are angry is just such an occasion. We are often angry because we want to make our rights known, to lift the roof a few inches. However, a verse from the Psalms is the background of Paul's advice to the Ephesians: 'Be angry, but sin not; commune with your own hearts on your beds, and be silent' (Ps. 4:4). Being silent is the best place to begin as we feel anger rising within us.

Being silent can be much more creative than the proverbial counting to ten, one hundred, or even one thousand. When someone begins to feel anger rising, they are at a most critical point. How they react to this feeling will decide the direction of their personality in that situation and perhaps others to follow. If they commit themselves to anger, they will find it difficult to reverse that direction. Let us take an example. A man comes home from work after a hard day. For some time he has been afraid that he might lose his job. Today he had been accused of negligence that was not his fault, intensifying his anxiety. He also had been up too late the night before. The combination of anxiety and fatigue has given him a splitting headache. As he approaches his home he sees to his horror that the whole left side of the family car is smashed in. Instantly he estimates the cost of the repair, balances it against his bank account, and sees the summer vacation disappear. His wife had smashed up the car three times in the previous year. Once it had been while driving the wrong way on a one way street, another while racing to get to an overdue appointment, and the third (just three weeks earlier), by opening her door into a passing car while she was parked.

The man feels helplessness, exasperation, and rage. He is now at a very critical point. Unfortunately he might not reflect on himself at all, or on the consequences of the decision that he will be unaware of making. He might be conscious only of the outrage parked in front of him.

The Bible repeatedly compares anger with fire. Again and again anger is 'kindled.' It also 'waxes hot,' 'smokes' and 'burns.' Each of us has a kindling temperature, a point at which our tolerance for frustration ends and gives way to anger. This point changes. One day it might be as low as gunpowder – almost anything makes us explode – but the next day we are able to tolerate almost anything. The crucial issue is the point at which our tolerance for frustration ends. This level is far more important than the objective external situation which triggers our anger. Nothing can make you angry. Your anger depends far more on you than on the outside circumstances that thwart your expectations. Is the breaking of a plate in the kitchen a cause for a good laugh, a momentary inconvenience, or a catastrophe of cosmic proportions? Is an insult an unforgivable assault on your person or a cause for compassion for the one who made it? Your tolerance level determines the answer and this is not static or fixed.

What sets the kindling point? It is not fixed by the external situation (the broken plate, the insult or the smashed car), nor by the mood that you happen to be in at the time. You can talk yourself into being angry. You do this by reminding yourself of the outrage of your violated rights and reviewing the other person's past record of unreliability. This serves both to lower the kindling point and add fuel to the fire once it is lit. However, you can also talk yourself out of anger in many instances. This is where it is important to commune with your own heart on your bed and be silent. Our exasperated husband must at this point talk to himself. To talk to himself he must be silent to his wife, for a moment at least. He is able to change the crucial variable – his own kindling temperature. To do this he must fight his way free from the total involvement that his anger demands of him. He must grasp some measure of detachment from his feelings. He is not his feelings and he does not need to allow them to dominate his life. He must be willing to relinquish anger's many satisfactions.

He can say many things to himself. He can remind himself of the painful times he and his wife have had when they have fought before. They said things just to hurt each other. Little was gained. Though the air was sometimes cleared, nothing was resolved. He can also remind himself that his wife has needs too in this situation. Perhaps she was hurt in the accident; certainly she is not happy about it. He can remind himself that he is not living in the best of all possible worlds, free from weeds in the garden, sweat on the brow, disease and finally death of the body. He has no reason to expect freedom from frustration; he had better learn to cope with it. If he is blessed with the invaluable ability to laugh at himself, he can then see the childish side of his rage, deflating his anger as a pin does a balloon. If he is able to recognize that his anger is partly rooted in his own tiredness and anxiety over his job he will see how self-indulgent it would be to inflict this on his wife. Lastly, if he is a Christian, he has the vast resource of being able to call on God for help. He can ask God's forgiveness for wanting to throttle his wife. He can also ask God to help him grow in humility, self-control, and love.

The requirement for making all this possible is of course silence. You cannot talk yourself out of your anger as you are shouting yourself into it. You are able to control yourself far more easily at the kindling point than after you have allowed your anger to take its course (Prov. 17:14). Each one of us would do well to ask ourselves God's gentle but withering question to Jonah, 'Do you do well to be angry?'

## Speaking Out

Perhaps the husband does not defuse his anger by taking an extra forty-five seconds for deliberation with himself, but instead covers the distance from the street to the kitchen door in three bounds and enters the kitchen like John Wayne entering a Texas bar. With a quick glance at his wife preparing the supper he allays the thread of fear in the back of his mind that she might have been injured. He then bellows, 'AGAIN! What are you trying to do . . . ruin us? That's the fourth time in one single year!' He pauses for a second to catch his breath and then launches into a historical survey of her past automotive incompetence. He owed it to himself. That is what husbands do at such times. He had been afraid, exhausted, and irritable. He had a headache. Now the car.

God's word says some searching things about how we use our tongues. Recall the well-known passage in the letter of James:

> For we all make many mistakes, and if any one makes no mistakes in what he says he is a perfect man, able to bridle the whole body also. If we put bits into the mouths of horses that they may obey us, we guide their whole bodies. Look at the ships also; though they are great and are driven by strong winds, they are guided by a very small rudder wherever the will of the pilot directs. So the tongue is a little member and boasts of great things. How great a forest is set ablaze by a small fire. (Jas. 3:2–5)

James uses three images to describe the way our tongue functions in our lives. It is the bit in the mouth of the horse, the rudder of a ship, and the match that sets fire. All are small things that produce great changes, far beyond their apparent potential. The bit and the rudder are small parts that steer the whole. The bit in the horse's mouth directs the horse; the rudder sets the course of the ship. The analogy is clear. Your tongue can steer *you*. Notice what happens when the husband has said only a very few words. What has been changed? The man himself. He feels a certain exhilaration and power as the sound of his own voice in rage bolsters his sagging pride. Cutting down his wife makes him feel a few inches taller. At work he has been a little man who has been pushed around a lot in recent months. At home he can be a big man and get away with it. As he had entered the kitchen door he felt angry; now he has committed himself to anger. Now he is caught up in it as a whole person. He has 'gone into print' with it, as it were. Now he must be able to defend all the accusations in subsequent debate, perhaps for years afterward, or else suffer a humiliating retreat. In other words, the rudder is hard over and the ship has begun to change course.

James' third image of the tongue is that of the match which can set a whole forest afire. The point here is that your tongue not only changes the course of your life, but it can change others' lives as well. As with a match in a forest, if the wind is right and the forest is dry a spark can ignite an inferno which can destroy millions of acres. One of the writers of Proverbs puts it this way, 'A soft answer turns away wrath, but a harsh word stirs up anger' (Prov. 15:1).

The point is that the husband's anger is likely to touch off a roaring blaze. His wife has not been enjoying herself either. In fact she has had a miserable day. She too had started it with a headache which had gotten worse as the day progressed. Both children had been at home from school with colds and had spent the entire day fighting, making it virtually impossible to do anything she had needed to do. She had to load both sick kids into the car to go get some medicine. The accident had happened on the way back. This time it had *not* been her fault, a possibility that had never occurred to her husband. An oncoming car had swerved out of its lane and side-swiped them. It had been a terrifying experience for her and for the children. She had not recovered from the moment when she had been sure that all three of them would be killed, or from her anger and confusion at the aggressive unrepentance of the other driver. Quite obviously she has had a ghastly day. Anybody could see that – except her husband. Now she has been attacked at the very moment that she needed his love, comfort, and support most. She knows that any wife attacked in this way has the right to retaliate. That is what wives do.

Her intuitive sense of battle strategy tells her that she can insure that he make a complete fool of himself if she saves her trump card (that this time it was the other car's fault) for later use. She can give him a bit more rope to hang himself. 'Just who do you think you are? I suppose you never had an accident?!' (He had had one two years before.) 'Just because you're about to be fired, don't take it out on me!' Or, she might vary the theme. She might cry, and say through bitter tears, 'You don't even love me. All you care about is the Ford. I should have known it when I married you. You only care about money and work, and you're not even any good at that!'

Now it is his turn to be hurt. What in the world does his *job* have to do with it? She sure knows how to kick a guy when he is down! As with most of us, he is not terribly threatened when someone accuses him of something which is manifestly untrue. But if someone hits him in a sensitive area, where the criticism is partly true and corresponds to his own anxiety, then the threat is far greater and the anger hotter. If she had accused him of being a terrorist, he could laugh. But he cannot dismiss the accusation of being an inadequate husband and provider. He feels particularly hurt because when she finally did play her trump card it became obvious to him that she had goaded him into accusing her in order to humiliate him. She too felt hurt because he so obviously had no thought for the pain that she had been through. Thus the argument could go on for hours were it not for the need to feed the children their supper. The best outcome of this incident is a heavily armed neutrality which is likely to be only a breather in the battle.

During the breather, when both retire to different rooms, Satan nurses their damaged pride. He is like the trainer of a boxer. The moment the bell rings to end the round, Satan rushes to offer sympathy, repair any injuries, and also to help the fighter figure out how to do more damage in the next round. He can unleash another whole battalion of specters to haunt them at this new stage of the quarrel. No longer are they involved in the cut and thrust of a fast verbal exchange, but it is now a more long-term effort in which they may be even less aware of what is happening within and between them. Now, self-pity raises its head along with resentment and conscious and unconscious revenge. The events which took place in a few seconds in the kitchen can now be painfully dredged up years afterwards.

In this drama of the quarreling couple, I have tried to emphasize that even though their reactions to each other might have seemed inevitable to them, in fact they were not. Neither were forced by the other to act and speak as they did. They were both under pressure, but this kind of pressure did not determine the course of their lives. The more aware they are of what is happening within them and between them, the more free they will be to act with a larger range of choices.

## Guard the Tongue

We need constantly to remind ourselves that we *can* exert control over the things that we say. We *can* guard our tongues. The earlier we try to control it the easier it is to control. Even at the peak of their fight, if a respected friend had called at the door either of them could have answered it with a tone of politeness and interest. Of course it would have been forced politeness, but the point is that we can control anger when there is a good enough reason to control it, even if it is already burning hot. We can exercise control. We must apply the principles of Ps. 4:4. We must aim at being able to be angry, yet without sin. To do this we must first learn to commune with our own hearts in silence.

David put these principles into practice in his own life. In Psalm 39 he does not tell us very much about the actual situation he is in, but speaks clearly about his internal wrestling with his feelings. He has obviously had a miser-able day and was in the presence of someone who infuriated him:

> I said, 'I will guard my ways,
>   that I may not sin with my tongue;
> I will bridle my mouth,
>   so long as the wicked are in my presence.'
> I was dumb and silent,
>   I held my peace to no avail;
> my distress grew worse,
>   my heart became hot within me.
> As I mused, the fire burned;
>   then I spoke with my tongue. (Ps. 39:1–3)

David, possibly under extreme provocation, found that hold-ing his tongue was just not enough. His anger mounted even as he spoke to himself while holding his tongue. The first three verses seem to be leading up to a scathing rebuke to the offending person, or a blistering prayer that God will erase the person from the face of the earth. This, in fact is the way we often describe ourselves, 'I tried to control my anger, but

it didn't do any good. I finally couldn't hold it in any longer
so I told that person what I thought of them.' However, David
does not cut loose. He prays one of the most beautiful prayers
in the Bible, asking God to give him humility:

> Lord, let me know my end,
>     and what is the measure of my days;
>     let me know how fleeting my life is!
> Behold, thou hast made my days a few handbreadths,
>     and my lifetime is as nothing in thy sight.
> Surely every man stands as a mere breath!
>     Surely man goes about as a shadow!
> Surely for nought are they in turmoil;
>     man heaps up, and knows not who will gather!
> And now, Lord, for what do I wait?
>     My hope is in thee.
> Deliver me from all my transgressions. (Ps. 39:4–8)

In praying such a prayer, David struck a blow at the root
of the anger itself. The root was his own pride. As the book
of Proverbs reminds us, 'A fool gives full vent to his anger
but a wise man quietly holds it back' (Prov. 29:11). By
quietly holding it back, David was able to gain perspective
on it and to see it as an opportunity for his own spiritual
growth. Although great injustice might have been done to
David, he saw the source of his anger not in the outrage
itself, but in an overinflated sense of his own importance.
Therefore he asked God to make real to him the transience
of his own fleeting life and his dependence on God.

Anger that is faced, owned, and then gotten rid of in this
way is anger that is gone. It has not been denied or repressed.
It has been controlled first and then demolished. That is not
to say that it will never recur, but it has been defeated this
time. Whoever deals with anger in this way has taken great
steps forward in personal freedom. They are not

programmed by either outside circumstances or inward moods and feelings. They control their own spirit. In the terms of Ephesians 4:26, they can go to sleep without letting the sun go down on their anger because their anger is gone. Notice also that David does not make a direct attack on his anger in the prayer. He does not pray, 'Oh Lord, take this anger away from me.' This kind of a prayer can serve to fasten our attention on the very feelings that we want to get out of our consciousness. Instead David prays about the root cause of the anger, asking God for the humility that would necessarily displace his anger. The biblical approach is always positive. Just as fear is defeated more effectively by positive trust than by attacks on the fear itself, so unrighteous anger is displaced by humility.

## Resentment

Unfortunately, we cannot end our discussion of anger at this point. There are times when we cannot talk ourselves out of our anger or even pray ourselves out of it. We can be silent, communing with our hearts and with God, but the anger burns on. We still feel deeply wronged; there is a knot in our stomach. Anger like this can last not only past the sunset, but for years. Anger that lasts becomes resentment. Often our anger persists as resentment because we rather enjoy and encourage it, although this is not always so. Sometimes it is like a person who takes hold of a live wire by mistake. Instead of being able to let go and jump back from it, the current contracts the muscles in their arm, their hand grips the wire involuntarily, and they are unable to let go even though they want to. In the same way we can hold on to resentment, unable to let it go.

Resentment is a more serious thing than a flare-up of anger. It works within us and poisons and twists our attitudes, actions and feelings. Recall in Ephesians 4:26 the basis for this discussion: 'Be angry, but do not sin, do not let the sun go down on your anger.' Paul uses two Greek words for 'anger.' The anger which the sun goes down on is a stronger form of anger than the one at the start of the sentence. Though the precise difference in the meaning of the Greek words is unclear, the context seems to indicate that anger that lasts turns into a prolonged bitterness or grudge-bearing. If anger lasts more than one night, it has lasted too long.

Once again, a verse in Proverbs gives wisdom: 'He who conceals hatred has lying lips, and he who utters slander is a fool' (Prov. 10:18). The writer rejects two common false solutions to resentment. If we conceal it, sleeping on it night after night and pretending it is not there, we are liars. However, if we lash out at the one we resent, we are fools. This verse identifies a polarization that we have seen repeatedly in this book – the choice between hiding all feelings of anger, and broadcasting them from the rooftops. We can either give sweet smiles and suffer ulcers in the name of Victorian respectability, or ventilate our aggression in the name of honesty. Neither one works, or is pleasing to God.

## Dealing with Resentment

If we should neither hide our feelings of resentment nor ventilate them, what do we do with them? The first step is to see resentment from God's perspective. He very clearly sees it as sin, and that it should be treated as sin. Resentment is a more serious offense against another person than a flare-up of anger. Momentary anger can be sparked by almost any inconvenience or frustration while resentment is almost always fed by a deep sense of the sanctity of our violated rights. In resentment we nurse our wounds. We give our minds the time to distill the precise ways in which we have been wronged. Our expectations are established firmly as inalienable rights.

At this point the Christian must do some very sober thinking. Exactly what are our rights? Before God we have no rights. God gives us our breath itself out of his mercy, not because we deserve it. We are living in a fallen world in which people are not always going to be nice to us. The apostle Peter warns, 'Beloved, do not be surprised at the fiery ordeal which comes upon you to prove you, as though something strange were happening to you' (1 Pet. 4:12). We must expect to have some of our expectations frustrated even when we are trying to follow God. Indeed, sometimes they will be frustrated *especially* when we are trying to follow God. According to Peter, this should not surprise us. The love to which God calls us is a reflection of his love for us. His love is not first of all reciprocal love. But it is love upstream, uphill, love into the teeth of hatred, rejection, and neglect. Jesus taught about this with embarrassing clarity:

> If you love those who love you, what credit is that to you? For even sinners love those who love them. And if you do good to those who do good to you, what credit is that to you? For even sinners do the same. And if you lend to those from whom you hope to receive, what credit is that to you? Even sinners lend to sinners, to receive as much again. But love your enemies, and do good, and lend, expecting nothing in return; and you will be sons of the Most High; for he is kind to the ungrateful and the selfish. Be merciful, even as your Father is merciful. (Lk. 6:32–6)

This does not mean that Christians should always back down if their legal rights by civil law are violated. Paul decided to assert his legal rights as a Roman citizen on several occasions (Acts 16:37; 22:27; 25:10–12). It does mean, however, that the violation of legal rights need not be a cause for hatred or resentment. God expects us to image his love in our relationships with one another. This is God's standard for us. Any falling short of it is sin. Nothing in the teaching of Jesus suggests that I need to love my wife only when she drives carefully or my husband only when he speaks quietly. We are to be less concerned with the outrages perpetrated against us than with the godliness of our own response to them. Lest we think that this standard does not apply to cases of deliberate evil, we have the extraordinary example of Jesus. As he was being nailed to the cross, he prayed for those who were carrying out the crucifixion.

Non-forgiveness is synonymous with holding resentment. There is no neutral ground between the two. It is wrong both to hide resentment or to ventilate it in slander. But there is a third alternative. 'He who conceals his transgressions will not prosper, but he who confesses and forsakes them will obtain mercy' (Prov. 28:13). If resentment is sin against God and the other person, the honest thing to do is to treat it as sin and confess it to God and maybe to the other person as well. To hide it is to be honest only to our sense of propriety; to slander others is to be honest to our feelings. However, neither propriety nor feelings are always worth being honest to. If we confess resentment as sin, we are being honest to God. Asking the forgiveness of the one we resent might seem to be an extreme measure. It is a step to take only at last resort after all other ways of getting rid of our resentment have failed. But if the resentment has stayed even after reasoning with ourselves and confessing it to God, then we must somehow eradicate a deep-seated attitude against another who bears the image of God. It is a more serious wrong against the other than a flare-up of angry feelings. There is an againstness in holding a grudge that moves the relationship into a qualitatively different area.

Apologies are never easy, but apologies for resentment are among the most difficult. This is because the same pride that drives us into resentment blocks our retreat from it. Think of the difference between the ways a squirrel and a cat climb a tree. The squirrel has the equivalent of our thumb on the back of its front paws which enables it to scamper down a tree as easily and neatly as it goes up it. The cat, on the other hand, has only claws on the front of its paws. It can climb up a tree very nicely, but it is a great indignity for a cat to come down. It must come down backwards, usually very slowly, twisting and clutching at the bark, looking over one shoulder and then the other without being able to see clearly where it is going to put its feet next. A cat might climb to the top of a tree and stay there in its smallest branches, yowling until the fire department comes to carry it down on a ladder. In our resentment we are more like the cat than the squirrel. We rush into anger at high speed and with great ease. And there we sit in the high branches, with the reminder, 'Anger lodges in the bosom of fools' (Eccl. 7:9). To get rid of resentment can be an awkward and humiliating experience. Like the cat, we too would rather wait until someone hears our yowling, sympathizes with us, and helps to carry us down from our perch with gentleness and dignity. In short, we wait for the other person to apologize to us.

Saying 'Please forgive me for holding resentment against you' murders our pride. And yet for that very reason it can bring healing not only in the relationship but in our own attitude. The power of the resentment is broken when our pride is broken. The healing of the relationship depends in part on the other's response to our confession, but our own attitude can be changed irrespective of their response. One must be careful here, however, of offering this solution as some cure-all or panacea. If, for example, resentment is a symptom of another deeper problem, trying to deal with the resentment alone will not resolve the problem. However, many people have found great freedom from resentment's hold in this way, along with a growing ability to resist domination by all kinds of feelings of anger.

Let me give two illustrations of what I mean. I knew an older woman who claimed to have deep respect for Jesus and his teaching, indeed for the whole Bible. But there was one exception: Jesus' teaching about forgiveness. This she thought was unkind and impractical. People often reject teaching in the Bible they cannot stand: in this woman's case, something very deep was involved. She had built a psychological prison for herself out of her own hatred and resentment. She showed me a stack of paper nearly two feet high by the side of her desk. It was a typewritten account of the wrongs she had suffered at the hands of other people over the past forty years. The manuscript was to be publish-ed when it was complete, but of course she had not been able to finish it. I have met few people who were as consistently unhappy as this woman. Resentment had poi-soned and twisted her world to the point where it was the major core of her identity. Who was she? She was someone who had been unfairly treated by everybody.

A very different example is of a young man I knew who complained of excessive selfishness, self-pity, and apathy. An underlying problem was burning resentment of his father which had gripped him for years. He sometimes felt that he would sacrifice his life if he could sufficiently hurt his father and avenge the cruelty he had suffered. He had as a Christian prayed that God would help him to forgive, but to no avail. Fortunately, he came to see that his place was first not to struggle to forgive his father's wrongs, his mind fastened all the while on the gravity of these wrongs. His place instead was to look to his own life and ask his *father's* forgiveness for his resentment. He experienced a great freedom when he sent a letter of apology for his own years of bitterness, even though the letter went unacknowledged.

To many this would seem backward and unfair. The man's father had wronged him; therefore his father should have apologized. This is quite true, but that was his father's problem. The young man's own problem was that he was not forgiving. We are all very competent at giving an account of other people's sins and difficulties, but as Paul wrote, 'each of us shall give account of himself to God' (Rom. 14:12). This is a fearsome prospect, but it is also a very liberating one as it was for this young man. It frees us from the slavery of perpetually standing in judgment over others, at our own expense. It puts us in the position to change ourselves (the only ones we can directly change anyway).

Before we leave the subject of confession, a few words of caution are in order. Confession is not an end in itself, but it is a *means* to the final goal of reconciliation. However, as we discussed in the last chapter, it is a very delicate matter in which it is easy to achieve the exact opposite of reconciliation. By adhering to the letter and not the spirit of the law, one can force confession in those cases where even a well-intended confession would lead to alienation. Many of the interpersonal problems we get into come from being caught inside our own narrow pictures of the relationship – its past difficulties and future possibilities. Often these pictures prevent resolution of the problems. Discussion with a trusted friend who is not so emotionally embroiled can be a great help to clarify or enlarge our picture of the situation as it is, and the possible courses of action in the future.

## The Time Factor

As we approach the end of our reflection on Ephesians 4:26–7, let us note the importance of the time factor. Paul writes, 'Be angry but do not sin, do not let the sun go down on your anger, and give no opportunity to the devil.' The time factor distinguishes anger from resentment. According to Paul, anger that lasts more than a day has become resentment. There is therefore a real urgency in doing something about anger quickly. Hosea reflects on this same transition: 'For like an oven their hearts burn with intrigue; all night their anger smolders; in the morning it blazes like a flaming fire' (Hos. 7:6). Our anger is not a static thing. If we let it sit within us, it can turn into something far more destructive to ourselves and others. A tragic example of this is found in 2 Samuel 13.

Absalom's sister Tamar had been raped and then abandoned by Amnon. Absalom tried to comfort his sister, 'hold your peace my sister . . . do not take this to heart' (v. 20), but 'spoke to Amnon neither good nor bad' (v. 22). One might have thought that that would be the end of it, but two years later Absalom got Amnon drunk and then had him murdered.

We need to move quickly – whether we are at the early stages of an explosion of anger or at the later self-righteous resentment and refusal to forgive. The longer we wait the more opportunity we give to the devil to reinforce the walls of protection that surround our pride. It is not easy to back down. Most of us have such large investments in our pride that we are very out of practice in backing down. However, if those of us who are Christians believe that all the Scripture is 'profitable for teaching, for reproof, for correction, and for training in righteousness' (2 Tim. 3:16), then we must apply this reproof and correction to ourselves first. We must remember that our very identity as Christians is that of people who have backed down before God, confessed our sin, and asked for his forgiveness instead of standing on our imagined rights or virtues. One of the most telling criticisms of Christians is that they seem to be people who say sorry – only once, at the point of their conversion, and then never again. We are seen as those who have too big a stake in being 'good' to ever admit it when we are bad. Of course this turns the gospel upside down. God not only calls us to back down before one another, but he gives us the power to do it. This power comes both from the awareness of having been forgiven by God, and also from the direct work of God's Spirit within us.

## Anger and Identity

Anger reminds us that we do not live in utopia, but in a very twisted world. People do not always treat us properly or with due respect; they do not always honor our rights or care about our feelings. They can mis-hear, misunderstand, take offence unnecessarily and say things they don't mean. It is in this imperfect world that we are to be patient, kind, and loving. God never said to love only those who love you and make you feel good. We are not told to be patient only with those who are easy to get along with. Patience is only shown to be patience when we are with those who are tiring, unteachable, or exasperating. However difficult this may seem, it is the way to life.

Our true identity is derived from the character of the Creator, as a shadow, reflection, or counterplayer to the Supreme Identity. In this is our joy, fulfillment, and discovery of abundant life. Two Scripture verses help relate our discussion of anger to our identity. First a line from the psalms describes the anger of a person against the work of God: 'The wicked man sees it and is angry; he gnashes his teeth and melts away' (Ps. 112:8). This man's unrighteous anger destroys him; it is something that dissolves the fabric of his life and personality. Contrast this to Proverbs 19:11: 'Good sense makes a man slow to anger, and it is his glory to overlook an offense.' It need not be fear that makes a person control their anger, but good sense. It is not their loss to overlook an insult or attack, but their glory. We are not just dealing with useful techniques of the sort that abound in modern popular psychology, but with ways of living that are rooted in the character of the living God who existed before the earth was made.

> The Lord is gracious and merciful, slow to anger and abounding in steadfast love. The Lord is good to all and his compassion is over all that he has made. (Ps. 145:8)

Being the image of God, it is our glory to image his character. It is our glory to be gracious, merciful, slow to anger, loving, and compassionate. Love does not keep track of wrongs done (1 Cor. 13: 5) and therefore store up anger. As we mirror his love, each in our individual ways, we act from our true selves, our way of life is in harmony with our very being.

As we take these things seriously in our lives, gradually change does take place. With God's help, the fool becomes wise. One who is quick to anger and long to smolder becomes one who is slow to anger and quick to let the spark die. This is not just growth in one's ability to cope with one emotion, but growth in being a self-directed person, someone whose 'I am' controls an increasing amount of their life in obedience to and with the help of the living God. This control is not rooted in fear, repression or denial, but on the foundation of God's truth. We cannot hope that anger will never come, but rather that when it does come we know how to deal with it in God's strength. Although recognizing anger is often disconcerting to our self-image and painful within our relationships, it can be a blessing. If we deal with anger as God has told us, then very often reconciliation can bring a greater closeness to God and others than if the anger had never taken place.

The unifying factor in our discussion has been the imaging of God's character in our own actions, feelings, and attitudes. The witness of the whole Christian teaching about anger shows us an extraordinary vision of human character as a result. It is both deftly balanced and profoundly challenging. Unrighteous anger is met with humility that reflects the mind of Christ himself. If practiced, this humility brings healing and wholeness in our relationships at every level. Righteous anger calls us to courage, compassion, and love of justice. If it were a larger part of the life of God's people, the foundations of our society would be shaken as they have in times past.

# SEVEN

# Servants and Martyrs:
# Identity and the Family

*Finally, as the children rejected their parents in the 1960's, parents rejected their children in the 1970's. Having children is now openly and respectably proclaimed a mere burden . . . By an appropriate irony, as older people increasingly shirk the responsibilities of caring for the young, the young similarly reject the burden of the old.*[1] (James Hitchcock)

*Our ideas, no less than our lovers and our possessions, are pieces of ourselves. The most exquisitely rewarding and excrutiatingingly painful example of this inevitable fact of human life is in our relations with our own children. These are not merely 'other' people to us, or even those who act simply as a genetic or legal bridge between our past and our future. These pieces of ourselves are in some very real sense our most exposed flesh; a hurt to them can be unbearable far beyond our own corporeal pain; joy in who they are can lift us far beyond reason.*[2] (Michael Beldock)

*The family is the '. . . locale of highly significant expectations for self-fulfillment and emotional satisfaction.'*[3] (Peter Berger)

Most of us live in at least two families during our lifetime. We grow up in a family of some sort as children, and most of us later get married, forming another family which might also have children. Our experiences in these two families differ markedly from each other. In one we begin totally dependent on our parents and, over a long period of time, form our own sense of identity. This dependent relationship is temporary. Eventually we take responsibility for our own livelihood as either a single or married individual. Our second family is our own in a very different sense. Others depend on *us*. The foundations of our identity are formed in our first family. In our second family, they continue to be formed and tested through opportunity and stress. In our second family we can exert greater control, make decisions, and set directions for ourselves and others. The second family involves staggering levels of responsibility.

In this chapter I will look at some of the confusions of identity within the family. First, however, we will evaluate the family as an institution, looking at some of its difficulties in our culture. In any Christian understanding, the family in the United States and in Western Europe is weak. Indica - tions of this surround us. In the United States at the time of my writing, one out of every three children conceived is aborted. Predictions are that by the year 2000, up to 50 percent of all children will live in a fatherless home by age eighteen.

The family itself, along with many of the factors crucial to its wellbeing, is being attacked from all sides. Many of those trying to uphold their families along vaguely Christian prin - ciples are filled with doubt and uncertainty. What can be expected if the husband and wife have no idea how to resolve differences? What can the family do for the teenager's sudden identity struggles when all along the communication has been poor, shared experience meager and forced, and the father largely absent? At a time when the home is asked to accomplish more to nurture identity than it ever has, it is now weaker in some of the most vital areas, and suffers a crisis of identity all its own. Is it any wonder then that the home is the scene for great suffering and disillusionment?

A major part of the problem is the well-documented disintegration of the extended family, the local community, the local church, and other institutions that traditionally have supported the family. The nuclear family is left alone (with the uncertain influence of the school) to provide a framework for the formation of a child's identity. Husbands and wives are often solely reliant on each other for stability – who else is there if they relocate every three to five years? The husband and wife must provide each other with their only stable and lasting adult relationships. The ideological pressures,[4] the social fragmentation, the longer gap between the child's physical maturity and the time when he or she can be independent from the parents, and the vast range of role choices, have created a pressure on the adolescent's identity largely unknown in other cultures and times. The family, itself undermined from many sides, is now being asked to perform more demanding and varied functions than it ever was before in times when it was stronger and supported more fully by the rest of the culture. In short, more weight is being put on a more fragile institution.

Why did the family arise in human culture? Answers abound today. A biologist might point out that since men and women are sexually available to each other virtually all the time, unlike other animals, they may have developed more lasting relationships than most animals. An ethnologist might seek parallels for the human family in animal behavior. A social anthropologist, by contrast, might argue that the lowest common denominator of families throughout the world is that the family performs social functions, such as a means to legitimize children. A feminist might say that the family as we know it now arose simply as an instrument of male oppression.

We will take a theological view of the origin of the family. The family as an institution was appointed by God to fulfill many of the needs of humankind. It was his idea, his design in order that creatures made in his image be fulfilled and help fulfill one another.

## God's Commitment to Marriage

Marriage is not primarily a custom, but is rooted in the creation of God. He created the human race in his image as male and female and ordained marriage for them. He instructed us about the relationship husband and wife should have with each other for their own fulfillment and to his glory. God is concerned not for marriage in the abstract, but for individual married couples and their growth in marriage.

There is no better place to begin our search for the origin of marriage than the second chapter of Genesis:

> Then the Lord God said, 'It is not good that the man should be alone; I will make him a helper fit for him.' So out of the ground the Lord God formed every beast of the field and every bird of the air, and brought them to the man to see what he would call them; and whatever the man called every living creature, that was its name. The man gave names to all cattle and to the birds of the air, and to every beast of the field; but for the man there was not found a helper fit for him. So the Lord God caused a deep sleep to fall upon the man, and while he slept took one of his ribs and closed up its place with flesh; and the rib which the Lord God had taken from the man he made into a woman and brought her to the man. Then the man said, 'This at last is bone of my bones and flesh of my flesh; she shall be called Woman, because she was taken out of Man.'

> Therefore a man leaves his father and his mother and cleaves
> to his wife, and they become one flesh. And the man and his
> wife were both naked, and were not ashamed. (Gn. 2:18–25)

Adam's problem was that he was alone. Both he and God
saw this as a problem. Note his reaction when God brought
one fit for him. He did not say, 'At last, someone to be my
servant!' He did not even say. 'Here is a woman!' What he
said was, 'She is like me!' 'This at last is bone of my bones,
flesh of my flesh!' The fact that the woman is the helper fit
for the man does not mean she was specially made to provide
the kind of help that he needed, in the way a brick layer might
need a hod carrier or a carpenter an unskilled assistant. If
Adam needed this kind of help, God would have given him
a horse or a tractor. However, the biblical meaning of a helper
fit or 'meet' for man is one who corresponds to him as a whole
person, not just to the requirements of his work. The woman
was appropriate for man, at his level, he could talk to her.
The goal of the relationship was not greater efficiency, but
primarily companionship. Matthew Henry wrote,

> The woman was made of a rib out of the side of Adam; not
> made out of his head to rule over him, nor out of his feet to be
> trampled upon by him, but out of his side to be equal with him,
> under his arm to be protected, and near his heart to be
> beloved.[5]

God then appointed a pattern for marriage. The man and
woman were to form a new family unit by leaving their
parents' home and living together under one roof. Their
relationship is no longer to be one of dependence on their
parents. They are to cleave to each other. This literally
means to stick to or to adhere to each other, pointing to the
commitment that marriage involves. The husband and wife
are also to become one flesh. They are joined sexually not

only for the purpose of producing children, but also to enjoy their sexuality as an expression of their union. Their bodies become in a unique sense the property of their partner (1 Cor. 7:4–5). Adam and Eve were naked and unashamed. This suggests not only a lack of shame at being physically naked, but also that they were able to stand before each other without pretense or disguise, without either trying to impress or hide. Each knew and accepted the other as they were.

By God's grace, marriages on our side of the Fall can still realistically aspire to both a close relationship with God and a high level of openness with each other. Marriage can be a real companionship where a couple enjoys sharing their diversity.

In a debate with the Pharisees, Jesus referred back to the second chapter of Genesis and expanded on it. He said:

> 'For this reason a man shall leave his father and mother and be joined to his wife, and the two shall become one.' So they are no longer two but one. What therefore God has joined together, let no man put asunder. (Mt. 19:5–6)

Jesus pointed to a union formed by God in human marriage that somehow transcends the decision the couple have made themselves. One can decide to get married, but according to Jesus, to decide to end a marriage is prying apart what God put together. One of the distinctive aspects of Christian marriage is that the marriage bond is indissoluble until the death of one of the partners. Any breaking of the bond before that time involves sin. The only conditions that seem to be sanctioned in the New Testament are for adultery and desertion. Marriage is a commitment to not back out no matter how difficult the marriage becomes. One cannot promise to never *want* to back out, but one can promise to stay in through thick and thin.

The bond that God makes in marriage cannot be photo-graphed, weighed, or measured. It is not a bond that reduces one to the other. The husband does not become the boy-servant for the wife nor does the wife become the cook, child-minder, and general slave for the husband. Individuality is not lost but is strengthened. The bond of marriage is like the bond that exists between the risen Christ and his people. It is a spiritual bond which is a mystery to us, but which points to the relationship between Christ and his people (Eph. 5:32).

God's commitment to marriage extends beyond creating it. He has also given us a way of life within the institution he made. His form of marriage allows great freedom. Elaborate rules, roles, and job descriptions for husband and wife are conspicuously absent from the New Testament itself. The Bible says nothing of who should earn the most money, cook the most meals, balance the checkbook, or change the most diapers. The form that God has given is flexible enough for Christians in many different times and cultures to be imaginative in the way they build their relationships.

The most complete picture of the shape of the marriage relationship is given in Paul's letter to the Ephesians. In the context of telling Christians to be filled with the Spirit, he tells them also to 'Be subject to one another out of reverence for Christ' (Eph. 5:21). This command of willing mutual submission is a general command to all Christians, not just those who are married. The emphasis on mutuality in Ephesians 5 complements the even longer passage on marriage found in 1 Corinthians 7. There he speaks of the husband and wife having mutual authority over each others' bodies (vv. 3–5), the same principles for husband and wife governing separation and divorce (vv. 10–16), and the identical responsibility to make vocational sacrifice for the sake of the other partner in the marriage (vv. 32–5). But having asserted the mutuality of the relationship, Paul then addresses the husband and wife separately, saying what subjection is to mean for each of them. He writes to wives first.

> Wives, be subject to your husbands, as to the Lord. For the husband is the head of the wife as Christ is the head of the church, his body, and is himself its Savior. As the church is subject to Christ, so let wives also be subject in everything to their husbands. Husbands, love your wives, as Christ loved the church and gave himself up for her, that he might sanctify her, having cleansed her by the washing of water with the word, that he might present the church to himself in splendor, without spot or wrinkle or any such thing, that she might be holy and without blemish. (Eph. 5:22–7)

The wife's submission is to her husband's servant leadership. Her submission is as a whole person, so there is no area of her life that is kept separate from that commitment. She is to submit 'in everything' just as the church is subject in everything to Christ as its head. So also the husband is to submit himself to his wife by loving her as Christ loved the church, giving up even his life for her that she might grow in holiness and excellence, or literally, that she would be made glorious. Paul is thinking less of the unlikely need for a husband to risk his life to protect his wife from an armed intruder than of the more likely sacrifice of his time, plans and even career for her good.

What does this look like as a relationship, when you put the two people together? Christians have differed considerably over this point, especially when it comes to the resolution of the conflicts between husband and wife.

We must not think that the submission is completely unqualified for either wife or husband. In the early days of the church, Sapphira was rebuked by God and struck dead for *not* disobeying her husband when the two of them had participated in a lie to the church (Acts 5:1–11). Similarly, the husband is not required to lay down his life for every whim or wrongdoing of his wife.

How are decisions made? One way could be called the 'chain of command' model in which the husband as head is seen as the maker of plans and giver of orders. This seems to take very little account of the mutual submission that characterizes Paul's concern. Jesus taught that we were not meant to 'lord it over' anyone (Mk. 10:42–5), how much less our wives?

Some have reacted against the authoritarian character of this chain of command idea and conceived of mutuality as a fifty-fifty relationship in which husband and wife take turns in, or do half of, everything. 'It's my turn to make the decision this time' or, 'It's your turn to do the dishes, I did it last time'. This sort of bargaining gets too preoccupied with each person's rights to accurately reflect the mutually self-giving character of the marriage commitment.

Another model is that the husband and wife should make decisions together, but when there is disagreement, the husband has the tie-breaking vote. The wife submits to his final decision, except when this would involve her in moral compromise. This comes closer to Paul's intention, if it is well understood and agreed on ahead of time.

The problem is that the apostle Paul does not actually give us a prescribed technique of conflict resolution in this passage – however badly we might want one. What he does give us is what our attitude must be, what the shape of our character looks like, and what sort of commitment we are making to each other. What makes a marriage pleasing to God? Humility, love and mutual submission. The husband has a servant leadership role and his commitment is to his wife's glory, but Paul refrains from spelling out exactly what that will mean when they disagree.

With humility, love and mutual submission, different styles of decision making can honor God and build the marriage. Without these qualities, no technique of decision making will be able to redeem the marriage. For certain, there will not be one partner who will always have the final say.

Some may say, 'But this is too idealistic, we are living in a fallen world, and we need a clear-cut strategy to be followed without equivocation.' Actually, it is the other way around. Because we are living in such a broken world, no fixed procedure can be trusted. Fixed strategies are too rigid and are too easily abused. They often do the opposite of what God intends. They are especially dangerous when we put our confidence in them instead of in the things that Paul points to as central – humility, love and mutual submission.

The husband and wife are servants of one another. She vows to follow the leadership of one who has committed himself to lay down his life for her welfare. He vows to love unconditionally one who has committed herself to follow him. Do you see the strength in this relationship? As two Christians look to God for help and direction, their marriage can weather any storm. At the core is the willingness to serve each other.

Mutual submission is mutual service. Service is not unique to the marriage relationship, it is at the center of the whole Christian life. The fifth and sixth chapters of Ephesians apply the principle of subjection to everyone – man, woman, child, slave, and master. Jesus spoke into a world where the Jew's main concern was for their own righteousness and the Greek's highest goal was to perfect their own personality. Jesus' words, defining true greatness in terms of humbly serving others (Mk. 10:43–4), were like a bomb-shell landing in the middle of a calm pool of self-centeredness. Mutual service is the foundation of Christian marriage, but is not unique to marriage. It has been the foundation of Christian living all along.

God's commitment to marriage also extends to leading specific individuals to get married and helping to sustain them. God's sovereignty was clear in bringing Isaac and Rebekah together (Gn. 24). His concern for even the details of a marriage festival is seen in Jesus' saving the couple from embarrassment at their wedding reception in Cana of Galilee (Jn. 2:1–11).

Foremost among God's many purposes in marriage is our sanctification and Christian growth. The permanence of the marriage relationship is one of the main factors that makes this growth possible. The apostle Paul puts it in this wide context,

> For this is the will of God, your sanctification: that you abstain from immorality; that each one of you know how to take a wife for himself in holiness and honor. (1 Thess. 4:3–4)

This passage tells us that marriage is part of the process of sanctification. As such it is subject to all the guidelines that apply to the Christian life – including the assurance that the Spirit of God is at work in it.

The problems that marriages encounter are not for the most part qualitatively different from those of any interpersonal relationship. They are more frequent and intense because there is more at stake and emotional involvement is greater. In the vast majority of our relationships we can walk away from problems. It might not be right to walk away, but practically speaking it is often quite easy. We can leave home if we quarrel with parents, quit a job if we cannot get along with a boss, move out on a troublesome roommate. Walking away from people is easy and natural in our transient and fragmented society. By definition however, we cannot walk away from marriage. This is one of the glories of marriage. It is also a tragedy that people do in fact walk away from marriages in difficulty. Parting is

simply not an option. This provides an unparalleled opportunity for trust to grow, a trust that can lead partners to be
naked as whole persons before each other without shame
or rejection.

If we do not entertain the possibility of leaving, we are
much more likely to commit ourselves to working through
problems, however painful it might be. We are also more
likely to see that the most fruitful problems for me to work
on are my own. I may discover that I am simply too proud
to have anyone cut across my will, or that I am unable to
be patient between five and seven o'clock in the evenings. I
may learn that I am too sensitive to myself to love someone
who shows me up or tears me down. By getting married I
might discover that what I had thought was my strength
and maturity turned out to be only a frail shell easily broken
by someone close enough to expose my childish needs for
constant approval. If we are to stay in the marriage, we must
painfully confront these things. It is surely far easier to lay
the blame on our incorrigible partner or on our mutual
incompatibility. However, if we stay, we have a God-given
environment to face personal problems that we would be
unlikely to face otherwise.

Look also at the other side: that I can be sure that my
partner will not abandon *me*. This assurance can give us the
courage to tackle problems that would otherwise have been
too risky. You do not have to always be on your guard.
There is a security and safety, an ability to relax together,
that God intends for us and which is available nowhere else.

Marriage is made to accommodate trouble. Just as a
seaworthy ship is made to ride heavy seas, so a sound
marriage will survive many failures on both sides. This
should not come as a surprise to Christians, but it does. The
conviction that a marriage must be perfect makes that
marriage a frail craft indeed, unable to sail on any of the
seas of this earth. Edith Schaeffer writes,

The deep underlying sense of the importance of family continuity must be stronger than the insistence on having perfection.
People throw away what they could have, by insisting on
perfection which they cannot have, and looking for it where
they will never find it.[6]

If we believe this we will put far more trust in the means of
achieving reconciliation – confession, forgiveness, and
reproof – than we will in the probability of perfection.

## Problems of Identity within Marriage

Popular opinion about marriage tends to polarize: some say
that marriage is everything, others that it is nothing. Both
are wrong. Those who say marriage is everything feel
(though they would not often say it) that not getting married
amounts to a deep personal failure. Christians in their
commendable enthusiasm for marriage sometimes unwit-
tingly spread this idea. They seem not to realize that it
contradicts the apostle Paul's extremely positive view of the
single life as a way to serve God more undividedly (1 Cor.
7:32–5). The opposite view is that marriage in its Christian
form is a curse. Some radical psychiatrists[7] and social critics,
joined by many who have had bitter personal experiences
of marriage, point to all the destructive possibilities that
marriage holds. The first pole leads people to naively see
marriage as the thing that will automatically resolve their
problems of identity. The second pole would discourage
many from the kind of fulfillment and growth that is open
to them through it.

Out of this vast discussion I will touch on only one thing
– the danger of drawing your sense of identity from your
marriage partner. The problem is not in having a sense of
identity as a family, but rather in having your sense of

identity rest in your family or in a member of it. Identity as a family is helpful and good because it enables each member to sense a shared experience and tradition. What is unhelpful is drawing one's identity from the supposed strength of one's partner. This is unintentional exploitation in the name of love.

This is a particular problem for those with a weak sense of identity. Erik Erikson uses the phrase 'identity hungry' to refer to those who would bend every relationship to undergird their sagging sense of self. A partner in a marriage can be the object of this kind of dependency. If I find my identity in my wife, it does not mean that our personalities necessarily complement each other. Instead, it means that I draw my sense of being a full person from her and I live my life largely through hers. Although I cannot stand up by myself, her confidence makes up for my insecurity and fear. It means that I do not see her as a separate person in her own right with needs, problems, hopes, and fears, but only as the fulfillment of my own needs. I am identity-dependent on her. The boundary between us becomes blurred and I begin to relate to her as a necessary but sometimes absent part of myself. For me, she is an escape from myself. For her, I place more dependence on her than she is able to bear.

Each of us has within us a self that wants to be a mouse and another that wants to be a Napoleon. Sometimes one has the upper hand and sometimes the other. If I am depending on my wife to fulfill my needs for security, then I want her to be weak when I want to be strong. She must be submissive like an appreciative and admiring mouse when I feel like being Napoleon. But when I am a mouse, overwhelmed with anxiety and fear of the world, then she of course must be capable and strong, undaunted, and fearless. Her role is to approve, accept or take over when needed. But trouble begins when my wife turns out to be a full-fledged person with her own opinions, will, problems, and needs.

The kind of identity dependence that I have described cannot tolerate disagreement. It releases feelings of betrayal, hatred and accusations of treason. Bitterness is avoided only when a still more unhealthy pattern comes into being. Some have called it 'confluence,' a word taken from the flowing together of two rivers. It is the loss of one's individual identity in the marriage relationship. Partners in confluence placate each other continually. The survival of both is in the other's hands. That need for survival is more important than the truth. Though outside observers might think such a marriage is very solid, the partners are apt to be clinging even more tightly to each other as they become increasingly alienated from the world around them.

A far more common result of identity-dependence is bitterness and disillusionment. Dr. Jack Dominion writes, 'The failure to achieve a minimum of emotional independence is one of the main causes of marital breakdown.'[8] Notice the vicious circle which starts so easily if, for example, the wife is identity-dependent on the husband. Perhaps she feels great anxiety if her husband is not physically present with her. She pleads with him to come home immediately after work and spend all his free time with her. He understandably feels trapped by this arrangement and looks for more excuses to work overtime and to do things that have to be done without her. She becomes angry and, when he does come home, tells him their marriage 'means nothing!' This of course increases his incentive to spend time away from home. Often the disintegration of the marriage is accelerated if one of the partners is still emotionally dependent on his or her parents. The parents then provide an inexhaustible supply of ammunition to be used by their child against his or her spouse. If a baby is born 'to keep us together,' the marriage may head for deeper trouble as yet another person makes heavy emotional demands on the parents.

The identity-dependent partner looks weak, but he or she really wants a master–servant relationship. I want my partner to serve my emotional needs whatever they might be at any given time. I want to be master. My partner needs to be at the beck and call of my insecurity. This is the very opposite of the New Testament picture of marriage. Each partner is to be the other's servant, putting the other's needs before their own in mutual submission.

Overdependence and Christian love are incompatible. Overdependence erodes the commitment that Christian love requires. A commitment of love makes overdependence impossible.

We have seen that overdependence can easily become a vicious spiral of panic, possessiveness, and resentment. Dietrich Bonhoeffer wrote, 'Let him who cannot be alone beware of community.' This applies supremely to marriage as the most demanding kind of community. But Bonhoeffer also warned of the opposite danger, 'Let him who is not in community beware of being alone.'[9] Complete independence and isolation is no answer to the problem of overdependence. It is only giving into the fear of rejection or responsibility. Bonhoeffer pointed to the dual danger involved here,

> Each by itself has profound pitfalls and perils. One who wants fellowship without solitude plunges into the void of words and feelings, and one who seeks solitude without fellowship perishes in the abyss of vanity, self-infatuation and despair.[10]

Let us visualize the alternatives by imagining three couples walking along a road. The first couple walk together leaning on each other. They move only with each other's support, as if they were using each other as crutches. If one falls they both fall and take a long time to get up again. The second couple walks quickly along on opposite sides of the road from each other. They are sometimes abreast of each other and sometimes one ahead of the other. If one falls the other might go back and help, but the other might not have noticed. The third couple walk together, arm in arm. They do not normally lean on each other, but if one trips or falls, the other is instantly ready with the strength and balance to provide support.

The third couple illustrates the only strong relationship. It pictures the commitment of love that Christian marriage entails. There needs to be a certain identity-independence in both partners so that each has the internal strength for commitment. The husband who comes home with an al-most irresistible need to shout out his frustrations at his wife may well need to sit down and listen sympathetically to the frustrations of *her* day. He will not do this if he sees her primarily as one who is supposed to fulfill his own needs and to compensate for his inadequacies. Nor will he do it if he has isolated himself from her without emotional involve-ment. He will only do it if he is committed to her enough to love her as she is, for better for worse, in sickness and in health, for richer for poorer.

A big start in gaining independence in a relationship is just to understand what has been happening. Often a couple is so involved in the relationship from the inside that they have little insight into why things are going wrong. Insight is never enough in itself, but with the determination to fight for a relationship and the confidence in a God who works within us, few of these problems are insurmountable.

## Naivete in the Dating Relationship

In some contexts naivete is enviable and refreshing. But naivete about the central dynamics of family and marriage only brings pain and disillusionment. The high percentage of divorces in the first year of marriage suggests an epidemic of naivete among young people about the nature of the commitment required to make a marriage work. This naivete often shows up in the dating relationship.

The dating and marriage relationships have similarities. Both can be very intimate. Both are exclusive relationships in the sense that a third person cannot have the same kind of relationship with either partner without invading and threatening the relationship. However, the crucial difference is that dating involves intimacy and exclusiveness without the final commitment to the other person. This intimacy is therefore likely to have a certain artificial and temporary quality to it.

For example, two people dating each other are apt to spend a lot of time together. It is often time that has no other purpose than simply to be together. They each get the other's undivided attention. If they get married, the same couple might spend less time together than before marriage. Also, they often do not have each other's undivided attention in the time they do spend together because it is time spent doing other things that need to be done in the course of living. The wife may expect her husband's pre-marriage level of attention to continue and be bitterly disappointed to find that while his time with her decreases radically, the time she spends for him increases as she shoulders all the responsibilities for creating a home. Meanwhile the husband, having gotten married, is ready to move on to other challenges that his career holds. This is the climate that has fueled the women's liberation movement. If frustrations of the early months of marriage are met from the platform of overdependence instead of commitment, then there is bound to be trouble. She will be sacrificed to his career or he will be held to ransom by her demands for time and attention. Both will feel the bitterness of betrayal. The fault was not with the institution of marriage nor in mutual incompatibility, but in their ideas about what marriage actually involved.

Of course no one is so well prepared for marriage that it holds no surprises or hurdles. The kind of problem we have just described needs to be seen not as a disaster, but is a unique opportunity for growth on the part of both partners.

A film once described to me illustrates this well. It was about a man whose marriage had become stale and dull. His plight was epitomized by a daily ritual. Each morning as he would leave for work his wife would ask him to take the garbage out. This task came to represent all the duty-bound drudgery that his marriage had become for him, day after day, year in and year out. He then started an affair with another woman, meeting first in her apartment at odd times to avoid suspicion. The affair became all that his marriage was not. It was exciting. He felt like a man again. He was appreciated, respected, and admired. The dream faded only the morning after he had spent a whole night with her for the first time. As he left for work the next morning the film ends with her words, 'Oh, you wouldn't mind taking the garbage out, would you?'

In marriage there is no way to avoid the drudgery in life or the need for hard, creative work in building the relation-ship. Without it we either postpone our own growing up or abort it permanently. One cannot solve all the problems of marriage before it begins any more than one can learn to swim without getting wet. My plea is to enter marriage with eyes as open as possible to what it will involve.

## Communication as Service

Making a marriage which fosters growth of the identity of both partners depends largely on whether they practice the kind of mutual service that we have already described.

Unless they understand what this mutual service involves, then the communication that goes on in marriage tends to undermine the relationship rather than strengthen it. Even a couple committed to the ideal of servanthood can still get the whole thing exactly backwards if they are primarily aware of how grievously their partner has fallen short of serving them. Your partner is the negligent servant; you are the martyr. Your sense of identity within the marriage can then be tied to this martyr role. Then it is from that platform that you communicate. Words soon become more punitive than reconciling. 'Death and life are in the power of the tongue' (Prov. 18:21).

One couple I know were in grave danger of giving up on their marriage. It had become a battle-ground of exploitation, manipulation, and suspicion largely because this servant role had become reversed. The inner logic that inspired both of their actions was the attitude, 'I counted on getting something good out of this marriage. I am getting only pain, so I will at least make sure that my partner suffers for the failure.' The husband knew that he was not perfect, but in his mind his own imperfections were fully eclipsed by the hard fact that his wife had committed adultery. This offense affected him in two ways. First of all, he felt that the adultery was so serious that it tilted the balance of responsibility for all their marriage problems heavily to her side. In the light of it he could not take seriously anything he might have done to provoke the affair or, for that matter, any of their other difficulties. Second, he became suspicious of her every move. He restricted her life and subjected her to marathon interrogations, 'but *why* did you say that, you must know!' 'Where were you all afternoon? It doesn't take that long to get back from shopping!' He felt that if he didn't look out for number one, nobody else would. His wife's adultery was so heinous that he could never be sure what she might do next. A man must take precautions.

Not surprisingly, his wife saw quite a different picture. In her own mind, her affair was a desperate gasp for breath. It was an assertion of the tiny spark of freedom that she still felt, but that she feared would be snuffed out. It seemed that her only other means of maintaining her freedom was to dismantle his already fragile sense of security by ridiculing him.

They had become two martyrs locked in combat. Each felt the other's failure so overshadowed their own that there was little point in trying to do anything from their own side. The only strategy was for each to try to punish, coerce, and manipulate the other into a change of heart. This proved ineffective in the extreme. Their words were vengeful, ma-licious, and destructive because they had to pass through the grid of their martyr roles. Both had taken the martyr's identity, not the servant's. Suggestions of failure always brought the response, 'Yes, I might have done that, but *you* . . .' and this would be followed by a list of more serious recriminations.

The common verdict on marriages like this is that the partners had grown to be incompatible, or that the pressure of life had exposed an incompatibility that had been there all along. This verdict is suggested in phrases like, 'we have nothing in common any more,' or 'it was a mistake to get married, we were too young.' The word 'incompatibility' used in this way implies that the marriage is irretrievably broken down and that only stubbornness would encourage it to continue. This solution, if you can call it a solution, is far too glib. Paul Tournier wrote,

> So-called emotional incompatibility is a myth invented by jurists short of arguments in order to plead for divorce. It is likewise a common excuse people use in order to hide their own failings. I simply do not believe it exists. There are no

emotional incompatibilities. There are misunderstandings and mistakes, however, which can be corrected where there is the willingness to do so.[11]

A more accurate assessment of a marriage like this is not that the partners have nothing in common, but quite the reverse. They have too much in common – the wrong things. The marriage is in trouble when pride, stubbornness, selfishness, and martyrdom are held in common. When neither partner will admit a mistake and both insist that 'my will be done,' then the kind of bitterness that leads to divorce arises.

There is hope for such marriages. If communication is to bring healing and growth within the marriage, then martyrs must become servants. A first step is to apply the biblical principles of reconciliation in the fifth chapter of this book. As Paul wrote in Romans 14:10–12, God is not as interested in your account of another as he is in your account of yourself. There will be progress in a marriage when one or both partners are able to see that their own failure to serve the other's needs is the most important thing for them – the failure they can do something about. This is no minor adjustment in a relationship. It is a reversal of one's sense of identity within the marriage to shift from a martyr to a servant role – a radical shift that demands courage, humility, and willingness to take risks.

Very often a third person is helpful in the role of a mediator to point the way to individual healing and to reconciliation within the marriage. Paul found this in trying to reconcile two of his friends in the Philippian church while he was miles away. He wrote,

I entreat Euodia and I entreat Syntyche to agree in the Lord. And I ask you also, true yokefellow, help these women. (Phil. 4:2–3)

To help heal this relationship, Paul appealed not only to the two women themselves, but to another, called 'true yoke-fellow' to help unravel their disagreement. This is not an admission of defeat, but rather a very wise and practical step to take. A mediator who will not just choose sides can help both to see the way to reconciliation, or at least the first few steps toward positive communication.

## Dynamics of Love

Love is a free giving of one's self for the good of others without demanding a return for ourselves. The life and death of Jesus Christ serve as a paradigm for love, and he promised to enable his followers to love in the same way. Love is not just a warm or good feeling. Love has a definite meaning and content.

The New Testament talks about love expressed in three ways – feeling, commitment, and action. They are not strictly separable since the fullness of love is a circle made up of all three. Neither is more basic than the others. All three are necessary for the fullness of Christian love. Let me give you some examples in which these aspects are prominent.

Love is a feeling. In his description of the conversation between Jesus and the rich young ruler, Mark says that 'Jesus looking on him loved him' (Mk. 10:21). Though the other aspects of love are not excluded, the main force seems to be that Jesus felt affection for the man.

Love is commitment. In the second great commandment, Jesus said, 'You shall love your neighbor as yourself' (Mt. 22:39). People tend to have a firm commitment to their own welfare. Do we not all jump back on the sidewalk when a fast car passes too close to the curb? Jesus says we are to have this same commitment to the welfare of our neighbor.

Another instance of love as commitment is, 'they loved not their lives unto death' (Rev. 12:11). This means that they were finally not committed to their own lives as much as to God for whom they gave them up.

Love is action. The most common expression of love in the New Testament is not of feeling or commitment, but love in action. God's love is an acting love. He loves the world, so he gives his son (Jn. 3:16). Our love is to reflect his.

> But if anyone has the world's goods and sees his brother in need, yet closes his heart against him, how does God's love abide in him? Little children, let us not love in word or speech but in deed and in truth. (1 Jn. 3:17–18)

The love is not just expressed in action, but love *is* the action. How else could love be so often commanded (see, Jn. 13:34)?

Christian love in its fullness is love expressed in all three ways. The fullness of love should be the Christian's aim whether in marriage or not, and this fullness of love is commanded by Jesus himself.

How, then, do we obey this command, especially where there is no love or where there is actual enmity? While neither feeling nor commitment nor action is more fundamental than the others, where there is no love we are to start with action. One of the clearest examples is in Luke's gospel.

> But I say to you that hear, love your enemies, do good to those who hate you, bless those who curse you, pray for those who abuse you. To him who strikes you on the cheek, offer the other also; and from him who takes away your cloak do not withhold your coat as well. Give to every one who begs from you; and of him who takes away your goods do not ask them again. And as you wish that men would do to you, do so to them. (Lk. 6:27–31)

Notice that the well-known command to love your enemies does not stand alone. Along with it come a string of commands to take various actions. We are to 'do good,' 'bless,' 'pray,' 'offer the other cheek' and so on. We are to treat the enemy as we would like to be treated. The full circle of love involves feeling, commitment, and action, but the way into this circle is through action. Action alone is not enough, but action is the way to start into love in its wholeness. It takes little imagination to see applications of this principle within marriage. A marriage in trouble usually has hundreds of tiny thoughtful things that have been put off or ignored.

Some object that it is hypocritical to do loving things when you do not feel the love in your heart. There are three answers. First, our honesty is to God. When our feelings do not correspond to God's will, we must often choose between the two. A choice to obey God is not hypocrisy, but a choice for a higher honesty of the sort that we discussed in the fifth chapter. Second, loving action must follow reconciliation. It does not replace confession or forgiveness where they are needed. It would be ludicrous to start doing kind things for someone you have wronged seriously without ever apologizing for the wrong done. Third, love in action to one's enemies is only a first step into the full circle of love. God does not want it to stop there, but wants us to love fully with the widest scope of the love of Jesus Christ.

Marriage is a true and wonderful gift of God when we approach it the way he has told us to. There are many other areas where our sense of identity affects our marriage and vice versa. I have only given a glimpse of biblical teaching on a very few of these areas in the hope that our marriages might, as they were intended, provide windows through which one can see something of the future kingdom of God.

## Children

A theme that we have developed throughout this book is that people tend to rest much of their security, purpose in life, their very identity on something or someone that is ultimately unable to bear that burden. We have seen how this is true of the identity-dependence of one marriage partner on the other. Another is the parent who is identity-dependent on the child. The child's identity develops naturally in early years around the parents'. Here we will focus on the other side – the way parents invest their sense of identity in their child and their child's future.

The principle of an investment in business is very simple. You put your money in a venture, accept some risk, and hope to get it back later with a return. While this investment principle is a necessary function of capitalism, it brings disaster in politics of the family. Take an example:

A sullen and disheveled boy sits in the corner of a police station after being arrested for stealing. In bursts his father with an air of terminal exasperation. With hands in the air he bellows, 'Now look at what you've done to us! After all we've done for you! You'll never know how much you've hurt your mother!' (A policeman who heard me use this example in a lecture said this kind of confrontation was so much the rule that he was shocked when a parent behaved differently.)

What has gone wrong? The father's response seems natural enough. He and his wife have spent thousands of dollars, hours of worry, endless sleepless nights, and years of hard work for their son. They have done it because they love him and want to be good parents. What do they get in return? A kick in the teeth like this! Public disgrace!

But what has the father's attitude toward his son been over the years? What is his main concern? He has made an investment of himself in his son and this investment has turned sour. He had expected to get something in return for his sacrifice. From the cradle to successful adult life his son was meant to be a credit to him. He gave his son opportunities he never had to become the success that he never was. The father's hurt was so great that there was no thought to his son's pain, his anger, guilt, fear, and shame. The father ignored all this in the blow to his own sense of identity.

It is important to realize that the father is more than disappointed. The father's own sense of psychological safety was undermined. He sees the situation as something that had happened primarily 'to us,' meaning to him and his wife. In the struggle of caring, loving, suffering, and hoping over the years it is easy for parents to let their own identity get wrapped up in their child in a way that is destructive. Their value as people begins to depend on the success of their child. The child must compensate for the parents' failure (or else maintain the parents' tradition of success) in order to sustain the parents' positive picture of themselves. Having outstanding children is one of the sol-idest currencies of competitive success in modern America. Parents can push children into whatever form of success is meaningful to the parent – usually academic, social, or athletic – to satisfy their needs rather than for the child's growth and enrichment. The parent can be more concerned with the way the child maintains the family image than how the child bears the image of God. Children become debtors through no choice of their own, somehow obligated to give parents the feeling of adequacy.

The parents' identity-dependence is often exposed most clearly when the child does not live up to expectations. A truly caring parent is still able to take the child's own needs seriously. An identity-dependent parent will retaliate out of a sense of betrayal. Those of us who are parents should ask ourselves this question: how do we react when our children misbehave in front of our friends?

We can see the same problem of invested identity in biblical accounts. Rebekah's favorite son was Jacob. He was 'her boy.' To get what she wanted for him she undermined her relationship with her other son, her husband, and God by a string of lies and intrigue by which she set a poor example for Jacob himself (Gn. 27). In the New Testament Matthew records Zebedee's wife, the mother of James and John, coming to Jesus. She knelt down before him and pleaded, 'Command that these two sons of mine may sit, one at your right hand and one at your left, in your kingdom' (Mt. 20:21). She wanted to be able to look at them in their power and glory and say, 'These are my boys, my very own sons!' It is instructive that Jesus did not reply directly to her at all, but to James and John. Their future was finally their business. Both Rebekah and James and John's mother seemed less concerned for the good of their sons than for their own pride in seeing them as celebrities in the kingdom of God.

The most destructive result of an invested identity is that it puts a burden on the child that he or she is too small to bear and too young to comprehend. Children were not given to sustain their parents' sense of the meaning of life. Nor do they understand when they fail and then are treated as if they betrayed the family cause. Such a child soon learns that he is less important than his performance.

Parents who have invested their identity in the child will tend to have a twisted attitude toward discipline. Discipline easily becomes very severe because the parent sees disobedience as a threat to their successful training. Invested identity can also lead to the opposite problem: the child who can do no wrong. So much is at stake in the success of the child that the parents would rather take all the blame on themselves than admit failure of the child. This child is coddled, protected, and endlessly justified in whatever they do. Because they are so much their pride and joy, they are deprived of the discipline they need.

In all cases of invested identity the child is unable to grow up as a person in their own right. Thye are enmeshed in a highly complex psychological web involving unspoken threats, rewards, and punishments, all of which is beyond the child's ability to understand.

## The Child as a Separate Image of God

Modern society abounds with popular wisdom about how to treat children. Everyone – from the great grandmother to the educational psychologist – has an opinion. Methods abound, with promises for sure-fire results. All systems for child rearing, especially the sure-fire ones, have their dangers, but nevertheless one does need some guidelines, some framework or structure of ideas within which one can be flexible. Here again we confront the polarities of Victorianism and Romanticism. We need to take note of them because their ideas affect the way we think about children today.

The classic Victorian approach at its extreme has the parents, especially the father, ruling the home with an iron hand. The child is a nuisance to be made to behave like a little adult at as early an age as possible. The primary role of the parent is to maintain authority and to instill in the child the right sense of discipline and duty.

The Romantic reacted against this. They begin with the assumption that the child is basically good and that the problem is the influences of adult civilization. Outside authority stifles their development and creativity, bringing inhibition, suppression, and repression. The Romantic with some acquaintance with Freud's theories might suggest that parents who discipline their children are acting because of repressed sexual anxiety, frustration, and guilt as well as the unconscious need to exert power. The implication is that there is no need for discipline if parents and teachers have enough love and imagination to provide freedom for children. In their literature one often encounters assertions like, 'parents in nurturing families know that their children are not intentionally bad.'[12] What about parents who are not so sure about this, who have observed their own children being bad on purpose for years? Such parents are made to feel guilty, for obviously they do not have a nurturing family.

The Bible has some very different things to say about children. First of all, every child is the image and likeness of God, created by God to reflect his character and to have dominion over the earth. Thus the child is a gold mine of creative potential, interest, curiosity, love, determination, and humor. But at the same time every child is fallen. Sin is a very real presence. No one ever had to teach a child to be selfish or stubborn. The two sides to human nature – the glory and the shame of humankind – are already visible in childhood. The child is the likeness of God, but a rebel at their own level, in futility throwing themselves into the task of replacing their creator.

God has given us the family as the context within which children grow up. Children are gifts of God to their parents. Parents do not deserve their children, nor are children their parents' property. Parents are responsible for children as stewards under God until they are ready to leave the home. Unlike marriage, which is 'til death us do part,' the special nature of the parent–child relationship is temporary. A child leaves father and mother and starts a new home. It is every parent's responsibility to prepare their child for that time.

This means that children are extremely important people in their own right, whatever they do or do not do, no matter whose expectations they fulfill or dash. Children are not extensions of their parents. God calls Christian parents to treat their children in a way that reflects both their great value and their status under God.

It should not surprise us that parents, following Jesus, are to be servants to their children. Paul's advice and example go together. He wrote to the Corinthians, 'for children ought not to lay up for their parents, but parents for their children. I will most gladly spend and be spent for your souls' (2 Cor. 12:14–15). Paul is speaking here about his spiritual children, but draws a principle from family life. The principle is that parents are to be in a primarily giving role, spending and being spent without looking for returns. Just as the husband who loves his wife ends up being the one to gain, so also the parents who spend and are spent for their children know the joy of this kind of giving. Parents are not to demand satisfaction and retaliate when they do not get it. They are to make a commitment of love to their children but not grow too dependent on them. Dependence leads to the martyr's retreat or retaliation.

Parents suffer with their children, worry for them, work their hearts out for them. When everything goes well they rejoice and are proud. When their hopes are crushed they are disappointed or ashamed. Parents want the best for their children. They want their children to share their world view, values, to get the best education possible, and a few hundred other things which they believe (rightly or wrongly) their children need. This is as it should be. However, the parents must finally be committed to the child – not just to the satisfaction that the child might bring. This is a terribly difficult line to draw. No parent is completely on one side of the line or the other. But we see where the invested line is drawn when a child defies the parents' wishes or values. Most of us have known a daughter who has been thrown out of her home for getting pregnant without being married or for marrying the wrong person. We may have heard about the son who was disowned, whose family even forbade the use of his name in the house because he used drugs.

Parents have a right to enforce their values, and the right kind of discipline is entirely consistent with treating a child lovingly and as an image of God. But they must accept the child at some level despite his or her violation of their values. Children are bound to disappoint their parents. We have all done it to our own parents many times. Children must be allowed to fail without the pressure of knowing that their failure would pronounce failure over their parents' lives as well.

The parenthood of God himself is our highest example. In the parable of the prodigal son, the father allowed his son to leave home without threatening him or rejecting him. Even though the son's expedition wasted a lot of the father's money, and certainly did not improve his reputation in the community, the father welcomed him back with open arms. He was not indifferent to what his son had done, but he received him home because of his love for and commitment to his son in whatever state his son was in. Those of us who are Christians have received this sort of parenthood from God. We are called to reflect it in some poor way to our children.

# EIGHT

# The Problem of Living With Myself

## (The View of Self in Romans 7)

*To know oneself is above all, to know what one lacks. It is
to measure oneself against Truth, and not the other way
around.*[1] (Flannery O'Connor)

*But thou wilt sinne and grief destroy;*
*That so the broken bones may joy,*
*And tune together in a well-set song,*
  *Full of his praises,*
    *Who dead men raises.*
*Fractures well cur'd make us more strong.*[2] (George Herbert)

We have looked at many sides of the question of identity,
trying to determine some of the dynamics at work in our
own personalities as we struggle along in this world. If we
are to clarify questions of our relationship to ourselves, we
are pushed by our own honesty to deal with larger
questions, beyond the limits of psychology.

Two aspects of our sense of identity are intertwined –
self-acceptance and internal continuity. The absence of self-
acceptance involves conscious self-hatred or else living unconsciously as one's own enemy. The absence of internal

continuity means confusion and insecurity about who we are. For the Christian, both sides of our identity are bound up in the dynamics of our relationship with God. In this last chapter, we will consider the example of Paul as he confronts both of these dangers in the strength of Christ. One of the most psychologically profound of the autobiographical passages in Paul's letters is the seventh chapter of his letter to the Romans. In it, he dealt with his own stance before the law of God and how this affected his picture of himself. We find Paul, with deep honesty, writing about Paul at his worst.

Paul wrote of not being able to understand his own actions, of a civil war raging within him, of being a wretched man, unable to carry out good intentions or prevent the actualization of bad ones.

[14]We know that the law is spiritual; but I am carnal, sold under sin. [15]I do not understand my own actions. For I do not do what I want, but I do the very thing I hate. [16]Now if I do what I do not want, I agree that the law is good. [17]So then it is no longer I that do it, but sin which dwells in me. [18]For I know that nothing good dwells within me, that is, in my flesh. I can will what is right, but I cannot do it.

[19]For I do not do the good I want, but the evil I do not want is what I do. [20]Now if I do what I do not want, it is no longer I that do it, but sin which dwells within me.

[21]So I find it to be a law that when I want to do right, evil lies close at hand. [22]For I delight in the law of God, in my inmost self, [23]but I see in my members another law at war with the law of my mind and making me captive to the law of sin which dwells in my members. [24]Wretched man that I am! Who will deliver me from this body of death?

[25]Thanks be to God through Jesus Christ our Lord! So then, I of myself serve the law of God with my mind, but with my flesh I serve the law of sin. (Rom. 7:14–25)

This negative self-evaluation has puzzled many Christians. How could Paul, who has just written Romans 6 and was about to write Romans 8, possibly describe himself in such despondent terms? Where is his sense of victory over the power of sin? Trying to account for this, some have suggested that Paul is describing here his pre-Christian days up to and including his conversion. However, the passage does not fit neatly into the Paul we see either before or after his conversion. He seems to have too much of a sense of defeat to be a believer, yet too clear a conviction of his own sin and God's perfection to be a non-believer.

There are, in fact, excellent reasons for seeing Romans 7 as a part of Paul's Christian experience – not necessarily his constant experience, but as the account of a mature Christian having an honest and painful look at his own failures. I see six reasons for this interpretation.

First, the passage contains an important change of verb tense. Verses 7–13 clearly do deal with Paul's initial conviction of sin and of the attitudes in and around the time of his conversion. These verbs are in the aorist tense in the Greek, denoting completed action. With the passage in question, starting at verse 14, the tense shifts to the present and continues this way until the end of the chapter. This strongly implies that Paul was referring to a continuing experience contemporary to the time of his writing.

Second, the situation changes from verses 9 and 10 to verse 14 and after. In the earlier verses, he is 'dead under the law'; after verse 14, he is alive and fighting, refusing to admit defeat because he knows that his side will eventually triumph.

Third, Paul's delight in the law of God, combined with the acute sense of his own sin, does not match the picture we have of Paul the Pharisee, breathing threats and murder against the disciples of the Lord and coolly holding the coats of the men who stoned Stephen. Before his conversion, Paul appeared determined and self-righteous, ignoring his own conscience. The man who wrote verse 14 and following was one whose conscience had laid him bare and left him without defenses.

Fourth, if verses 14–23 refer to Paul's pre-Christian days, then verses 24–5a must refer to his conversion: 'Wretched man that I am! Who will deliver me from this body of death? Thanks be to Jesus Christ our Lord!' But this would be a crassly dramatic re-living of his conversion, a theatrical touch quite out of character with the apostle's other writing.

The fifth reason why verses 23–5a do not seem to refer to Paul's conversion is that after saying, 'Thanks be to God through Jesus Christ our Lord!' he immediately returns, in verse 25b, to the very conflict that had dominated the earlier verses. On the other view, he was meant to have turned his back on this conflict forever. But he says, 'I, of myself, serve the law of God with my mind, but with my flesh, I serve the law of sin.' This shows that there was no dramatic trans- formation to a new attitude, but that his conflict was a part of his Christian experience.

Sixth, and finally, Paul's self-description matches the experience that countless Christians have known as Chris- tians. Unfortunately, the Christian is not immune to feelings of defeat, confusion, and internal conflict. These feelings are not constant, nor are they to be sought after, but they are often a part of Christian experience.

Assuming that Paul was writing as a Christian in Romans 7:14ff, let us examine the conflict that he describes. One senses a real anguish in Paul's mind as he evaluates his own inability to put his intentions into practice. He is confused about himself (v. 15); he does not understand his own actions. He does not do the good he intends. It seems he *cannot* do the good that he intends. But the problem is worse: he does the *opposite* of his good intentions, the very things that he hates. The fault does not lie in the law of God because God's law is spiritual and good (vv. 14, 16). Both he and the law of God agree that Paul's *actions* are the problem.

We must not miss the importance of what Paul wrote. He was one of the great moral teachers of all time, but here described the impotence of moral intentions. What a contrast to Socrates, who believed that 'to know the good is to do the good.' Paul saw that there was no automatic correspondence between knowing what is right and doing it. He arrived at the humiliating conclusion that 'the evil I do not want is what I do' (v. 19). Good intentions are necessary and commendable, but, being sinners, we know our intentions are not enough. Paul wrote, 'So I find it to be a law that when I want to do right, evil lies close at hand' (v. 21). Evil is right beside us, even when we intend to do right. Paul found this to be so predictable that he called it a law in the same sense that we would speak of the law of gravity.

We can see the truth of Paul's observation if we look carefully at what happens when we try to put Christian principles into practice. One of the places we can most clearly see the law of evil in operation is in the way we use our tongues. It is easy to say 'Well, I am not going to say that – it would only be gossip and unkind.' Then, before you know what has happened, you have either let the gossip slip out or managed to get the same information across indirectly. This is why New Year's resolutions are an international joke. Few can take them seriously because the truth of Paul's conclusions is widespread in human experience. Despite our good intentions and our will power, there is a power of sin at work within us that drags us down.

The conflict then is between Paul's good intentions and the law of God on one side, and Paul's behavior on the other. Who is winning this struggle, or is it a stalemate? Paul deals with this question in verses 17, 20, 22, and 25. His argument is that since we reject our own behavior and God rejects it too, there must be an alien force working in us, against us and against God. In verse 17, he says that it is 'no longer I that do it,' and this idea is repeated in verse 20. The implication is that once Paul did stand with the force of evil but now he no longer stands there. He now stands on the side of God, over and against his own actions which are affected by the unwelcome law of sin. There is a self that looks disapprovingly at his behavior, that fully admits sin, but that somehow distances itself from it. This seems a strange way of talking. What or who is this self? Paul uses several different terms to describe it. His 'inmost self' delights in the Lord (v. 22). Then again he says, 'I, of myself, serve the law of God with my mind' (v. 25). Paul's love of God and his law is not just one of many conflicting voices within Paul. It is at the core of his selfhood – despite his uncooperative behavior.

Paul contrasts this inmost self to what he saw in his 'members' where he saw another law 'at war with the law of my mind and making me captive to the law of sin which dwells in my members' (v. 22). This is similar terminology to what he used in chapter six of Romans. There he enjoined us not to yield our members to sin, but to 'yield ourselves and our members to God.' It seems that the Christian no longer has the option of yielding him or herself to sin because he or she belongs to God. The Christian can, however, yield his or her members to the cause of sin. The 'members' are our gifts, powers, abilities, and feelings. Despite a Christian commitment, we can present these to evil and destruction. The inmost self is with God, but one's actions can work against him. This distinction is also sug- gested in Paul's prayer beginning in Ephesians 3:14 where he asked that the Christians would be 'strengthened with might through his Spirit in the inner man' (v. 16). It is beyond the scope of this book to consider what these ideas mean in the market place of twentieth-century theories of personality. We must, however, be prepared to take Paul's teaching seriously. There is an 'inner person' where the Spirit of God is at work and which is in some way the seat of the Christian's intention to love and serve God.

There is profound encouragement in this teaching. When we are experiencing the kind of frustration with ourselves that Paul describes, we can better resist the temptation to discredit everything that God has done in us. God's work is not simply a thin veneer over our own deeper selfishness and pride even though when we are discouraged, it seems this way to us. This is Satan's analysis of Job, an analysis which proved spectacularly wrong.

The book of Job is the account of the struggle over who understood Job – God or Satan. God had said that Job was his servant. Satan countered that Job's faith was based merely on all the good things that God had given him – 'Does Job serve God for nought?' (Job 1:9). He suggested that if all of Job's possessions were taken away, Job would show his true colors by cursing God. Satan claimed that the inmost Job was filled with greed, pride, and self-interest. His relationship to God was only a superficial, external thing resting on God's payoffs. This kind of self-analysis can seem very plausible to us when we are discouraged. It might have even seemed plausible to Job had he heard it. But Job showed he was willing finally to serve God for nought, to even serve him without the answer to his questions about evil and justice in the world. He maintained his basic trust in God in such a way that God himself said in the final chapter that Job was 'my servant Job.' Despite Job's doubts, struggles, suffering, and anger, God's work was certainly in the depth of who Job was. It weathered the removal of almost everything Job had – even his health and many members of his family. His faith was not just on the surface of his consciousness, but in his inner self. His allegiance to God outweighed his attachment to his possessions, his position in society, and even the death of his children.

Satan's argument in the book of Job strangely parallels that of some modern psychological theories. These theories of psychology see humankind's basic self as understood best from the perspective of our animal origin. What is most real and basic in us is something we share with animals. These are the drives for survival, sex, hunger, power, territory, aggression, the seeking of pleasure, and the avoiding of pain. The places where we differ from animals are relatively superficial by comparison – a thin veneer produced by civilization. Therefore the distinctively human qualities such as the concern for morality, justice, religion, aesthetics, creativity, love, and purpose can be seen as a thin gloss over the life of the naked ape – caused only by the accumulated accident of human culture.

As a consequence of these theories, much of psychology is particularly ill-equipped to help in understanding the most distinctively human attributes and problems.

Christians who are influenced by these views may be blinded to the wonderfully encouraging message of Paul. When they see in themselves what Paul saw in himself, many Christians are tempted to say, 'I give up.' 'I've tried Christianity and it didn't work for me.' But this is not true of the Christian, no matter how disgusted we are with ourselves. It is not true that it 'did not work.' Paul faced the worst in himself, did not flinch from it and yet was not destroyed by it. Sin wages war in our members, but we must not identify our inmost self with our worst thoughts and feelings. In some strange way, it is no longer 'I' as a fully integrated person who does these things, said Paul, but a law in me alien to my new nature in Christ. In my inmost self I stand against it.

Is Paul avoiding responsibility for his own sin? After all, it is his sin and not anyone else's. Was he being like a child who says, 'I didn't hit you, it was my hand'? I do not think so. Paul accepted full responsibility for his sin – it was still 'me' that does the sin. The 'I' was still the agent of the sin (v. 25). He makes no claim to innocence, nor does he seek to cast blame for the law of sin anywhere else. Yet at the same time, he keeps confidence that God is at work in a radical way within him. He does not give up in self-disgust.

Indeed, Paul's sin bothered him intensely. He wrote 'Wretched man that I am! Who will deliver me from this body of death?' (vv. 24–5). But his response was neither despair nor self-indulgent moral apathy. He was disgusted with himself, called out for deliverance and knew that deliverance had been granted. Paul's cry of gratitude lifts him out of the danger of despair and self-pity. 'Thanks be to God through Jesus Christ our Lord!' (v. 25). He knew where deliverance was coming from. His note of triumph transcends the anguish. He knew that he had been forgiven and accepted by God even though God knew him at his worst. He knew also that the work of God did not stop at that. God was working in him in his inmost self, to change, to transform, and renew him and that God's work was not superficial. Paul was quite appropriately overwhelmed with gratitude.

Believers have had this experience all along. Isaiah, when confronted with a vision of God in the temple, said 'Woe is me, I am undone' (Is. 6–5). He felt disintegrated and un-clean. Perhaps this sort of conviction about oneself is that quality of life that Jesus spoke of when he said that the poor in spirit were blessed and would inherit the kingdom of heaven (Mt. 5:3). Brutal honesty about one's sin and con-sequent confusion and disgust is not alien to Christian experience. It is quite normal and can be the road to humility and wisdom.

It is a great source of encouragement that the apostle Paul himself could experience such disillusionment with himself and still be used in such a monumental way in the kingdom of God. He was not some plastic superstar, but a man with moral integrity before God and a firm trust in his promises. He had learned a self-acceptance that encouraged striving, a peace that bred vitality. Another servant of God voiced these ideas in a slightly different way. John Newton, the slave trader turned abolitionist, put it this way,

> I am not what I ought to be; I am not what I would like to be; I am not what I hope to be. But I am not what I once was; and by the Grace of God, I am what I am.[3]

# Notes

## Introduction

[1] W.H. Auden, 'The Age of Anxiety', *Collected Longer Poems*, Faber and Faber, London, 1974, p. 350.

[2] Alexander Pope, From Epistle II, 'Of the Nature and State of Man With Respect to Himself, as an Individual', *The Norton Anthology of English Literature* 3rd Edition, Ed. M.H. Abrams et al., New York, 1962, p. 2192.

[3] Francis Schaeffer, *Whatever Happened to the Human Race?*, Fleming Revell Company, Old Tappan, New Jersey, 1979, Chapters 4–5.
*The God Who is There*, InterVarsity Press, Downers Grove, Ill., 1968.
Os Guinness, *The Dust of Death*, InterVarsity Press, Downers Grove, Ill., 1973.
C.S. Lewis, *Mere Christianity*, William Collins and Co., Ltd., Glasgow, 1975.

[4] Herman Dooyeweerd, 'The Secularization of Science', unpublished paper translated by Robert Knudsen, p. 4.

## Chapter One
## Identity Under Attack

[1] M. Brewster Smith, *Psychology Today*, Feb. 1976, p. 74.

2   Peter Berger, Brigitte Berger, Hansfried Kellner, *The Homeless Mind*, Penguin Books, Ltd., Harmondsworth, Middlesex, England, 1977, p. 166.

3   Erik Erikson, *Identity*, Faber and Faber, London, 1968, p. 217.

4   Ibid., p. 137.

5   Aleksandr Solzhenitsyn, 'The Listener' BBC, London, March 4, 1976, p. 261.

6   William Kilpatrick, *Identity and Intimacy*, Dell Publishing Co., Inc., New York, 1975, p. 25. This book is a very helpful discussion of the relationship between values and the self.

7   Allen Wheelis, *The Quest for Identity*, W.W. Norton and Co., Inc., New York, 1958, p. 174.

8   James W. Fowler, *The Stages of Faith*, Harper and Row, New York, 1981, p. 277.

9   Ernest Becker, *The Birth and Death of Meaning*, 2nd Edition, Free Press, New York, 1971, p. 33.

10  Ibid.

11  Erik Erikson, op. cit., p. 40.

12  Matthew Arnold, Stanzas from 'Grand Chartreuse' quoted from Robert Langbaum, *The Mysteries of Identity*, University of Chicago Press, Chicago, 1982, p. 52.

13  Erik Erikson, op. cit., p. 220.

14  R.C. Zaehner, *Drugs Mysticism and Make Believe*, Collins, London, 1972, p. 17.

15  Jacob Bronowski, *The Identity of Man*, Penguin Books, Ltd., Harmonds worth, Middlesex, England, 1967, p. 4.

16  Ernest Becker, op. cit., pp. 119–126.

17  Ibid., p. 124.

18  Erik Erikson, op. cit., p. 40.

19  Hans Mol, *Identity and the Sacred*, Basil Blackwell, Oxford, 1976, p. 36.

20  Rollo May, *Psychology and the Human Dilemma*, D. Van Nostrand Co., New York, 1967, p. 4.

21  For a helpful exposition of this thesis, see *The Sorcerer's Apprentice*, by Mary Stewart Van Leeuwen, InterVarsity Press, Downers Grove, Ill., 1982.

22 Ernest Becker, op. cit., p. 126.
23 William Kilpatrick, op. cit., p. 161.
24 *Time Magazine*, June 19, 1978, p. 24.
25 Ibid.
26 Sam Keen, *Voices and Visions*, Harper and Row, New York, 1974, pp. 183–4.
27 For a further development of theme see: Os Guinness, *The Gravedigger File*, InterVarsity Press, Downers Grove, Ill., 1983; Jacques Ellul, *The Technological Society*, Vintage Books, New York, 1964; E.F. Schumaker, *Small is Beautiful*, Harper and Row, New York, 1975.
28 Allen Wheelis, op. cit., p. 87.
29 Merrill Abbey, *Preaching to the Contemporary Mind*, Obingdoz Press, 1963, p. 179.
30 William Irving Thompson, *At the Edge of History*, Harper and Row, New York, 1971, p. 37.
31 Os Guinness, *The Gravedigger File*, InterVarsity Press, Downers Grove, Ill., 1983, pp. 74–5.
32 Peter Berger, *Facing up to Modernity*, Basic Books, Inc., New York, 1977, p. 30.
33 Gail Sheehy, *Passages*, Bantam Books, E.P. Dutton and Co., Inc., New York, 1977, p. 245.
34 Erik Erikson, op. cit., p. 42.
35 Rollo May, op. cit., p. 42.

## Chapter Two
## Identity Lost

1 Ernest Becker, *The Birth and Death of Meaning*, Free Press, New York, 1971, p. 187.
2 Karl Menninger, *Whatever Became of Sin?*, Hawthorne Books, Inc., 1973, p. 135.
3 This argument is developed by Ernest Becker in *Escape from Evil*, Free Press, New York, 1975.
4 H. Richard Niebuhr, *Christ and Culture*, Harper and Row, New York, 1956, p. 154.

5 Quoted from Henry Fairlie, *The Seven Deadly Sins*, University of Notre Dame Press, Notre Dame, Indiana, 1979, pp. 31–2.

6 Quoted from Ernest Becker, *The Denial of Death*, Free Press, New York, 1973, p. 15.

7 Ibid., p. 17

8 Ibid., p. 26.

9 Daniel Boorstin, *The Image*, Atheneum, New York, 1961, pp. 15–16.

10 Elizabeth O'Connor, *Our Many Selves*, Harper and Row, New York, 1971, p. 25.

11 David Belgum, 'Hypocrisy and Mental Health', in O.H. Mowrer, *Morality and Mental Health*, Rand McNally and Co., Chicago, 1967, p. 312.

12 Karl Menninger, op.cit., p. 198.

13 O.H. Mowrer, *The New Group Therapy*, D. Van Nostrand Co., Inc., Princeton, New Jersey, 1964, p. 29.

14 A catalyst for my own thinking about shame and its importance has been *Shame and the Search for Identity*, by Helen Lynd, Harcourt Brace and World, Inc., New York, 1958.

15 James Thurber, 'The Secret Life of Walter Mitty,' in *The Thurber Carnival*, Penguin Books, Ltd., Harmondsworth, Middlesex, England, 1945, p. 71.

16 Jean-Paul Sartre, *Being and Nothingness*, Methuen and Co., Ltd., London, 1976, pp. 259–60.

17 James Taylor, 'Country Road,' in *James Taylor*, Ed. Herbert Wise, Wise Publications, London, New York, 1971, pp. 52ff.

18 William Kilpatrick, *Identity and Intimacy*, Dell Publishing Co., New York, 1975, p. 237.

19 Ibid., pp. 222–3.

# Chapter Three
# Identity Found: A Healed Relationship

1 Ernest Becker, *Escape from Evil*, Free Press, New York, 1975, p. 136.

2  Examples of this would be: Alan Watts, *Beyond Theology*, World Publishing Co., Cleveland and New York, 1964; see also his *The Book*, Collier Books, New York, 1967; Kent and Nichols, *I Amness*, Bobbs-Merrill Co., Inc., Indianapolis, New York, 1972.

3  Helen Lynd, *Shame and the Search for Identity*, Harcourt, Brace and World, Inc., New York, 1958, p. 50.

4  Laura Ingalls Wilder, *Farmer Boy*, Puffin Books, Penguin Books, Ltd., Harmondsworth, Middlesex, England, 1975, pp. 166–7.

5  William Kilpatrick, *Psychological Education*, Thomas Nelson Publishers, Nashville, Camden, New York, 1983. Kilpatrick deals more fully with the question of the authority for self-acceptance in chapter three.

6  Francis Schaeffer, *True Spirituality*, Tyndale House Publishers, Wheaton, Ill., 1983, chapters 8–11, p. 105.

7  George MacDonald, quoted by William Kilpatrick, op. cit., p. 180.

8  See the final chapter of this book for an expanded discussion of the self in Romans 6 and 7.

## Chapter Four
## Identity Found: A Restored Reflection

1  Michael Novak, *Ascent of the Mountain, Fight of the Dove*, Harper and Row, New York, 1978, p. 60.

2  John Fitch, 'On Becoming a Self' unpublished paper, p. 3.

3  Arthur Miller, *The Death of a Salesman*, Viking Press, New York, 1968, p. 126.

4  Gail Sheehy, *Passages*, Bantam Books, E.P. Dutton, and Co., Inc., New York, 1977, pp. 94ff.

5  Bonaro Overstreet, *Understanding Fear in Ourselves and Others*, Perennial Library, Harper and Row, New York, 1971, p. 80.

6  Roberto Assagioli, *The Act of Will*, Wildwood House, London, 1973, pp. 211ff.

7   G. Kittel, *Theological Dictionary of the New Testament*, W.B. Eerdmans Publishing Co., Grand Rapids, Mich., Vol. I, pp. 487–8.

8   Ernest Becker, *Escape from Evil*, Free Press, New York, 1975, p. 164.

9   Rollo May, *Love and Will*, Collins, Fontana Library, 1972, p. 15.

10  A discussion of the question of psychological determinism is found in Stephen Evans, *Preserving the Person*, InterVarsity Press, Downers Grove, Ill., 1977.

11  Macaulay and Barrs, *Being Human*, InterVarsity Press, Downers Grove, Ill., 1978. Chapter four of *Being Human* deals more fully with our active role in the Christian life.

12  G.C. Berkouwer, *Sin*, W.B. Eerdmans Publishing Co., Grand Rapids, Mich., 1971, pp. 249ff.

13  William Kilpatrick, *Psychological Seduction*, Thomas Nelson Publishers, New York, 1983. Kilpatrick deals with the tension between the Christian faith and humanistic psychology on the matter of self-acceptance with some thoroughness.

14  Rollo May shows this to be a widespread pattern in *Love and Will*, p. 32.

15  Newman and Berkowitz, *How to Be Your Own Best Friend*, Random House, New York, 1971, p. 50.

16  William Kilpatrick, op. cit., pp. 56–73.

17  Dietrich Bonhoeffer, *Letters and Papers from Prison*, Macmillan, New York, 1962, p. 221.

## Chapter Five
## Reconciliation: Toward a Higher Honesty

1   Blaise Pascal, *Pensées*, E.P. Dutton and Co., Inc., New York, 1958, #101, p. 33.

2   C.S. Lewis, *Fernseeds and Elephants*, William Collins Sons and Co., Ltd., Glasgow, 1976, pp. 39–43.

3   Jay Adams, *Christian Counselor's Manual*, Presbyterian and Reformed Publishing Co., Philadelphia, 1973, p. 67.

<sup>4</sup> This passage is often taken to teach that it is permissible not to forgive others if they are unrepentant. This is not the force of the passage, since it points to a brazen abuse of confession – worse than no confession at all – and still says to forgive.

Another point arises from our emphasis that our actions are to mirror God's. It is clear from Jesus' teaching that God does not forgive all men and women indiscriminately and irrespective of their response to him. Why then must we forgive the unrepentant when God does not? There is a discontinuity here to be sure, but it is a proper discontinuity for which there is a good reason. God is the ultimate judge. The moral balance of the universe rests with him. We on the other hand are only tiny, dependent creatures who are sinners and are asked to forgive those who, just like us, have fallen short. We are in no position to stand as judges and refuse our personal forgiveness when we have been forgiven so freely. There is a discontinuity between us and God – morally and meta-physically.

Another confusion is over trusting someone again after they have violated that trust. Forgiving is not the same thing as re-trusting. Harm can be done to us and we can forgive it, not holding it against the one who hurt us, and yet we might not trust ourselves to that same person in the same way again until we see evidence of change. A wife who is beaten by her husband may forgive him, but she might also move out to a place where she can have protection until she has reason to hope that he has changed.

<sup>5</sup> C.S. Lewis, op. cit., p. 42.

<sup>6</sup> The commands to forgive in the New Testament focus on the individual. They are not intended to override all enforcement of justice in the public world (Romans 13:4). Pope John Paul II personally forgave Mehmet Ali Agca, who had shot him, but the attempted assassin remained in prison. This seems a proper expression of both principles.

<sup>7</sup> Martyn Lloyd-Jones, *Studies in the Sermon on the Mount*, W.B. Eerdmans Publishing Co., Grand Rapids, Mich., 1967, chapter 16.

<sup>8</sup> Ibid., p. 180.

9 Dietrich Bonhoeffer, *Life Together*, SCM Press, Ltd., London, 1970, p. 83.

## Chapter Six
## Anger

1 Ernest Becker, *The Birth and Death of Meaning*, Free Press, New York, 1971, p. 171.

2 Konrad Lorenz, *On Aggression*, Bantam Books, Harcourt, Brace and World, Inc., New York, 1967, p. 272.

3 Theodore Rubin, *The Angry Book*, Collier Books, New York, 1974, p. 203.

4 Ibid., p. 184.

5 Rollo May, *Man's Search for Himself*, Signet Book, New American Library, Inc., New York, 1967, pp. 128–9.

6 Rollo May, *Power and Innocence*, W.W. Norton and Co., Inc., New York, 1972, p. 23.

7 A recent survey of some of this work is Carol Tavris, *Anger, the Misunderstood Emotion*, Simon and Schuster, New York, 1982.

8 Leonard Berkowitz, *Psychology Today*, July, 1982.

9 This raises a number of controversial questions, among them the church's discipline of its members and parents' discipline of their children. It is confusing to call this discipline 'punishment' in the sense of just retribution for evil done. Neither kind of discipline should be *un*just, but doing justice is not the primary motivation. The primary motivation is training – by providing a deterrent to future sin and a positive incentive to growth in righteousness.

10 Bonaro Overstreet, *Understanding Fear in Ourselves and Others*, Harper and Row, New York, 1971, p. 134.

11 Quoted from Norman Wright, *The Christian Use of Emotional Power*, Fleming H. Revell Co., Old Tappan, New Jersey, 1974, p. 105.

12 This argument is woven into the whole of Rollo May's *Power and Innocence*.

[13] Ibid., p. 167.

[14] Leo Madow, *Anger*, George Allen and Unwin Ltd., London, 1972, pp. 7lff.


# Chapter Seven
# Servants and Martyrs: Identity and the Family

[1] James Hitchcock, *The New Oxford Review*, Sept. 1981, p. 13.

[2] Michael Beldock 'The Therapeutic as Narcissist,' in *Psychological Man*, Ed. by Robert Boyers, Harper and Row, New York, 1975, p. 111.

[3] Peter Berger, quoted in Hans Mol, *Identity and the Sacred*, Basil Blackwell, Oxford, 1976, p. 136.

[4] See chapter one of this volume.

[5] Matthew Henry, *Matthew Henry's Commentary*, Vol. I, Fleming H. Revell Co., New York, p. 20.

[6] Edith Schaeffer, *What is a Family?*, Fleming H. Revell Co., Old Tappan, New Jersey, 1975, p. 32.

[7] R.D. Laing and David Cooper, *The Death of the Family*, Penguin Books, Ltd., Harmondsworth, Middlesex, England, 1971.

[8] Dr. Jack Dominion, *Marital Breakdown*, Penguin Books, Ltd., Harmondsworth, Middlesex, England, 1968, p. 42.

[9] Dietrich Bonhoeffer, *Life Together*, SCM Press, London, 1971, pp. 57, 58.

[10] Ibid.

[11] Paul Tournier, *Marriage Difficulties*, SCM Press, London, 1971, pp. 11–12.

[12] Virginia Satir, *People Making*, Science and Behavior Books, Inc., Palo Alto, Calif., 1970, p. 17.


# Chapter Eight
# The Problem of Living with Myself

[1] Flannery O'Connor, *Mystery and Manners*, Farrar, Straus and Giroux, New York, 1981, p. 35.

2 George Herbert, from 'Repentance,' *The Poems of George Herbert*, text by F.E. Hutchinson, p. 42.

3 John Newton, quoted in *In Search of God*, by David C.K. Watson, Falcon Books, London, 1974, p. 101.

# Index

Acceptance:
  awareness of, 84
  of humankind by God, 82–4,
    88, 90, 98–101, 131
  of salvation, 77, 79. *See also*
  Self-acceptance
Adams, Jay, 151
Alienation:
  and existentialist view of
    humankind, 12–13
  remedy for, 141 and sin,
    36–7, 69, 140
Anger, 171–217
  benefits of, 187–9
  Bible on, 190–91, 196, 199
  causes of, 177–8, 191, 188–9,
    196, 199
  Christian view of, 176
  destructive quality of, 173–4,
    182
  expression of, 180–82
  and forgiveness, 180
  guilt and, 190, 196
  and identity, 215–16
  and isolation of self, 188, 194–5
  in popular psychology, 172,
    191
  and prayer, 185

and revenge, 179, 180
  righteous, 177–82, 198, 217
  unrighteous, 182–90, 192, 207
  violence and, 173–4, 183
*The Angry Book*, 173
Anxiety, 21–2, 25, 187, 197
Arendt, Hannah, 147
Arnold, Matthew, 12
Assagioli, Roberto, 109

Bach, George, 174
Becker, Ernest, 9, 10, 14, 17, 39
Belgum, David, 47
Berger, Peter, 29
Bergman, Ingmar, 67
Berkowitz, Leonard, 175
Bible:
  on anger, 190–91, 197, 199
  in conflict with psychology,
    94–5
  on emotions, 63–64
  and moral values, 5–6
  sense of identity and, 5
Bonhoeffer, Dietrich, 135–6,
  165, 233
Boorstin, Daniel, 39–40
Bronowski, Jacob, 13
Bunuel, Luis, 150

Camus, Albert, 67
Chekhov, Anton, 106
*The Cherry Orchard*, 106
Chessman, Caryl, 188
Children:
    discipline of, 245, 249
    as an image of God, 246–9
    parental investment in, 243–6
Choice, 21, 66, 67, 80, 123
Church, breakdown of, 22
Community, 22
Confession, 140–47, 163, 169,
    210, 214
Conflict:
    and anger, 193
    part of Christian experience,
        253–9
    patterns of coping with,
        139–40
Conformity, 23, 103–9
Coolidge, Calvin, 25
Creativity, 35
*Crime and Punishment*, 52
Cults, 104

Darwin, Charles, 13
Dating relationship, 235
Death, 38, 84
*The Death of a Salesman*, 24,
    104
Dependency in marriage,
    230–34
Descartes, 74–5
'The Discreet Charm of the
    Bourgeoisie,' 150
Disintegration of self, 4–5, 8, 16,
    47–9, 64, 66–7. *See also*
    Integration of Self
Dominion, 5, 7, 35, 60, 63–4,
    69–70, 125–6
Dominion, Dr. Jack, 232

Emotions, 62–5, 66–7, 190
Enlightenment, 14, 15
Erikson, Erik, 5, 11, 29, 231
Existentialism, 13, 17, 56,
    75
Experience, 2

Failure, 94, 103, 252–4. *See also*
    Shame.
Faith, 116–17
    and acceptance of salvation,
        77, 79
    direction of, 89
    and honesty, 98
Fall of humankind, 33, 35–6,
    40–41, 54, 93
Family, 24, 219–23
*Farmer Boy*, 82
Feelings:
    of anger, 178, 183, 195
    emphasis on, 28, 65–7
    of guilt, 42–3
    of love, 240
    place of, 62–3
Feminist movement, 27
Ford, Henry, 25
Forgiveness, 147–9
    and acceptance by God, 81,
        84, 100–101
    and anger, 180
    asking for, 142, 213–14
    certainty of, 80
    as God's solution to
        humankind's
    problem, 80, 147–9
    and imitation of Christ, 112,
        157, 169
    opposed to being excused,
        142, 155
    and resentment, 210–14
Freud, Sigmund, 121

Galileo, 13
Generosity, 113
Gospel:
　meaning of, 77
　psychological implications of,
　　100
Guilt, 41–3, 50
　and anger, 190, 197
　exposure of, 94
　and shame, 50–52, 92–4

Hatred of self. *See* Self-hatred
Henry, Matthew, 222
Heroes, 17–20, 110–20
　loss of, 17–20
Heroism. *See* Heroes
Hesse, Herman, 30
Honesty, 43–50, 94–101, 258
Hope, 85, 94–101
Humanistic Psychology
　movement, 130
Humility, 113–14, 127, 207,
　217
Hypocrisy, 47–8, 160, 242

Identity:
　anger and, 215–17
　attempts to manufacture,
　　23–4
　beyond, 8–11
　Christian growth and,
　　129–33
　crisis of, 2, 26
　cults and, 104
　defined, 1
　Enlightenment and, 15
　Existentialism and, 13, 75
　and the Fall, 35–7, 41, 42–50
　family and, 219
　forgiveness and, 150
　God and, 9–11, 76, 215–16

integrity a path toward, 99
jobs and, 27, 126
loss of, 35–72, 106, 232
loss of love destroys, 71
marriage and, 105–6
models and, 7, 19, 59–60
moral values and, 5–6, 58–9,
　146
negative impact of
　technological society on,
　21
New Romanticism and, 28–9,
　66, 75
New Victorianism and, 24–8,
　75
possessions and, 105–6
as a psychological concept, 8
self-worship and, 131
sense of, 4–8, 15, 22, 36–7,
　104–5, 135, 187, 189,
　231
and sex, 30
and shame, 57–8
sides of, 4–5
source of, 75–6, 126, 219
through other people, 104–5
and transcendence, 8–11, 16
and truth, 74–7, 99
undermined by scrupulosity, 68
Image of self. *See* Self-images;
　Likeness of humankind to
　God
Imitation of Christ, 111–15, 128,
　210, 240
Independence, 108–9, 234
Integration of self, 4, 8, 102–37
　*See also* Disintegration of self
Integrity:
　and honesty, 50, 100
　and internal continuity, 250
　and love, 129

as path to identity, 98–9
and security, 50

James, William, 37

Keen, Sam, 20
Kilpatrick, William, 18, 70, 134

Law of God, 123
Lewis, C.S., 18, 91, 142, 153
Likeness of humankind to God:
  in children, 246–9
  Christian claim regarding, 32
  dominion and, 7, 35, 60–61,
    126
  forgiveness and, 155–7
  growth in, 107–8
  love and, 71
  natural, 34
  and need for identity, 11
Lloyd-Jones, Martyn, 163
*The Lonely Crowd* 23
Lorenz, Konrad, 172
Love, 7
  biblical commandments of,
    131–3
  and commitment, 69–70,
    240–41, 248
  and correction, 165–7
  difficulty of, 209
  disintegration of, 69–72
  of enemies, 181, 242
  humility and, 127
  and the imitation of Christ,
    112, 210, 240
  recovery of, 126–9
  of self, 129–33
Lynd, Helen, 81

MacDonald, George, 97
MacLaine, Shirley, 38–9

*A Man for All Seasons*, 6
Margolis, Susan, 19
Marriage, 105, 221–334
May, Rollo, 16, 30, 121, 174–5,
  189
McLuhan, Marshall, 92
Menninger, Karl, 48
Mercy, 77–8, 88
Miller, Arthur, 26, 104
Models, 7, 17–20, 23, 50–60,
  69, 81, 107–9, 110, 126.
  *See also*
  Heroes
Mol, Hans, 15
Moral values:
  forgiveness and, 80
  God the basis of, 11
  guilt and, 41–3, 69
  honesty, 43–50
  sense of identity and, 5–6, 58,
    146
More, Thomas, 6
Mowrer, O.H., 48

*Narziss and Goldmund*, 30
New Romanticism, 28–31, 65,
  75, 246–7
New Victorianism, 24–8, 30, 75,
  246
Newton, John, 259
Niebuhr, H.R., 36

Obedience, 123–6
O'Connor, Elizabeth, 46
Overstreet, Bonaro, 108–9,
  186–7

Parents. *See* Children
Paul, Apostle, 251–5
Peace, 1, 4, 168
Perls, Fritz, 174

Personality:
  disintegration of, 47–9
  self-awareness and, 34–5. *See
    also* Self
*The Pilgrim's Progress*, 20
*Playboy* magazine, 30
Pride, 145, 206, 211, 229
Psychology:
  and mechanistic view of
    humankind, 14
  reductionism in, 16
  and Romanticism, 30–31
  salvation by, 131
  and tension with biblical
    thought, 99
  and theories of the self,
    257
  treatment of anger in,
    172–6

Rebuke, 159–68
Reconciliation:
  and anger, 185
  challenge of, 168–70
  components of, 139
  confession and, 142–5,
    213
  forgiveness and, 146–7,
    156–7
  in marriage, 239, 242
  and peace, 168
  role of rebuke in, 159
Redemption, 77–9, 84. *See also*
  Salvation
Relationships:
  and anger, 193–4, 216–17
  dating, 234–6
  to God, 11, 37, 40, 135,
    251
  of husband and wife, 222,
    224–7, 233

'identity-hunger' and, 5, 11,
    231
  and reconciliation, 138, 210,
    213
  and sin, 37, 153
  and transcendence, 8
Repentance, 97, 98–9
Resentment, 180, 196, 207–15
Rights, 208–9
Roles:
  martyr, 238, 239
  mediator, 239
  personal relationships and,
    4
  servant, 239
  sex, 55
Rubin, Theodore, 173
Russell, Bertrand, 6, 36

Salvation, 80, 84, 88, 147–8
Sartre, Jean-Paul, 36, 56, 99
Schaeffer, Francis, 92
Science, 12–14
Scrupulosity, 68
'The Secret Life of Walter Mitty,'
    53–4
Self:
  anger and, 186–9
  denial of, 128
  emotions and, 62–4
  hatred of, 5, 68, 93, 250
  and independence, 108–9
  inmost, 255–8
  loss of, 6
  love of, 130–33
  and love of God, 255
  in marriage, 230–32
  and material world view,
    12–15
  and 'members,' 255, 257
  nature of, 74–76

parents and the sense of, 108
sin and, 255, 257
transcendence and, 9
Self-acceptance:
Christian, 84–5
and God, 11, 84–5, 97, 100
and repentance, 96–7, 100
rests on honesty, 99, 100
and self-love, 130
and sense of identity, 5, 7,
135, 250–51, 259
and shame, 58
and truth, 100. *See also*
Acceptance
Self-confidence, 90–91, 102
Self-control, 63, 65, 215–16
Self-deception, 48, 85, 96, 99,
129
Self-denial, 128
Self-hatred:
feelings of, 5, 250–51
scrupulosity and, 68
and shame, 93–4
Self-images, 3–4, 8, 41, 93,
107–9, 133
Self-love, 130–31
Sermon on the Mount, 9
Service:
the center of Christian life,
227
communication as, 236–40
and imitation of Christ,
114–15, 127
of parents to children, 248
within marriage, 227, 233
Sex, 30, 55, 222–3
Shame, 50–52, 81, 93, 118–20
Sheehy, Gail, 105

Sin, 34, 36–66, 69, 93–4,
95–101, 124, 140–47,
160–65, 203. *See also*
Forgiveness
Society:
breakdown of institutions in,
22
changes in, 20–23
rebellion against, 18–19
Solzhenitsyn, Aleksandr, 6
*The Stranger*, 67
Suffering, 113
Sullivan, Harry Stack, 188

Taylor, James, 66
Thompson, W.I., 27
Thurber, James, 53
Tournier, Paul, 238–9
Transcendence, 8–17
Truth:
identity and, 74–7, 99
and self-acceptance, 99

Value. *See* Moral values
Victorianism, 24, 75. *See also*
New Victorianism

Warhol, Andy, 18, 19
Wheelis, Allen, 8, 24
Wilder, Laura Ingalls, 82
Wisdom, 133–4, 184
Work, 25–7, 28–9
World views:
Enlightenment, 12, 14–15
materialistic, 14
loss of God from, 16–17

Zaehner, R.C., 13